Music in the Old Bones

୨୧

Music in the Old Bones

❧

Jezebel Through the Ages

Janet Howe Gaines

Southern Illinois University Press
Carbondale and Edwardsville

Library of Congress Cataloging-in-Publication Data
Gaines, Janet Howe, 1950–
Music in the old bones : Jezebel through the ages /
Janet Howe Gaines.
p. cm.
Includes bibliographical references and index.
1. Jezebel, Queen, consort of Ahab, King of Israel.
2. Jezebel, Queen, consort of Ahab,
King of Israel—In literature. I. Title.
BS580.J45G35 1999   99-24189
222'.5092—dc21   CIP
ISBN 0-8093-2274-9 (cloth : alk. paper)

To Barry

Who taught me to
"pluck till time and times are done
The silver apples of the moon
The golden apples of the sun."

Contents

๑๑

Plates   ix
Acknowledgments   xi
Introduction   xiii

Part One
Biblical Interpretations

1 Reclaiming Jezebel   3
2 The Queen's Transgressions   30
3 Last Gasp of the Goddess   70

Part Two
The Eternal Jezebel

4 Prose Adaptations of the Jezebel Story   97
5 Jezebel in Poetry   140
6 The Smell of the Greasepaint: Jezebel in Drama   163

Works Cited   193
Index   203

Plates

☙❧

Following page 69

1. *Eve,* Lucas Cranach the Elder, oil on panel
2. *Early Goddess,* from *Emblemata Nova,* by Michael Maier (1618)
3. *Jezebel and Ahab Met by Elijah,* Frederick Leighton, oil on canvas
4. Ivory plaque, woman at the window, from the Nabu Temple, Khorsabad (Iraq)
5. "Jezebel is killed by horses and eaten by dogs" and "Athalia is slain by horses," from the Amiens Picture Bible
6. *The Death of Jezebel,* Luca Giordano, oil on canvas
7. Cover illustration, from *Jezebel,* by Denise Robins (1977)
8. Cover illustration, from *The Black Hills Jezebel; or, Deadwood Dick's Ward,* by Edward L. Wheeler (1881)
9. "'Hear me!' Jezebel Cried," illustration by Corwin K. Linson, from *Jezebel: A Romance in the Days When Ahab Was King of Israel,* by Lafayette McLaws (1902)
10. Bette Davis and Henry Fonda, in *Jezebel* (1938)

Acknowledgments

჻

THERE ARE MANY PEOPLE WHO HELPED TO MAKE THIS BOOK POSSIBLE. I want to thank my friends and students at the University of New Mexico, especially Elisa Mendalas, Rob Rosenberg, and Tiffany Sanchez, for suggesting novels and popular culture references to Queen Jezebel. I am also grateful to my friend Victor Luftig and his friend John Whittier-Ferguson for tracking down James Joyce references. Jeanne Roberts helped enormously by reading an early manuscript and making valuable suggestions. Special thanks go to my teenage children, Gwendolyn and Jason Gaines, for solving computer problems far beyond my expertise to handle. Most of all, I want to thank my husband, Barry Gaines, for finding Jezebel material in libraries around the world, for editing and proofreading the text, and for continuously supporting me as I worked. Without his help, this book would have never been completed.

Introduction

ତୁଇ

Can these bones live?

—Ezekiel 37.3

T HE BONES OF JEZEBEL WERE NEVER BURIED. HER ASSASSIN, KING JEHU, neglected to order her immediate interment. Instead, Jezebel's bones lay abandoned in the streets of Jezreel, deliberately left there to be trampled by horses and devoured by dogs. The rebel Jehu's ascent to Israel's monarchy in 842 BCE (Before the Common Era) was supposed to mark a return to God's order and justice after years of sinfulness under Queen Jezebel and her husband, King Ahab. Yet the promise of a fresh start under Jehu was never fully realized, and today Jezebel's bones rattle like a skeleton in our own family closet.

As the biblical story opens, God's laws have been violated in the Promised Land, and Queen Jezebel is the accused culprit. She is a foreigner, hailing from Phoenicia, but now living and ruling in xenophobic Israel. Though the Bible provides no details of Jezebel's upbringing in her native land, it is certain that she was a polytheist who greatly threatened the single-God requirement of Yahweh worship. In Phoenicia there were goddesses as well as gods, unlike the situation in male-dominated Israel, land of strong patriarchs and a lone masculine deity. It is also quite possible that Jezebel was raised within a despotic monarchy where rulers boasted of broader administrative power than in ancient Israel. So when Jezebel arrived as a young woman to wed King Ahab, her worldview and expectations of her role as sovereign were at odds with those of her adopted country. As a result, she became a convenient scapegoat for misogynistic biblical writers who tagged her as the primary force behind Israel's apostasy. Someone had to bear their vituperation. Why not the alien woman who engaged in blasphemous worship customs and seemed to be the power behind Ahab's throne?

In the ninth century BCE, King Ahab brought the Phoenician princess to Israel as his bride. His actions suggest a worldview that encompassed the hope of drawing diverse groups of Semites together in harmony and prosperity. Marrying the daughter of a powerful neighbor, attempting later in his reign to form alliances in the Middle East, and eventually uniting his daughter with the king of Judah point to Ahab's breadth of outlook. His political policy was devoted to establishing his country's military and financial security. Religious tolerance and conciliation with foreign powers seem part of the overall plan instituted by King Ahab and Queen Jezebel, a couple gifted in statecraft. Proof of their success is perhaps best shown after the fall of Ahab's dynasty, when mutual cooperation among the nations ceased. Today their regional unification policies would surely win Ahab and Jezebel a respected, if not an honored, place in history. Yet they are depicted in the Bible as reprobates.

Jezebel's misfortune is that her lot is cast with ancient Israel, where prophets and biblical writers determined that the country's religious needs outweighed all secular considerations. Surrounded by polytheistic nations, the biblical writers tell stories aimed at stamping out competing gods and vilifying people who worship or even tolerate such deities. So while progressive Ahab and Jezebel might, in different circumstances, have been regarded as sagacious leaders and deliverers of their people, they are instead the focus of institutionalized wrath. The compilers of existing biblical records have total contempt for Jezebel; she is a representative of all that threatens their patriarchal authority and cherished monotheism. Unqualified disapproval of Jezebel is the verdict of historians who favor a strong theocracy devoted to the God of Abraham alone. Coexistence with outsiders is heresy to those who insist that tolerance will undermine and taint Yahweh worship in Israel. Jezebel is thus the nemesis of the devout.

With her husband, Jezebel is accused of bringing evil idolatry into Israelite society and contaminating the purity of the Yahweh cult. Yet worship of a single god had never been absolute among the Chosen People. The first commandments from Sinai demand obedience to one divine authority, implying the extent to which the writers of Exodus worried about polytheism. Furthermore, the golden calf incident in the desert before the people enter the Promised Land is hardly the first instance of disobedience among the ancient Hebrews. Stories before and after Jezebel's tell of the people's religious lapses. Transgressions against divine law must therefore be resoundingly condemned by each generation of scripture writers. When the monarchy was firmly established in Israel and the people went astray again, Jezebel provided a logical focus for the prophets' harangues against sin.

Jezebel was not condemned just because of her worship customs. She was also damned for violating domestic law when she circumvented Israel's time-honored property codes. According to biblical accounts, Jezebel—possibly without her husband's knowledge—plotted to murder a subject named Naboth to confiscate his land. The crime of stealing another's patrimony was compounded because it was a foreign woman, Jezebel, who showed blatant disrespect for Israel's laws. Feminine influence was equated with evil, for Jezebel's wickedness undermined patriarchal authority to enforce society's rules. The queen became emblematic of woman's capacity to wreak havoc on the social order.

Jezebel was so disruptive to Israelite social and religious ways that she is called a harlot in 2 Kings, though the writers never provide examples of adulterous behavior. One explanation of the promiscuity accusation is that biblical authors sometimes connect pursuing false gods with chasing false lovers. A relationship with a foreign deity is similar to an extramarital affair; both are immoral and offer only sham affection or protection. Perhaps this concept was in the minds of the scripture writers repelled by the pantheon of deities constituting Jezebel's dowry. Through the ages, Jezebel's very name has carried sexual connotations, been linked with prostitution, and become a term of derision and abuse. People today know that to call someone a "Jezebel" is to level a serious insult.

Whatever her crimes, Jezebel paid dearly for them. Always in conflict with the mighty prophet Elijah and scorned by the writers of 1 and 2 Kings, she was executed when the new king, Jehu, ordered that she be hurled out of her balcony window. Since that day, her name and reputation have been vilified and reviled, despite details of her heroic death scene, for which all but Jezebel's most obdurate critics cannot help but praise the queen's dignity and courage. While celebrating his victory over the House of Ahab, Jehu left Jezebel's bones where they dropped. When he finally relented and commanded burial for the queen, it was too late— she had already become a meal, offal for the town dogs. Animals devoured her body; only a few bones remained.

The queen is still a source of fascination. Each year the Jezebel montage expands. Jezebel is firmly ensconced in today's popular culture, and the hypnotic heroine's enduring influence is often put to plebeian use. In Los Alamos, New Mexico, the name Jezebel was used on a World War II missile that, along with the nuclear bomb, was part of the arsenal developed to defeat hated enemies. The evil woman's name was to be unleashed as a weapon of war. Further, in 1998 President Bill Clinton was embroiled in scandal and faced impeachment hearings over a sexual relationship with youthful Monica Lewinsky, a former White House intern. For months independent counsel Kenneth Starr, unpopular in opinion polls, collected evidence about the affair. *Newsweek* reported that Lewinsky and Starr had never met because, in the words of a noticeably biased source close to the investigation, "you don't want to schedule an appointment between Jezebel and the pope" (Klaidman 47). During the 1999 Wimbledon tennis tournament, an HBO commentator labeled enticing Anna Kournikova the "Jezebel of Sweat." Additional evidence of Jezebel's popular culture appeal is even reflected in current advertising campaigns. The queen's bad-girl reputation, the power of her name, is so enduring that it is exploited by merchandise executives looking for ways to increase their profits and sell products. For example, advertisements for Renee of Hollywood's sexy Jezebel push-up, padded bra boast of dramatically enhancing cleavage and giving women perfect silhouettes. The Jezebel bra ads, seen in standard print media, such as the Spiegel catalog, are usually accompanied by provocative pictures of young women who certainly appear to be enjoying the benefits of an augmented décolletage. When purchasing Jezebel lingerie, shoppers are also buying into the Jezebel myth.

Popular culture references to Jezebel are evident today, but literary references are ubiquitous. In every generation, writers return to the tale of the biblical queen, retelling or reshaping it. A strategically placed Jezebel reference can launch a series of emotional reactions in readers. Some writers use her name as a catapult to new stories far removed in time and place from ancient Israel. Since the Deuteronomists first put reed to parchment and created their version of Jezebel's reign, she has become a symbol of sin. More recently a few writers have questioned the Bible's harsh judgment, but most have accepted its rendition of events. Is Jezebel really tyrannical, unscrupulous, and rapacious? Or is she, along with husband Ahab, deliberately misunderstood and misrepresented by biblical authors who are dedicated to polarized thinking and who use Jezebel to typify darkness in their black-white theology? Does she possess a marked gallantry of spirit, as even the Bible grudgingly suggests? Today the debate marches forward as people continue to be fascinated by Jezebel.

When the story of a naughty woman is told, chances are good that she will eventually be called a Jezebel. Though some may esteem the ancient queen's courage, most typically she or her modern namesake is reviled in literature. Whatever the genre—sermon, novel, poem, play—the Jezebel character is siren and shrew. She leads men astray, causing their downfall and her own. She usually has admirable beauty, self-possessed grace, and surety of purpose, but she plies these qualities for wicked ends. In postbiblical sources, she is the culprit behind an unascertainable number of pernicious plots. For many she is an evil Everywoman, and her end as dog food is her just reward. On very few occasions is the queen released from unsavory connotations. It would be impossible to list all the references to Jezebel in literature; the total number is unknown and probably unknowable. One thing is certain, however: the number keeps growing. In every generation, when artists wish to return to the familiar theme of the wicked woman, the name Jezebel crops up again and again. And again. Such is the Bible's potent legacy as its influence spreads through the centuries.

Today we can still hear Jezebel's ancient heart pound and her old bones clatter. They tap out a rhythmic, musical beat that continues to serenade us with its spark and crackle. Her life testifies to how damage to a reputation can linger through the millennia. The sermons of John Knox, novels of James Joyce, poems of Percy Bysshe Shelley, dramas of William Shakespeare, and films of Bette Davis all refer to the ancient queen. She has fascinated almost everyone who has ever known about her, and most find her a difficult woman to like. Yet perhaps it is time to reconsider the motives of the original storytellers and to explore the complicated nature of the queen. Her portrayal in 1 and 2 Kings and in the numerous retellings of her story leaves little to admire, except perhaps for her decision to die regally—without useless protest and in full dress costume. In the last moments of her life, when Jezebel applies makeup and dresses her hair, she emerges as much more than the priestess of paintpots. She is figuratively clad in her virtue.

As Jezebel's bones lie in a heap in the streets of Jezreel, they beg to be picked over again. Fleshing out her skeleton is an arduous task, for the entire Judeo-Christian tradition has already passed judgment on her. Many people curse her bones but still enjoy gnawing on them. Examination of her extraordinary reign supports poet F. R. Higgins's conclusion about the remains of the ancient queen of Israel: "There's music in the old bones yet." In listening to that dissonant music, perhaps we can hear new chords and expand our understanding of the inharmonious melody that is Jezebel's life.

Part One
Biblical Interpretations

∾

1

Reclaiming Jezebel

&❦

She moves a goddess,
and she looks a queen.

—Homer, *The Iliad*

WHEN IT COMES TO REPRESENTING EVIL, THE NAME THAT RESONATES through the centuries is Jezebel. The three syllables comprising her name have always been synonymous with sin. She is, without question, universally regarded as one of the wickedest women of all time. Her name may be grouped with a motley assortment of real and imaginary femmes fatales, including Cleopatra, Clytemnestra, and Lady Macbeth. The Judeo-Christian tradition vilifies Jezebel as an idolater who leads men and nations into pagan worship customs. She is a shameless fornicator, a painted hussy. While the devil is certainly more condemned in the Bible as a source of humankind's trouble, Satan is a supernatural being. And though Eve is forever connected to man's fall, she is a figure of legend. Jezebel is a historical person. She is a mortal queen born during the lifetime of Homer, some believe, and assassinated in Israel during Jehu's insurrection of 842 BCE. She is the influential daughter, wife, mother, mother-in-law, and grandmother of kings. Her power over men stems from her ability to tempt sexually, plot cleverly, and dominate completely. For two millennia—in literature, art, and music—she has epitomized wanton wrongdoing.

Jezebel's story in the Hebrew Scriptures (also called the Old Testament) may be briefly summarized. She is the daughter of a Phoenician king who is also a high priest of the god Baal. As a princess, Jezebel is probably a priestess of Phoenician deities; she is certainly raised to honor the gods and goddesses of her country. Her father gives her in marriage to Ahab, king of the ten northern tribes of Israel (c. 875–853 BCE). Her hold on men leads readers to conclude that she is beautiful, though the Bible makes no mention of her appearance. She grows up at one of the most liberal courts of the day and causes quite a stir when she goes to Israel's capital, Samaria, a provincial town when compared to her home of Tyre (Sur) and Sidon. Ahab is apparently smitten by his bride, for the Bible says that immediately after their wedding, he does her bidding. Ahab's military prowess, as recounted in the Bible, indicates that he is no weakling easily henpecked by a woman. Yet directly after the marriage vows are spoken, Ahab builds a temple to Baal in Israel, presumably so that Jezebel can continue her idol worship.

When she marries, Jezebel changes her nationality but not her religion. She clings to her native deities, an understandable inclination for the daughter of a high priest. She therefore comes into conflict with God's prophet Elijah, who conducts a contest on Mount Carmel to see which deity is more powerful, the Jews' Yahweh or the Phoenicians' Baal. In the next episode, Jezebel deliberately breaks Hebraic law while trying to help her husband acquire a vineyard belonging to one of their subjects, Naboth. The king and queen have three children, but the story concludes with the end of their dynasty. Ahab fails to remain loyal to God and dies in battle; Jezebel's children are portrayed as evil idol worshipers who die without glory; and the queen herself is thrown to her death from a balcony when God's newly anointed King Jehu enters Jezreel. Thus the Bible asserts that a bad lot comes to a bad end, and justice reigns again in Israel.

In the scriptures, there are only a few verses about the life of Jezebel. Five references in 1 and 2 Kings report her marriage to Ahab, her conflict with Elijah, her plot against Naboth, her influence upon her children, and her death. The biography of Jezebel begins in 1 Kings 16 and continues, off and on, through 2 Kings 11. In none of these verses does the writer have a kind word for the queen. Despite the military and economic success of Ahab's reign, the only real concern of the biblical writer is the couple's religious apostasy. Reports of Jezebel's deeds are scathing, designed to teach lessons against idol worship, and the royal duo becomes the prototype for an evil king and queen. Yet even in the Bible stories, the queen is always shown to be strong, independent, and brave. From head to foot, she is indeed a queen. She lives life on her own terms and faces death with a mixture of courage and disdain for her assassins. So, is she ultimately valorous or villainous, heroine or harridan? Any attempt to reclaim Jezebel as a shining example of womanhood is a difficult task, to say the least. History has condemned her. Yet by reexamining biased biblical accounts and information compiled about the age in which she lived, we can search for traces of Jezebel's true nature.

Who are the biblical purveyors of information on Jezebel, and why do they condemn her for all time? Are the authors or editors conveying factual material, an objective record of what occurred in Israel? Today we expect historians to provide an analysis of people, places, and events as they actually were and to interpret the significance of these things for our own age. Whether we actually get such unprejudiced reportage is open to question, but we do hope for it. Compilers of biblical stories did not share this modern view of how history should be written. The parts of the Bible that are called *historical* start with Deuteronomy, which serves as an introduction and theological guidepost to the other books. Joshua, Judges, 1–2 Samuel, 1–2 Kings, 1–2 Chronicles, Ezra, and Nehemiah—works lumped into the historical category—therefore possess a misleading label. Biblical writers and redactors, whose work sometimes was the result of a process spanning several centuries and including many sources, were motivated by a desire to tell a didactic tale rather than to relate a verifiable body of facts. High drama was more useful to their purpose than dry certainty, so centuries of oral myth and written legend, marvels and miracles with great emotional impact, and fanciful descriptions possessing striking beauty were woven into the so-called historical books, in which the narratives of Jezebel are now located. Her tale thus blends the contemporary categories of history and literature. As a combination of the two genres, it comprises a sort of revisionist history, in which Jezebel receives no plaudits from the writers.

The composition known as the "Deuteronomistic history" was composed by an anonymous group of people, almost certainly men, who can be referred to by various titles. *Deuteronomic historian, redactor, compiler,* or simply *author* are all acceptable appellations for those who, over the generations, wrote and edited the work. This massive history contains the story of Israel from its entrance into the Promised Land until its exile in Babylon. The lessons stress the people's struggle to remain faithful to Yahweh and obedient to the teachings of the Torah (the first five books of the Bible) in a land that is filled with temptation to follow other gods. This theme is especially poignant in the books that today are artificially separated into 1 and 2 Kings, originally a single work that continues the narrative found in the books of Samuel. Here the tales of Jezebel reflect the writer's devotion to God and hatred of the Canaanite deities that Queen Jezebel represents. The theological framework of 1 and 2 Kings identifies idol worship as a leading cause of the eventual fall of the monarchy. King Ahab is just one in a long line of rulers who fails the Deuteronomist's test of moral and religious righteousness, and Ahab's wife, Jezebel, is his partner in crime. She, among all the nameless and faceless political wives of the Bible, has a distinct voice and personality. The historian embellishes her persona to suit his pedantic purpose and creates a Jezebel who is one of the worst Bible villains. She is characterized by the writer as the epitome of evil, the blasphemous foreign termagant who seduces her man and her adopted nation into apostasy by flaunting her alien customs of worship. Elevating God's prophets and denigrating Jezebel is consistent with the Deuteronomist's ideology.

Jezebel's life is presented as unsavory history in the Bible and in extrabiblical sources. Yet history is a construct, a flowing river into which we can step to view different moments of recorded time. Decisions about what part to study reveal that some bends in the river are more significant than others. Jezebel's life provides a framework for viewing not only the times in which she lived but also the ramifications of her existence. Its purpose being didactic, the Bible is hardly objective history. While biblical narratives may be based on actual events, the moral lessons that the stories teach are more important (to the original writers and to generations of readers) than the dispassionate recitation of facts. By stepping into the river of history during the reign of polytheistic Jezebel, one can witness a monumental shift in the flow of human events, a moment that alters the course of the river forever. The Deuteronomist hoped that Jezebel's life would represent the last gasp of the goddess. With her death, monotheism scored one of its greatest victories and eliminated one of its most powerful threats. The day Jezebel died was meant to change the world.

By the ninth century BCE, monotheism was hardly new in the Middle East. When 1 Kings relates that Jezebel marries King Ahab, the Jews have long been settled in their own country and are living under Mosaic law. But all is not well in Yahweh's land. In addition to military challenges from foreign powers, there are internal threats to the security of the state religion. Other deities compete with Yahweh, as they always have, and find followers even in the heart of Israel. Arriving from a foreign country, Jezebel carries her alien gods with her, including the chief Phoenician god Baal. Jezebel is not the first foreign woman to wed a Jewish leader, nor even the first to turn her husband's heart away from God, but her life and death prove to be a turning point in Israelite history. Later prophets would continue to lambaste their flocks with admonitions against false gods, and later kings would stray from the monotheistic path, but no female threat as great as Jezebel, follower of the Phoenician goddess Astarte (also closely linked to Asherah), would again rule in the Promised Land. When Jezebel dies, the goddess and the possibility of a divine feminine influence perish with her. Since Western civilization is based in large part upon biblical precepts, the death of Jezebel and the goddess she represents has had an incalculable impact upon life as we know it.

Phoenician Influences on Jezebel

As soon as the Bible mentions the queen, her Phoenician ancestry points to the cause of her problems in Israel. In the Phoenician language, her name may have originally meant "Where is the Prince?" and was the cry of Baal's subjects (Metzger and Coogan 368). The spelling of the Phoenician term for "Where is the Prince?" is altered by the Israelite redactor in order to obtain the Hebrew spelling for *Jezebel,* a new word that may convey the biblical writer's sentiment "Where is the excrement?" Given the manner of the queen's death, this interpretation seems reasonable. The last sentence of 2 Kings 9 urges readers to remember that "the corpse of Jezebel will be like dung spread on the fields." The Hebrew version of her name is therefore likely to be a conscious twist of a traditional Phoenician term honoring Baal (Ziolkowski 15). Whatever its etymology, today the name Jezebel is synonymous with wickedness, and modern dictionaries maintain that it connotes evil.

Jezebel's father, Ethbaal (891–859 BCE), was king of the maritime trade center Tyre and its neighboring port city Sidon. These twin cities were the hub of Ethbaal's kingdom, well known for excesses in personal and religious practices (Herm 75). Because of the Phoenician people's idolatry, biblical sources frequently use Tyre and Sidon as symbols of unholiness (e.g., Joel 3.4; Isaiah 23; Ezekiel 26.1–28; Amos 1.9–10; Zechariah 9.2–4). The deity Baal's name is preserved within that of Eth*baal*. Baal is also a general term for lord, and even some very prominent Jews give their children names that appear to honor the god, at least in their alternate spellings: Saul's son is Ish*baal*; Jonathan's son is Merib*baal*. Coming from a royal house, Jezebel seemed a good match for Ahab, son of Omri and second king of the fourth dynasty in Israel. The marriage would unite the two regions, possibly coalesced already by common interest in Baal.

The Phoenicians were Semitic. In the Bible, the Bronze Age inhabitants of the entire region were originally called Canaanites, but the Phoenicians were part of an early migration that resulted in settlements along the fertile strip of seacoast near Mount Carmel. During the last half of the second millennium BCE, the general mass of Canaanites was differentiated from the segment of the population dwelling along the coast (Harden 37). Phoenicia existed until 146 BCE when Rome destroyed Carthage, a Phoenician colony. After being sacked, the land was divided between Rome and Greece.

Phoenicia lay between the thirty-second and thirty-sixth parallels, a length of approximately three hundred eighty miles. Its width was only about twelve or fifteen miles. Today the terrain remains much as it was in Jezebel's time. Along the coastal strip is a mountain chain, rarely more than a few miles from the sea, and ample streams of freshwater flow down from the nearby highlands. The lowlands are fertile but not expansive. Pomegranates, apricots, figs, almonds, oranges, lemons, plums, peaches, cherries, bananas, and grapes grow. Lumber is still available, though the famed cedars of Lebanon are less plentiful today due to deforestation. An extraordinary array of flowers and plants—including hyacinths, anemones, jasmine, honeysuckle, clematis, mandrakes, and ferns—are found in Jezebel's homeland (Rawlinson 101). The desert of Israel must have indeed looked barren and inhospitable to Jezebel.

Being a coastal people, the Phoenicians took up fishing and sailing. Commercially they became a world power, importing and exporting their specialties. In the Bible, King Solomon of Israel obtains the prized cedars of Lebanon for his Jerusalem temple, and he seeks highly skilled Phoenician artisans to assist in crafting the temple's lavish decorations. Phoenicians learned how to work in copper, bronze, and precious metals, gathering the raw materials they needed by trade. They excelled in manufacturing gold and silver jewelry and were excellent potters. Phoenician textiles, colored with the purple dye of the murex shell, were coveted everywhere. Phoenicians also cultivated flax for linen, to the extent that their meager land allowed. Mediterranean nations, notably Greece, Spain, and settlements along the northern coast of Africa, became trading partners. The degree to which Israel traded with Phoenicia makes it plausible that, at the time of Jezebel's marriage to Ahab, she went to a new homeland that was already familiar with Phoenician goods and customs.

However favorably history may record the Phoenicians' industriousness, the Deuteronomic historian has a different opinion of these worshipers of idols. There can be no doubt that during Jezebel's lifetime religion played an important role in Phoenician life. In each city and colony, the central attraction was the temple, erected on the highest ground. Rulers were also priests; coins displayed figures of gods; prows of Phoenician ships had as figureheads images of deities.

The Deuteronomic historian finds such graven images intolerable. Immediately, in the same biblical sentence that recounts Jezebel's marriage to Ahab, the king is said to go astray: "And it came to pass, as if it had been a light thing for him to walk in the sins of Jeroboam the son of Nebat, that he took to wife Jezebel the daughter of Ethbaal king of the Zidonians, and went and served Baal, and worshipped him" (1 Kings 16.31). (All references to the Hebrew Scriptures are taken from the Jewish Publication Society [JPS] version, *The Holy Scriptures,* based on the Masoretic text.) The first time Jezebel's name is mentioned, it is in conjunction with sinful behavior. In the verse that follows, Ahab, presumably under Jezebel's influence, builds an altar to Baal in Samaria and provokes God more "than all the kings of Israel that were before him" (16.33).

Jezebel also represents the power of the city-state in the millennia before Christ. Approximately twenty-five cities comprised Phoenicia, but each retained its separateness, and they never amalgamated into a unified political entity. Sidon was the oldest of these city-states, established over three thousand years ago. Each city looked after its own interests, the territory around it comprising the "kingdom." Major cities, such as Tyre and Sidon, probably had some hegemony over the others from time to time, but there was never a single Phoenician capital, much less a confederation or a nation.

Security was certainly a concern in the city-states. When the Hebrews marched into Canaan at the time of Joshua, Phoenician city-states were already famous for commerce and the arts. The towns were heavily fortified, too strong to be conquered by the newcomers. Nevertheless, Phoenicia lay on the land route between the powerful nations of Egypt to the south and Assyria to the north. Its walled cities needed to be able to withstand siege. War would cut off trade routes, squeezing Phoenician cities like grapes in a winepress. All the nations that the Phoenicians dealt with were land powers, so Phoenicians played their nautical advantage and sent ships to trade with and colonize towns in Europe, Asia, and Africa. Maintaining independence was a top priority and meant not being absorbed into the vast Assyrian or Egyptian empires (Frost 511). Jezebel's ideas about unlimited power or the divine right of kings, demonstrated in the Naboth incident, were probably in keeping with principles embraced by city-state governments flourishing along the corridor between the great desert and the Mediterranean Sea. There the ruler was despot.

Jezebel's convictions about despotic rule and pagan worship influence her whole family. After Ahab's death, their son Ahaziah ascends to the throne and immediately offends God by worshiping Baal. At the end of 1 Kings, Ahaziah "did that which was evil in the sight of the Lord, and walked in the way of his father, and in the way of his mother . . . wherein he made Israel to sin" (22.53). King Ahaziah becomes desperate to know if he might recover from injuries sustained in his fall through his upper-chamber window lattice (2 Kings 1.2). Near death, he blasphemes by calling on the "lord of the flies," Baal-zebub. Though Jezebel is not directly mentioned in Ahaziah's death scene, the redactor may be attempting to demonstrate the Phoenician woman's long-term sinister power. When her dying son feels compelled to consult a false god, Jezebel's enduring influence is implied.

Jezebel's Marriage to Ahab

Jezebel's marriage was a political alliance. The union of Ethbaal's daughter with the son of Omri, king of Israel (886–875 BCE), potentially benefited both countries. First, it encouraged economic growth by opening trade routes that would increase the likelihood of domestic prosperity. Second, and more important, however, it provided valuable military cooperation against neighboring enemies sharing common frontiers with Israel and Phoenicia (Robinson 84). So Jezebel was packed off to Omri's new capital of Samaria in the northern kingdom of Israel. Whether she went with alacrity or resentment is unknown and at present unknowable; the biblical storyteller was unconcerned with the princess's feelings. What is clear is that Omri's reputation was forever stained by his association with his son's queen. King Omri is discussed only briefly in the Bible, but he is censured strongly. The brilliant dynasty that he founded is irreparably injured by Jezebel's presence in it.

Extrabiblical sources elaborate somewhat on Omri's reputation among foreign powers, and evidence indicates that Omri is one of Israel's most able rulers. Though Omri is forced to make embarrassing concessions to the powerful Assyrians (Peake 296), he holds on to power. Omri's exploits are recorded in cuneiform on the Assyrian Black Obelisk, an impressive tribute that refers to Israel as Omri's country long after his death and his kingdom's fall. The obelisk contains a relief showing Jezebel's assassin, Jehu, submitting to Shalmaneser III, king of Assyria. Omri is a much-admired regional leader, as the obelisk's inscription indicates. By arranging his son's marriage to the Phoenician king's daughter, Omri also demonstrates that he is a farsighted diplomat.

Soon after becoming king, Omri purchases "the hill Samaria of Shemer for two tablets of silver; and he built on the hill" (1 Kings 16.24). Thus Israel has a capital in the north to correspond to Jerusalem, the capital of Judah in the south. Establishing this governmental center is the only real accomplishment by Omri that the biblical author notes. Ahab and Jezebel maintain ties to the former capital at Jezreel, probably continuing to use it during the winter (Ben-Sasson 123), but they also conduct court business at Samaria.

Despite founding a new capital, Omri is quickly condemned at 1 Kings 16.25: "And Omri did that which was evil in the sight of the LORD, and dealt wickedly above all that were before him." Perhaps Omri's greatest sin, which the Deuteronomic historian cannot forgive, is that this king is father to Ahab. And Ahab is husband to Jezebel. Omri is thus the founder and sponsor of a dynasty profoundly connected to idolatry in general and goddess worship in particular. The union of two princely houses must always be regarded as a blending of cultures; their economic, military, cultural, and religious ties become stronger. It is precisely this spiritual interaction that the Deuteronomist cannot tolerate. Since one of the main purposes of including the Jezebel story in the Bible is to establish firmly the superiority of Yahwehism and patriarchal authority, Omri is guilty by association with his daughter-in-law. Hector's rebuke of Paris for his marriage to Helen of Troy in book 3 of *The Iliad* could also apply to Omri and Ahab:

> Can *you* be the man, I ask, who . . . hobnobbed with foreigners and carried off a beautiful woman from a distant land and warlike family, to be a curse to your father, to the city and to the whole people, to cause our enemies to rejoice, and you to hang your head in shame? (65)

Other Israelite kings take foreign wives, but no non-Hebrew woman compares to Jezebel in the specificity of charges against her. Exogamy is commonplace because it helps to circumvent potentially adverse relations with rivals and to cement good trade. Conventional wisdom and past experience of the Israelites point to the political feasibility of such unions. The Bible provides numerous examples of foreign wives who pose no threat to monotheism. Joseph is married to an Egyptian woman, and no adverse repercussions follow because she does not interfere with her husband's theology. When Aaron and Miriam criticize Moses because of his Cushite wife, it is clear that he still enjoys God's favor. Therefore, some biblical narratives present instances of benign marriages to foreigners. When the wife has no power to threaten the Israelite deity or the business of state, little complaint is made about exogamous marriages.

Solomon's story is different. The Deuteronomist insists that Solomon's

> wives turned away his heart after other gods; and his heart was not whole with the Lord his God, as was the heart of David his father. For Solomon went after Ashtoreth the goddess of the Zidonians, and after Milcom the detestation of the Ammonites. (1 Kings 11.4–5)

In Solomon's story, exogamy leads to the inevitable clash of opposing cultures.

Obviously, when marrying into an Israelite household, high or low, it is not always easy for a foreign woman, such as Jezebel, to forsake her previous way of life. The Bible's harangues against the immoral influences of foreign brides make sense only if the women remain attached to the religious values of their native lands (Meyers 184). Many women who help sway their husbands' allegiance away from Yahweh remain nameless. Their sins are not as fully illustrated as Jezebel's. It is Ahab's queen who has a name and a narrative to demonstrate how she exerts unwholesome influence on her spouse, thus making her unique among the biblical wives of political convenience.

Jezebel is also singular in the force of her personality. Unlike foreign spouses before her, she seems to have high intelligence and administrative ability not commonly demonstrated by biblical wives. In her formative years, she has the opportunity to acquire definite concepts of kingship, based on the non-Hebrew model she observes at the Phoenician court. In Israel Jezebel makes and carries out plans pertaining to matters of state, and she maintains her husband's favor over the years. Since Ahab is credited with having seventy Samarian sons (2 Kings 10.1), he obviously has many wives and concubines, as is the royal prerogative. (*The Oxford Study Bible* points out, however, that these seventy sons may be "leading members of the royal family, not literally sons of Ahab" [384].) Yet no wife other than Jezebel is ever named, and it is Jezebel's sons who succeed to the throne of their father and Jezebel's daughter who marries the sovereign of Judah and becomes queen in the southern kingdom. Ahab and Jezebel operate as a genuine husband-and-wife team. Such partnership is not easy for a woman to achieve, given the circumstances of a large royal harem. Jezebel's abiding influence testifies to the strength of her character (Frost 507).

Undoubtedly, it is partly this personal strength that leads to Jezebel's influence over Ahab. She works indefatigably to get her way. Those who cherish today's separation of church and state may underestimate the degree to which religious and political life were inextricably enmeshed in the first millennium before Christ. When nations made alliances, their gods had to coexist as well (Peake 296). Worshiping foreign gods was likely to be a natural outgrowth of the compact with foreigners.

When Jezebel goes to Israel and marries a follower of Yahweh, she does not forsake her native gods, as Ruth the Moabite chooses to do. Jezebel takes her priests and prophets of Baal with her, and her worship ceremonies require shrines where she can practice religion in her customary way. A pivotal point in Jezebel's defense against the claim that she corrupts King Ahab and his people is that Baal already has followers in Israel who would also want to use such sanctuaries. Elijah, the foremost prophet during Ahab's reign, bemoans the Israelite custom of Baal worship. With the passing centuries, interest in other gods continues, as Isaiah, Amos, and Hosea frequently lament. Worshiping alien deities does not begin or end with Jezebel, but her reign is certainly a high watermark for the influence of the Baals.

Perhaps Ahab is practicing religious tolerance toward nonbelievers in the northern kingdom rather than making concessions to an overbearing wife by allowing Baal worship in Israel. If this is the case, Jezebel is not such a villain and Ahab's actions acknowledge the polytheism already practiced by some Israelites. Not all commentators believe Jezebel is the culprit:

> As a considerable part of the population was of Canaanistic stock in this area (Judg.1:27f), Baal worship had a great appeal. It seems likely that the erection of a Baal sanctuary was not due to weakness on Ahab's part, but was considered policy: to give the Canaanite element in the kingdom a religious center at Samaria, such as the Israelite elements had at Bethel and Dan (1 Ki.12:26–29). But that Jezebel made her royal husband an apostate from the religion of Yahweh, as the author of the Books of Kings would have us believe, is unlikely. (Bewer 49)

Omri's capital at Samaria thus symbolizes religious tolerance. A temple to Baal may even have been part of the original building plan for the city. Another theory is that Ahab feels divided loyalties between his attachment to the ancient religious traditions of his people and his attraction to the ways of Canaan (Robinson 205). Whatever the cause of Ahab's liberal attitude toward Baal and other gods and goddesses, it is blasphemy to the Deuteronomist. The biblical goal is to wipe out the acceptance of idolatry and firmly to establish monotheism, a Father-God belief system that cannot by definition tolerate other gods, as the commandment from Mount Sinai (also called Mount Horeb) stipulates:

> Thou shalt have no other gods before Me. Thou shalt not make unto thee a graven image, nor any manner of likeness, of any thing that is in heaven above, or that is in the earth beneath, or that is in the water under the earth; thou shalt not bow down unto them, nor serve them; for I the LORD thy God am a jealous God. (Exodus 20.3–5)

The Talmud (an ancient compendium of rabbinical teachings and commentaries on the Bible) issues general warnings about falling under the spell of idol worshipers. For instance, R. Abbahu admonishes, "There are three [evils] before which the Curtain is not closed: over-reaching, robbery and idolatry" (*Talmud, Baba Mezia* 59a). Furthermore, the Talmud cautions that "he who follows his wife's counsel will descend into *Gehenna* [Greek term for hell]. . . . Ahab's downfall is thus attributed to his allowing himself to be led astray by Jezebel" (*Talmud, Baba Mezia* 59a).

Talmudic legend definitely amplifies biblical accounts of Jezebel's active role in causing Ahab's apostasy. In the Bible, Jezebel contributes significantly to Ahab's religious downfall: "But there was none like unto Ahab, who did give himself over to do that which was evil in the sight of the LORD, whom Jezebel his wife stirred up" (1 Kings 21.25). In the Talmud, R. Levi expounds only the first part of this verse for six months, omitting the end concerning Jezebel. Then Ahab appears to the rabbi in a dream and asks, "In what way have I sinned or transgressed against you? For you expand upon the verse's beginning, but ignore its conclusion." Thereafter, for the next six months, Levi repeats the entire verse and reflects upon Jezebel's effect on her husband (Bialik and Ravnitzky 132, citing *Talmud,* Sanhedrin 10, 28b).

The issues of dreaming about biblical figures and needing to punish idolatry are cited in Talmud tractate Berakoth 57b when the rabbis claim that a man may receive important messages while sleeping: "There are three kings [who are important for dreams]. If he sees David in a dream, he may hope for piety; if Solomon, he may hope for wisdom; if Ahab, let him fear for punishment." In fact, Sanhedrin 102b explains that Ahab's very name (אחאב in Hebrew) means that he is an undependable brother (אח) to heaven but a loving father (אב) to idolatry.

There are conflicting reports in the Talmud about just how enthusiastically

Ahab gives financial support to other gods. For example, in one section (*Talmud,* Sanhedrin 10.2, 28b), Ahab gets dressed with the assistance of his treasury secretary Hiel (mentioned in 1 Kings 16.34). The Talmudic story says that, after adorning himself, Ahab asks if he looks handsome. Hiel responds, "Each day, more and more." Then Ahab donates to the shrines of false gods a sum of money that he judges as being equal to his worth. Jezebel does not appear in this scenario, but one can argue that her influence lingers even when she is not in the room. Sanhedrin 100b further asserts that Jezebel has her husband weighed every day and then sacrifices to her idols an amount equaling his weight gain. On the other hand, one of Bialik and Ravnitzky's anthology entries retells a Talmudic story of how Jezebel entices Ahab to sin against God, though he refuses to submit totally to her will:

> Every day she used to weigh out gold shekels for her shrines of idolatry—you say of such a man that he was equally balanced between good and evil! He was not! But Ahab was generous with his money—with his means he used to benefit disciples of the wise. Hence, half his sins were forgiven him. (Bialik and Ravnitzky 132)

Though Jezebel may not be thoroughly successful in influencing Ahab's use of money, tradition teaches that she attempts to corrupt him in other areas. The biblical account of Jezebel does not give evidence of her sexual promiscuity, but the metaphor of an adulterer being equated to an idolater is sometimes found in the Bible. For example, the prophet Hosea is commanded, "Go take unto thee a wife of harlotry and children of harlotry for the land doth commit great harlotry, departing from the LORD" (Hosea 1.2). A country desiring false gods is symbolically represented by a woman lusting after additional sexual partners. Therefore, the concept of unlawful sex and unlawful idol worship are linked in the Bible. In Jezebel's case, it is in postbiblical commentary that she becomes a seductress, an interpretation predicated perhaps upon biblical precedent for such thinking. In the Talmud (Sanhedrin, 39b), Raba recounts that Jezebel draws pictures of prostitutes on Ahab's chariot. Ahab, the rabbi concludes, is "frigid by nature [passionless], so Jezebel painted pictures of two harlots on his chariot, that he might look upon them and become heated." The queen herself is not adulterous in this passage, but she certainly condones such behavior in her husband and thus contributes to his corruption.

How much influence could Jezebel really expect to have as queen of Israel? What is the traditional contribution of a king's wife circa 860 BCE? Jezebel's actions as recounted in the episodes with Elijah and Naboth are atypical of the behavior of biblical women. Yet her active role may actually be consistent with regional customs inside Jezebel's time period but outside her adopted country, Israel. In Mesopotamia, a monarch's consort routinely supervised her household and had broad authority. She was permitted to oversee a range of palace matters, involve herself in diplomacy, and show religious devotion apart from the beliefs of her husband/king (Metzger and Coogan 636). Thus, when Jezebel advises Ahab, acts in his stead, or handles domestic problems as she sees fit, her behavior is not outrageous. Her Phoenician opinions about what is appropriate procedure conflict with Israelite law and habit, but her authority to behave independently was not unconventional in the general region.

In Israel, where masculine authority took its cue from a masculine deity, the formation of the monarchy marginalized the role of women (Meyers 196). Due to the service and administrative demands placed on the monarchy, new public institutions developed, all of them in the hands of men. The importance of the home, where women dominated, diminished in the patriarchal state, and the status of women deteriorated. As the perceived importance of women's contributions to society eroded, the next logical step was to associate women with the negative side of life. By the time of Jezebel's reign, a misogynist worldview had superimposed an image of sin and seduction upon the strong and vital woman. In fact, relegating women to the fringes of authority may be regarded as a natural by-product of Israel's monarchy.

The Deuteronomic historian definitely does not appreciate female independence, nor does female independence find widespread acceptance throughout the ages. Jezebel is criticized by commentators from Talmudic to modern times for having too much power and for knowing how to use it. Nobel Peace Prize winner Elie Wiesel adds his voice to the generations of biblical scholars who condemn Jezebel and assume that Ahab is a puppet caught in seductive strings:

> In that royal family, clearly it was the woman who reigned. Jezebel ruled over her husband and therefore over the nation. It was she who made the most important—and bloodiest—decisions; it was she who ordered the slaughter of the true prophets of the Jewish people, she who built altars to Baal, she who manipulated people against people, and all against the God of Israel. If that Jewish kingdom became indifferent to its own mission, it was her doing. Ahab was too much in love to protest—and she made him more and more dependent on her. . . . Clearly, Ahab was so addicted to her that he allowed her to run the business of government. (49–50)

The scholar protests too much. Even if Ahab and Jezebel act as co-regents, and the Bible never makes such a huge concession to the queen's direct authority, Ahab would need to approve of her plans, as Wiesel later concedes. His conclusion, however, is that "we are told that [Ahab] was a great commander, but only when she was not around; he was a weakling, but only when she was around" (50). The traditional view of Jezebel reflects society's standard assessment of what women should do: keep out of the masculine business of setting religious and governmental policy.

The Gallery of Wicked Women

The Bible discusses a plethora of women who tempt men into performing evil deeds. Yet some of the strongest condemnations of women come not from the Bible but from Ecclesiasticus, or the Wisdom of Jesus Ben Sira. Ecclesiasticus is probably the oldest book of the Apocrypha, a collection of ancient works written in the biblical tradition but never canonized. His composition dates from circa 180 BCE, is frequently quoted in the Talmud, and is an example of wisdom literature resembling Proverbs, except that it is the work of a single author, unlike Proverbs. "Ecclesiasticus" is its Latin title, meaning "church book," a name probably given to the work because it was so widely used in early Christian liturgy. Greek Church Fathers called it "The All-Virtuous Wisdom," and Pope Innocent I and St. Augustine held the book in high esteem. Ecclesiasticus can be viewed as advice for young men studying in Ben Sira's school. First written in Hebrew, the book was translated into Greek by Ben Sira's grandson. The original Hebrew text is lost, but a fragment of it was discovered in the Cairo Geniza archives at the end of the nineteenth century. Sections of chapters 39–44 were also excavated at Masada, and portions have been discovered among the Dead Sea Scrolls. Much of Ben Sira's material is lofty prescription for how to lead a good life, but also contained in this innocent-looking volume with the interesting history is some of the earliest and severest condemnations of women.

Ecclesiasticus deals with four types of women: the good wife; the bad wife; the adulteress, or prostitute; and the daughter. Ben Sira is a misogynist, negative in his descriptions of all females (Trenchard 38). Some (Di Lella 28; Weber 545) excuse and defend Ben Sira's offensiveness by pointing out that his attitudes toward women are just a product of the times in which he lived. In this view, Ben Sira is not an extremist, just a typical Jewish man living in an age in which women had few rights and were considered the property of their fathers or husbands.

In Ecclesiasticus the good wife is defined only by her relationship to her husband; she has no independent existence. She behaves nothing like Jezebel. A wife deserving of praise is silent and modest. Her beauty arouses her husband, but it is also a potential problem because it invites opportunities for others to seduce her. A woman can be useful to her husband, and without a wife, he may suffer negative social stigma. A good wife has virtues, but her goodness is calculated only by how much comfort she can bring her man:

> A loyal wife brings joy to her
> husband,
> and he will complete his years
> in peace.
>> (Ecclesiasticus 26.2)

(All references to books in the Apocrypha and New Testament are taken from *The New Oxford Annotated Bible*, based on the New Revised Standard Version [NRSV] text.) In a society where Ben Sira's attitude is common, a strong woman like Jezebel does not meet the qualifications for a good wife and will not be accepted.

Ben Sira's most extensive discussion of women focuses on the bad wife, causing the reader to remember Jezebel. On the subject of naughty husbands, Ben Sira has so little to say that one might conclude that they do not exist. Misbehaving wives talk and drink too much, but Ben Sira does not consider that a husband who acts in this fashion would humiliate and cause pain to a virtuous woman. It is interesting to note that bad wives support their husbands financially, publicly disgracing men and causing them to lose face in the community. Troublesome women are adulterous, hot tempered, outspoken on matters that do not concern them, domineering, untrustworthy, and deserving divorce. In Ecclesiasticus 25.13, Ben Sira exclaims that one can tolerate "any wickedness, but not the / wickedness of a woman!" A female is even compared to a serpent, that biblical bringer of trouble:

> There is no venom worse than a
> snake's venom,
> and no anger worse than a
> woman's wrath.
> (25.15)

Ben Sira never mentions a biblical woman by name, but considering how Jezebel loses her temper in the 1 Kings episodes with Elijah and Naboth, she could certainly be an example of what he considers "a chafing yoke; / taking hold of her is like / grasping a scorpion" (Ecclesiasticus 26.7).

In Ben Sira's writing, women are also troublesome due to their loose morals. The biblical Jezebel is widely considered to be promiscuous. Her harlotry is mentioned by Jehu in 2 Kings 9.22, and her image through the ages is that of a concupiscent fornicator. Ben Sira strongly condemns prostitutes and warns men not to fall into their snare:

> Do not give yourself to
> prostitutes,
> or you may lose your
> inheritance.
> (Ecclesiasticus 9.6)

Also in chapter 9, Ben Sira condemns girls who sing, women who have shapely figures, and virgins as examples of females who lay traps for innocent men. All of these women are described as potential seductresses who trample a man's strength of will. Women are blamed for men's sexual escapades. A woman who commits adultery is viewed far more negatively than a man who is guilty of the same sin (as 23.16–26 demonstrates).

Ben Sira also has extremely harsh words concerning daughters, who are viewed as far more burdensome than sons. Daughters, whether they are married or not, are an economic hardship. Girls are a source of family shame because they are sexually intemperate, and fathers must keep special watch over daughters' behavior:

> Do you have daughters? Be
> concerned for their
> chastity,
> and do not show yourself too
> indulgent with them.
> Give a daughter in marriage, and
> you complete a great task.
>
> (7.24–25)

Jezebel is not only somebody's wife in the Bible; she is also somebody's daughter. Her father, Ethbaal, offers her up in marriage as a pawn to unite two peoples.

Jezebel is a prime representative of females, in biblical and extrabiblical sources, who are blamed for causing men to sin. Not all women, of course, are the source of masculine downfall. Some provide valiant assistance in the establishment of monotheism in the region, and they are praised as heroines. The Deuteronomic historian develops a series of stories focusing on the leadership role of women in the saga of God's preeminence in the Promised Land: (1) Deborah, a prophetess of Yahweh who guides Barak and the people to victory over Israel's enemies; (2) Jezebel, a queen associated with evil Baal worship in Israel; (3) Athaliah (Jezebel's daughter), a queen connected to Baal worship in Judah; and (4) Huldah, a prophetess of Yahweh during the time of righteous King Josiah (Christensen 402). Here the gallery of wicked women sandwiches two advocates for idol worship in between two loyal followers of Yahweh.

The redactor portrays Jezebel as controlling and manipulating. Misogyny is not a universal biblical attitude, however. Not all determined, strong women are evil. In the story of Isaac and Rebekah (Genesis 25–27), she is the risk taker who schemes and plots to obtain parental blessing for her favorite son. Isaac is far more passive. In this respect, Jezebel is similar to the matriarch Rebekah, while Ahab resembles the patriarch Isaac. Yet Rebekah is not vilified for working to control the course of events. She may possess dubious morality in helping Jacob trick his father, but she remains faithful to God and worships no other. Moreover, her machinations are helpful in fulfilling what could be viewed as the divine plan of having Jacob, the better of two flawed choices, inherit the position of clan leader.

Jezebel, ultimately judged as the opposite of Rebekah, uses her power to thwart God's will.

The foibles of men who are married to strong women receive scant attention in the Bible. Infrequently mentioned in biblical narratives is the correlative of the dominant female—the docile, submissive, indecisive male. If female characters, such as Rebekah, are deceitful, one explanation is that they operate from an "inferior social position and political powerlessness in patriarchal society" (Fuchs 137). This situation even applies to a queen, such as Jezebel. Because she lives in Israelite society, she too is hampered by its restrictions on feminine authority.

Biblical women may be categorized into three groups (Greenspahn 50). First are evildoers, such as Jezebel. Second are silent and nondescript ladies, such as kings' concubines and protagonists' sisters, who are basically ignored and represent womanhood. Here the storyteller is interested in women not as individuals with thoughts and feelings but only as voiceless symbols of their class or as appendages to men and extensions of masculine volition. Third are women who are treated positively. These female characters may have power over men, but it is not evil influence. Esther, for example, manipulates her husband, King Ahasuerus, but she acts for the good cause of saving the Jewish people from extermination by Haman.

Eve is the first woman in the Bible and the first, according to Christian tradition, to exert a wicked influence on man. Many lament the doctrine of the Fall because women are blamed for ruining what is ostensibly Paradise. Joseph Campbell does not accept the dogma that humanity was better off before the disobedience in the Garden of Eden: "This identification of the woman with sin, of the serpent with sin, and thus of life with sin, is the twist that has been given to the whole story in the biblical myth" (47). Since the day Eve handed Adam the forbidden fruit, women have been identified with evil. Adam (like his "brothers" Isaac and Ahab) is passive and takes what Eve offers. According to the biblical story, Eve does not cajole Adam into doing something against his will. She evaluates the serpent's message, seems to consider the risks, and makes her decision based on the fruit's merits. Then she offers Adam the fruit, and he accepts it. A grand temptation scene in which she seduces Adam to rebel against God is not in the narrative: "And when the woman saw that the tree was good for food, and that it was a delight to the eyes, and that the tree was to be desired to make one wise, she took of the fruit thereof, and did eat; and she gave also unto her husband with her, and he did eat" (Genesis 3.6). Her action is certainly disobedient to a deity who prizes dutiful compliance, but Eve's deed is the result of free will rather than innate depravity.

In fact, humankind benefits enormously from Eve's free-will decision to eat the fruit. She exercises moral and intellectual independence and chooses knowledge over ignorance. The punishments leveled against mortals are also signs of humanity, and man's domination of woman is placed in the context of an imperfect world. Such things as being aware of sexuality and working for a living are essential ingredients of being alive, and many of us would not trade them for the dubious honor of living in a "paradise" where we have no labor to perform and no understanding of what sort of beings we are. At the end of Genesis 3, the man names his wife Eve (חוה), which stems from the same root word *life* (חי). Adam (אדם) comes from the word for earth (אדמה). The message is clear: man is connected to the earth, but woman is forever linked to life.

If the Bible story does not convincingly denigrate Eve, where does the tradition of associating woman with original sin begin? Since when is Eve the culprit responsible for man's downfall? Jezebel and other women are seen as daughters of Eve, but who first sullied woman's reputation? The answer again lies with the author of Ecclesiasticus. Contained in this little volume is a short but historically critical condemnation of Eve. As the climax of a poetic treatise on the characteristics of the bad wife, chapter 25.24 states, "From a woman sin had its / beginning, / and because of her we all die." This is the earliest extant example of Jewish writing that blames Eve for man's troubles. Ben Sira held women responsible for sin, and though Ecclesiasticus was never canonized, its effect is felt to this day.

In part, goddesses from later centuries are associated with sin because womankind is held responsible for humanity's waywardness. The notion of a Jezebel-type woman as the instigator of sin does not exist in other cultures and mythologies, according to Joseph Campbell. He observes that

> the closest thing to it would be perhaps . . . Pandora's box, but that's not sin, that's just trouble. The idea in the biblical tradition of the Fall is that nature as we know it is corrupt, sex in itself is corrupt, and the female as the epitome of sex is a corrupter. Why was the knowledge of good and evil forbidden to Adam and Eve? Without that knowledge, we'd all be a bunch of babies still in Eden, without any participating in life. Woman brings life into the world. Eve is the mother of this temporal world. Formerly you have a dreamtime paradise there in the Garden of Eden—no time, no birth, no death—no life. (47)

Eve brings us our human existence, for all the happiness and misery that it may offer (plate 1). Yet in Christian civilization, Jezebel and the goddess worship she embodies are traditionally seen as an extension of Eve. The two women are condemned because they are thought to tempt men to perform evil.

In extrabiblical legend, Eve is not Adam's first wife. There is a prior, more evil partner for man. Her name is Lilith, and she is only mentioned once in the Bible, and then not in all English translations, though the Hebrew text clearly refers to her by name, לילית. In the New Revised Standard Version of Isaiah, a postexilic editor describes the terrible end that will come to the nation of Edom, representative of God's enemies. Edom's name shall be "No Kingdom There" (34.12), and it will be the abode of wild animals:

> Wildcats shall meet with hyenas,
> goat-demons shall call to
> each other;
> there too Lilith shall repose,
> and find a place to rest.
>
> (34.14)

Perhaps the Lilith myth originated in Babylonian demonology, where she is associated with a storm devil. Lilith is also portrayed as a killer of pregnant women and infants. Eve represents womanhood and motherhood, and though she is held responsible for man's sinfulness, Lilith is unquestionably more depraved. Another translation of Ben Sira tells of Lilith deserting Adam after she unsuccessfully demands equality. She says to Adam, "We are equal because we both come from the earth" (Ecclesiasticus 23a–b). Modern feminist interpreters focus on Lilith's more positive traits, such as independence and confidence, and they stress that Lilith is defamed by traditional masculine writers who wish to subjugate women (Nathanson 437). Perhaps Lilith is connected to Jezebel in this respect. Both are less tractable than Eve, and both are resoundingly censured by storytellers through the centuries.

Unlike Jezebel, Eve and Lilith do not exactly qualify as foreign women. There is no concept of "foreignness" in Creation stories. Shortly thereafter, nationalism is introduced as a theme in the biblical narrative, and the idea of the "other," the non-Hebrew, is immediately conspicuous. In Genesis, Egypt quickly emerges as the land of the "other." Egyptians are outsiders, and outsiders are idol worshipers and fornicators. A good example is Potiphar's wife, who attempts to seduce the young, handsome Hebrew hero Joseph. In the beginning of the Joseph narrative, he is a seventeen-year-old cocky kid, spoiled by his father, hated by his brothers because he is a braggart and a tattletale. Yet, in Egypt, he grows into an admirable man and an able national leader. The first evidence of his maturity and morality comes with his refusal to have sex with Potiphar's insistent wife. No sycophant is Joseph, using association with women in high places to gain advantage. His rhetorical question "How then can I do this great wickedness, and sin against God?" (Genesis 39.9) and his refusal of this foreign woman's sexual invitation land him in pharaoh's dungeons. Because of events that transpire in prison, however, Joseph is able to fulfill his destiny of saving the Hebrews (and the Egyptians) from famine. Potiphar's wife thus indirectly assists in the divine plan that Joseph describes to his brothers in Genesis 50.20: "ye meant evil against me; but God meant it for good, to bring to pass, as it is this day, to save much people alive." The storyteller means for readers to condemn Potiphar's wife as an evil seductress, yet good comes from the tribulations endured by Joseph. Potiphar's wife and Jezebel have things in common. They are both foreign women associated with evil. Yet Jezebel is never described as even an indirect instrument for good.

In the Book of Judges, God's plan is also carried out by two foreign women who deceive a Hebrew man. The scene of the treachery shifts from Egypt to Philistia, but once again we have idol worshipers who manipulate a follower of Yahweh. Ironically, everything the women do helps God kill the Philistine adversary. Samson, a giant collection of male hormones, cannot find an Israelite woman who pleases him and insists that his parents arrange a marriage to a Philistine bride. Samson's two women—an unnamed first wife, "a woman in Timnah" (Judges 14.1), and his second paramour, Delilah—coax Samson into revealing secret information to the enemy. Yet in both situations, he annihilates the Philistines and thus fulfills God's wishes, an important distinction between these episodes and the tales of Jezebel. Like Samson's women, Jezebel is a foreigner who lures a man into committing misdeeds, but 1 and 2 Kings draw no conclusions about the positive effect of Jezebel's intrigues.

The Bible states that the whole scheme involving Samson's first Timnah spouse "was of the Lord; for he sought an occasion against the Philistines" (Judges 14.4). In his rage over being duped into telling outsiders the answer to his riddle and having his wife given to another, Samson destroys many of his foes and burns their crops. Later, after Samson's divorce, he is seduced by another woman usually considered to be a foreigner, Delilah. (The Bible does not specify her nationality; she could be a Jew living in Philistine territory.) She is certainly a collaborator. Her Dagon-worshiping Philistine compatriots pay Delilah eleven hundred pieces of silver to "entice [Samson], and see wherein his great strength lieth" (Judges 16.5). Samson reveals to Delilah his Nazirite oath not to cut his hair. The enemy shaves it off while he sleeps, symbolizing the temporary severance of Samson's special relationship to God. Samson is taken prisoner. As his hair grows back, indicating a return to God's favor, Samson literally brings the enemy's house down. He breaks the supporting columns of the arena where the Philistines have gathered to gawk at him. Samson dies in the wreckage, killing many opponents at the same time. "So the dead that he slew at his death were more than they that he slew in his life," concludes Judges 16.30. In these two cases, which serve as foils to the Jezebel story, good comes out of evil perpetrated by foreign women.

Ironically, the Bible does present women who are guilty of the same crimes as Jezebel but who do not receive the same criticism. What is condemned in Jezebel as mendacity is applauded in others as helpful when it benefits Israel. Lying is not denounced when it is a mitigating circumstance in alleviating Israel's woes. The dishonesty motif permeates most stories where women appear (Fuchs 137). Whether the ladies are condemned or praised, they are likely to deceive and trick men. Duplicity appears as an inevitable feature of femininity. When Esther schemes and deceives her husband, it is to entrap Haman and put an end to his dreams of geno- cide. Her banquet trick when she invites her husband and Haman to dine with her (chapters 5–7) is a white lie represented as a good deed that saves the Jewish people from extinction, but it is a trick nonetheless.

Like deceit, seduction is not always viewed negatively. When Tamar tricks Judah into having sex with her and when Ruth lies down beside Boaz, these seduc- tion scenes are considered proper fulfillment of the levirate marriage laws from the Torah (Deuteronomy 25.5–10). In the Bible, Ruth is the antithesis of Jezebel. Both are foreigners; but Ruth chooses to follow the God of Israel, while Jezebel worships in her own way. Ruth is portrayed as the ideal woman because she for- sakes her own country and customs in favor of Hebrew practices, never waver- ing in loyalty to her new people. In the Bible, both Ruth and Jezebel are loyal to their Jewish husbands, but only Ruth is rewarded for familial devotion. Jezebel flouts patriarchal authority and threatens monotheism by continuing to worship Phoenician gods, causing the compiler to vilify the queen. Ruth's conversion to Yahweh is sincere, and she proclaims to Naomi, "your people shall be my people, and your God my God" (Ruth 1.16). Ruth also upholds Mosaic law by making a levirate marriage. Jezebel abuses the law by encouraging perjured testimony in the Naboth incident. Ruth embodies perfect devotion and is blessed with a son, who becomes part of the royal lineage leading to David and Jesus. Jezebel is cursed by having three children—two who, like their mother, are executed as heretics and one who sins and dies in office.

Ruth, the perfect wife, is the opposite of a prostitute, but even harlotry is for- given when the women, as in the stories of Rahab and Mary Magdalene, are believers. Rahab is convinced that the Hebrews' Lord is the one true God. She has heard about the parting of the Red Sea and says, "I know that the LORD hath given you the land" (Joshua 2.9). She therefore assists Joshua's spies and ensures the vic- tory at Jericho. Moving to the New Testament, the Gospels do not mention Mary Magdalene's being a prostitute; Luke 8.2 indicates simply that she is among "a number of women who had been set free from evil spirits and infirmities." Yet folklore and Christian tradition, promoted primarily by Pope Gregory the Great (b. 540), assign her the reputation of one who gives up past sexual intemperance to follow Jesus, providing an illustration of divine forgiveness of errant ways. Pope Gregory combined the Magdalene's character with that of two other biblical women, one a nameless prostitute. The advantage of the fiction about Mary Magdalene's prostitution is that she becomes an example of sinner turned saint (Haskins 134). Legends about Jezebel's infidelities are never excused because she remains an outsider and nonbeliever.

Even a crime as serious as murder is sometimes not condemned in the Bible. Ironically, considering the sexist tenets of the times, two women assassins are God's heroic tools in fulfilling divine will. Dying at the hands of a woman was considered the ultimate disgrace for a soldier, and both Jael and Judith distinguish themselves by murdering Israel's enemies. When the Bedouin woman Jael welcomes Sisera into her tent, lulls him into a false sense of security, and hammers a spike into his head, she is called "blessed above women" (Judges 5.24). Likewise when Judith of the Apocrypha decapitates the drunken Assyrian commander in chief, Holofernes, in his bed, she is venerated, the ideal Jewish woman who is thoroughly devoted to God. At several points, the storyteller lavishes praise on Judith. Before committing the crime, she prays that her deed will "bring glory to Jerusalem" (Judith 13.4), and afterward the astonished Ozias declares that blessings should rest on her "more than any other woman on earth" (13.18) because she risked her own life to save God's people from humiliation by their foes.

Yet when Jezebel is accused of the same kinds of crimes—deception, seduction, prostitution, and murder—the narrative is always vitriolic. There is a clear double standard regarding these matters. Jezebel is judged harshly because she is seen as a foe of Israel. When other women commit these same offenses on behalf of "good" causes—such as helping Israel against enemy attack, supporting masculine-oriented legal principles, or showing divine forgiveness of sinners—their behavior is accepted as proper and even extolled.

Whether their deeds assist Israel or not, today names like Delilah and Jezebel are synonymous with deception and trickery. When foreign women in the Bible are not given names or distinct personalities, it is sometimes because they are being used collectively as representatives of a corruptive influence. The personalities of these women are not fleshed out because they are not germane to the writer's purposes of establishing Father-God preeminence and showing idol worship to be the cause of Israel's woes. Defining women by their relationship to men is a device found in many stories of the Hebrew Scriptures and the New Testament. The Torah proclaims the necessity of avoiding marriages to non-Hebrews:

> neither shalt thou make marriages with them: thy daughter thou shalt not give unto his son, nor his daughter shalt thou take unto thy son. For he will turn away thy son from following Me, that they may serve other gods; so will the anger of the LORD be kindled against you, and He will destroy thee quickly. (Deuteronomy 7.3–4)

The gallery of wicked women presents as prime examples of this category Solomon's foreign wives and concubines (plus harem members discussed in Nehemiah and Ezra). Yet two women who are named, Jezebel and Delilah, are more conspicuous because they are more thoroughly developed than their silent sisters. Jezebel, in particular, speaks. Her words are intended to condemn her. Furthermore, Jezebel's daughter, Athaliah, presents a somewhat more detailed portrait of a woman with a name. After Athaliah's death in 2 Kings 11, the people destroy the House of Baal. Evidence of Jezebel and Athaliah's evil influence is presented in Kings, whereas other foreign women remain mute, faceless tempters.

Psalm 45 is a mystery, then, if the traditional interpretation of the poem's being about Ahab and Jezebel is correct. The psalm presents its female protagonist in a very favorable light and does indeed bear indications that the characters are Ahab and his wife. For instance, verse 9 refers to "ivory palaces" for which Ahab is famous, a probable allusion to 1 Kings 22.39, which describes "the ivory house which [Ahab] built." The lady in the psalm is a royal foreigner, and verse 11 advises the beautiful woman to "forget also thine own people and thy father's house." Most specifically, however, is verse 13's reference to the woman as a "daughter of Tyre, the richest of the people." Since Jezebel's father is king of Tyre and Sidon, Jezebel certainly fits the description. The psalm lavishes praise on the queen, "All glorious is the king's daughter within the palace" (verse 14). Perhaps Psalm 45 is a court poem, an epithalamium written at the time of the marriage to honor the bride and bridegroom, before trouble interrupts Jezebel's tenure as queen. The union is greeted at first with rejoicing, and the far-reaching, tragic results of the marriage are not anticipated when the lyric is composed. Another theory is that Jezebel is never so reviled during her life as she is by the time the Deuteronomic historian retells her story. *The Interpreter's Bible* maintains:

> Ahab's greatest crime in the eyes of the Deuteronomists was that he married Jezebel the daughter of Ethbaal, priest-king of Tyre. Whether this marriage was so regarded in the north is open to doubt, since Ps. 45 bears every indication of being a love song in which Ahab and Jezebel appear to be the hero and the heroine. (3: 144)

Furthermore, Jezebel's concept of kingly authority, for which she is rebuked in the Naboth episode, is supported in this poem: "Thy throne given of God is for ever and ever" (verse 7). In Hebrew literature, this is one of the strongest expressions of the divine right of kings, though it does not automatically follow that a king can do whatever he wants, regardless of the law.

The New Testament also offers examples of wicked women who commit crimes similar to Jezebel's. The death of John the Baptist occurs at the hands of a misguided girl. She dances at Herod's birthday celebration, pleasing the king so much that he vows to reward her by granting any request (Matthew 14.7). At the prodding of her mother, Herodias, the girl demands the head of the prophet, and a distressed Herod must vouchsafe her wish. Though she is not named in the Gospels, Josephus identifies the girl as Salome. Her famous dance is often revisited in art and literature, notably in two eponymous pieces—Richard Strauss's opera and Oscar Wilde's play. Like Jezebel, Salome and her mother are never forgiven for murdering a man of God, and centuries of readers are reminded of their scandalous behavior.

The memory of the Hebrew Scriptures' Jezebel is also resurrected and vehemently lambasted in the New Testament book The Revelation to John 2.20–23. John's letter to the church at Thyatira berates a prophetess-teacher who encourages the servants of Jesus to fornicate and to eat food that has been sacrificed to idols. She too is named Jezebel, the second person in the gallery of wicked women to bear that name. Thus, the New Testament writer "feeds upon a malicious myth about an ancient Sidonian queen" (Selvidge 118) who also challenged divine authority. Given the opportunity to repent, this new Jezebel does not. The Son of God promises, through John, to "kill her children with death" (Revelation 2.23), a fate she shares with her counterpart in Kings. Though the seven letters to Asian churches chastise sinners in general, the prophetess Jezebel is the only person singled out by name. For the New Testament writer, the name Jezebel is sufficient to connote a woman who leads her people astray. Ninth-century illuminated manuscripts illustrate this new Jezebel and correlate her idolatry with adultery.

In androcentric literature, such as the Bible, female characters must obey patriarchal conventions. Favored women, including the matriarch Sarah, are often silent. When her only son is taken away for possible sacrifice, for example, Sarah's personal reactions remain undocumented by the male storyteller, whose purpose does not include an examination of her feelings or thoughts. Sarah's lack of protest probably demonstrates her faith in divine mercy. Her silence certainly upholds the expectations of the biblical writer and poses no threat to the established order.

If, unlike Sarah, a woman is more independent or rebellious, she is portrayed as degenerate, unless her actions support the male-sanctioned religion. Biblical women from Eve in Genesis to Jezebel in Revelation are despised when they stray from masculine concepts of decorous conduct. At the heart of good behavior is the acceptance of monotheism. Sin may be overlooked or lauded when it serves Yahweh. Hence, some women may be heroines even though they lie, manipulate, commit adultery, or kill. Examples range from the mild misdeeds of Esther (deception) to the more serious sins of Rahab (prostitution) to the tremendous transgressions of Jael and Salome (murder). Additionally, following foreign gods is always potentially damning, except when the idol worshipers assist Israel. Queen

Athaliah and the foreign wives of King Solomon are depraved because their worship of alien deities turns their Israelite husbands' hearts from God. Yet even some idolatrous women, such as Potiphar's wife and Delilah, are unwitting instruments of God and have positive accomplishments that advance monotheism in spite of the women's intentions to the contrary.

Jezebel from the Hebrew Scriptures stands alone in this gallery of wicked women. Others are bad, but she is worse. The Deuteronomic historian wishes her to represent all that is depraved in woman. From the first mention of her name, she is associated with pagan idols. She massacres God's prophets, suborns false witnesses against Naboth, and dies at the hands of God's newly anointed King Jehu. Her immorality is infamous; she is portrayed as the Queen of Tarts, the Slut of Samaria. Yet the opportunity to reinterpret the Jezebel story is today welcomed by feminists because the queen presents a challenge and a chance not only to recover the reputation of one woman but to undermine masculine presuppositions about the whole story. Then society can begin to reevaluate fundamental patriarchal assumptions about what personality traits and behaviors constitute bad women (Quick 44).

Some modern feminist critics have tried to be less harsh to Queen Jezebel. Feminist criticism contends that literature is just one of many modes of expression used by patriarchal society, the purpose being to keep women subordinate to men. Therefore, literature's portrayal of gender roles is thought to condition women (and men) to accept as normal a society in which women are inferior. Feminist critics examine history and conclude that the literary canon, created by men, has downplayed or ignored important women. Others who study literature from a feminist perspective challenge conventional interpretations of women's behavior. Still others explore the gender biases embedded in language, revealing how diction allows writers to impose their worldview. What is subtly instilled in the reader is the writer's notion of the natural order of the universe, often with men divinely ordained as superior.

For example, the name Jezebel is typically invoked to characterize a woman who flaunts what the Deuteronomist regards as absolute truth. Usually, however, this "truth" is an earth-bound, patriarchally defined verisimilitude in the guise of eternal, transcendent truth (Quick 45). There is a case to be made for Jezebel that is more favorable than the one recorded in the Bible and in most biblical scholarship. Her situation is more complicated than may first appear, and she has often been treated cruelly since the Deuteronomic historian originally condemned her. It is clear that the biblical stories intend Jezebel to be a villain associated with goddess worship; and throughout the ages, her reputation remains sullied. Divinity defined in feminine terms is traditionally abhorrent to male-oriented monotheism and to societies that are based on biblical concepts of morality. Never in biblical stories is she caught in an adulterous act; in fact, she is a loyal wife to King Ahab and extremely interested in defending his interests and assisting him in fulfilling his desires. Yet the Bible, folklore, and even contemporary adaptations of the Jezebel story—in song, cinema, and literature—generally portray her evilness.

The work of deconstructionist critics may also be of interest when analyzing the Jezebel story. Deconstructionism holds that much of what we are able to discern comes to us through language, but language is ambiguous and changeable. Thus it is impossible to discuss meanings in an absolute sense. Language polarizes our thinking into pairs of opposites (man/woman, black/white, etc.), with one term in the pair being better than the other. The aim of deconstructionism is to demonstrate that this hierarchy of worth is not timeless or universal. The traditionally desirable reading of the Jezebel story upholds a particular religious, cultural, and political view. When influenced by deconstructionism, readers cannot ignore factors that lead to conclusions not usually regarded as "correct." A deconstructionist critic maintains that language itself conveys more than the writer can know or control. Insisting that we acknowledge the way language supports conventional sex, race, class, and other biases, the deconstructionist viewpoint may be useful in challenging the Deuteronomist's religious paradigm as purveyor of immutable truth.

Despite feminist and deconstructionist interpretations, reclaiming Jezebel remains difficult. Viewing her requires a special framework because her actions are not always laudable. Jezebel is neither as engaging as matriarchs like Sarah and Rebekah nor as heroic as fighters like Deborah and Esther, nor is she as cherished as wives like Ruth and Bathsheba. Unlike Potiphar's wife or Delilah, no good comes from her deeds. We are not compelled to take Jezebel's side because she is weak and voiceless in a male-dominated society that ignores her needs and opinions. On the contrary, Jezebel speaks and is heeded by her husband and countrymen. She is simply on the wrong side of a male God and patriarchal law as she inveigles the Jews. Any attempt to be evenhanded in discussing Jezebel is likely to result in acrimonious responses from the devout who accept Bible teachings.

It is therefore hard for readers to identify with and feel sympathy for Jezebel. Her strength has traditionally been deemed inappropriate because she uses it to challenge masculine authority and break Mosaic law. In the early days of Hebrew civilization, after the Exodus from Egypt, the people worked to establish their new national identity and stressed how it differed from surrounding cultures. Zeal to encourage appropriate national characteristics and loyalties among the Jewish people make the scriptures seem xenophobic and ethnocentric. In the new framework for viewing Jezebel, however, readers may admire her strength without approving of her unlawful actions. What is required of readers is an understanding of Jezebel and her Phoenician upbringing. In Jezebel's background were omnipotent kings. Scholars believe that Jezebel's father had virtually unlimited authority to do as he pleased. Thus, Jezebel behaves rationally, given her experience, training, and education. Her ideas are different from those of Israelite society, but that does not automatically make them inferior. The concept of the divine right of kings finds much support in European history, for example. Readers may ultimately reject the image of Jezebel as the Sultana of Slut and acknowledge that she possesses strong principles and acts bravely upon them.

Readers do not have to reject God if they demonstrate religious tolerance of Jezebel's worship customs. The queen's religious practices are different from the Israelite norm, but that does not immediately invalidate them. Today, as in Jezebel's time, there are countless religions on planet earth, many of them not embracing monotheism. Of the three religions based on the Hebrew concept of God, the Deuteronomic historian would only approve of one—Judaism. The writer of the Jezebel narrative intends to discredit and destroy all goddesses and gods except Yahweh, and a broader view of world religion is contrary to that purpose. The framework required for affirming Jezebel demands enough of an open mind to concede the merit of other forms of worship. The idea of religious tolerance is hardly new, but it is essential if we are to understand the queen. Traditionally, Jezebel and the goddess she represents have not been tolerated by Bible readers and scholars.

Readers of the Jezebel story are jumping into the river of history at a significant moment. The life of this extraordinary woman marks an important point in history. The influence of the Deuteronomic historian has reached into the present century. To call a person a Jezebel is to impugn that person's honor and to endanger her good reputation. Even individuals who possess only a nodding acquaintance with the Bible know of Jezebel's treachery. Yet a closer examination of the queen provides opportunity for approval, as well as censure. She lives her life according to her own convictions, steadfastly maintains her religious independence, exercises what authority she possesses, and dies bravely. Yet Jezebel is almost universally hated. She stands condemned for all time unless we can at last begin to study, understand, and reclaim her.

2

The Queen's Transgressions

&C&

Any Jew who does not believe in miracles is not a realist.

—David Ben-Gurion, proverbial expression

THE ANCIENT HEBREWS WERE A NOMADIC PEOPLE. THEY WERE HUNTERS and herders who followed their flocks to green pastures and sources of fresh, potable water. The stories in Genesis clearly point to the travels of God's people. Abraham (still called Abram in this section of the Bible) is commanded to leave his native land and be guided by God to a new place: "Get thee out of thy country, and from thy kindred, and from thy father's house, unto the land that I will show thee" (Genesis 12.1). God's words are an imperative not a suggestion and come from a deity who expects obedience. In return for fulfilling divine orders, Abram and his people are promised an impressive reward. The patriarch is told that he will be the father of an important nation: "And the LORD appeared unto Abram, and said: 'Unto thy seed will I give this land'" (12.7). At some unspecified time in the future, Abraham's descendants will have rest from their wanderings.

Many generations and strong leaders pass before God's pledge to the patriarch is kept and the Hebrews are at home and at peace in the Promised Land. The stories of Joseph (Genesis 37–50) and Moses (Exodus 1–Deuteronomy 34) tell about the emergence of the new nation. Seeking food during a long drought, Joseph's brothers eventually go down to Egypt, where, unbeknownst to them, the sibling they had sought to destroy has risen to the position of viceroy and is responsible for distributing the food he has ordered to be stored for the famine. The Hebrews stay in Egypt because they are welcomed at first, but later they become enslaved by a pharaoh who has forgotten Joseph's accomplishments and friendship. There the people languish, forced into hard labor until God hears their groans and selects a man to lead them into freedom. The Exodus during the time of Moses marks the birth and infancy of the new nation that must mature and become worthy of its freedom. After tribulations in the desert, during which a national identity is forged, the Hebrews must take the Promised Land by force, for it is already inhabited by Canaanite peoples. At this juncture, a giant shift in Israelite civilization begins to occur; a nomadic people must transform itself into an agrarian people.

The Conflict of God and Baal

The Hebrew God is born of the nomadic experience. In the blistering hot and arid climate of the desert, the Big Empty, the burning winds blow and the parched horizon stretches farther than the eye can see. Nothing in the desert can be regarded as permanent. Watering holes where people and cattle refresh themselves in the spring may be completely dried up by the end of summer. Entire valleys may be covered by drifting sands; rocks crumble and disappear. In this wide-open wilderness, only the sky is constant, its clear blue dome and scorching sun visible by day and its thousands of brilliant stars by night. Here the silence blares so loudly that no one can fail to hear it, as the great prophet Elijah will discover at Mount Horeb. In this barren land, life is stripped to its most elemental form, and necessities cannot be taken for granted. Life itself is precarious. The landscape is treacherous, a rocky and virtually lifeless terrain that well represents the challenges faced by the people who wander into it. Single-minded devotion to simple duties is required for survival.

In this setting emerges Yahweh, the invisible and jealous masculine God of the Hebrews. Shrouded in mystery, even his many names tell very little about him. Moses continually wants to see God's face, to know his name. God reveals that his name is Yahweh (יהוה), which roughly translates into "I am." He is called Elohim (אלהים), a masculine plural term translated as "God" and borrowed from the Canaanite god El. Though known by many epithets throughout the Bible, the closer one approaches this Hebrew deity, the further he seems to recede into the purely abstract. He takes concrete form only in the stern 613 laws of the Torah, so the Jewish religion emphasizes action more than a complicated belief system. God expects obedience to his word and will tolerate no competition from other gods. The single God of the ancient Israelites demands austerity and exclusivity. He is a creative God who needs no assistance from a female consort in order to generate life. Yahweh chooses the ancient Hebrew people to announce the message of his power to the world. In the early generations of the covenant between God and the Chosen People, he is theirs alone. Yahweh is also a god of battles, assisting his people in their military conquests and often demanding that all enemies—men, women, and children—be slain so that his people will not be contaminated by foreign worship customs. As long as the people are faithful to him, they have divine protection. Absolute allegiance is the only possible course. Compromise is unthinkable.

When the ancient Hebrews entered Canaan and began to settle down in the Promised Land, they had to abandon their former nomadic way of life from the desert. Once rovers who followed food and water sources, they now had to become farmers who permanently established themselves in one fertile, hospitable location near a steady supply of water. At this juncture, an inevitable conflict between two ways of life ensued: hunting and gathering versus tilling the soil. As these two methods of ordering society clashed, so did their gods. When they came into contact with the original inhabitants of Canaan, the Israelites were susceptible to acquiring alien customs. Learning the art of Canaanite farming facilitated the Hebrews' successful transition to cultivating the soil, but assimilating Canaanite religious practices was strictly forbidden by Yahweh.

What types of gods did the Hebrews encounter in Canaan? The characteristics of planting-culture divinities differed sharply from those of the desert Yahweh. *Baal* is a generic name most frequently used in the Hebrew Scriptures for the supreme Canaanite deity, but it is actually a neutral term meaning "lord" or "husband," and each village probably had its own baal who husbanded the land, fertilized it, and provided abundant rain and sun for crops. What the Bible terms the "high places" on the mountaintops were typical locations for altars to Baal. There the first and last rays of the sun would strike the holy place, and Baal was always associated with the sun. The Baals were also worshiped in the rest of nature—near springs, rivers, and woods. The local people erected small, probably unassuming temples to Baal in the cities. We do not know if they set aside a particular day for Baal worship, as the Israelites did for God.

Planting cultures also had fertility gods connected with fruitful growth and regeneration, and Baal embodied the generative principle of nature. Baal, the lord of all Canaan, was a creative god who brought things to life. The blatant sexuality of the god may have been responsible for his popularity with the people. As a fertility god, Baal was the deity representing free love. While Canaanites worshiped their gods with sacrifice, prayers, hymns, processions, votive offerings, and annual festivals, one of the most common methods of supplication was through sexual acts that would today be considered licentious. Prostitution of women and men was considered a way to honor a fertility deity. In some places, including the Phoenicia of Jezebel, it was customary that a maiden before her marriage prostitute herself in the temple or give herself to a foreign guest, thus reenacting the fertile earth receiving newly planted seeds. This act of sacrificing virginity would also be regarded as similar to the offering of first fruits from the field (Rawlinson 207), but worship was certainly not a succession of wild orgies for their own sake. Religious sexual acts expressed profound survival concerns. When the sexuality of gods was honored, so the fecundity of human beings was ensured. Life itself was thus preserved for another year (Frost 512). The existential questions of humankind were addressed by gods who presented themselves to worshipers as manifestations of the impulse to life and vitality. As the earth gave birth to new life in the annual cycle of the harvest, so worshipers paid tribute to gods who quickened the bodies of people and were associated with the circle of productivity: crops grow in the summer, are reaped in the fall, die down in the winter, and germinate again in the spring. How strange the Hebrew God must have seemed to Jezebel. He forbade some types of sexual expression that her people regarded as essential to the continuance of life.

Tribute was paid to Baal for the use of natural resources because displeasing the god would result in crop failure. To thank him and to ward off his wrath, the people offered up not only sexual acts but also sacrifices as part of the worship ritual. Food and drink were given to the god, but Baal appears to have been a sanguinary deity who also demanded both animal and human sacrifice. Thousands of clay pots excavated in the region contain skeletons of animals and small children, usually under two years of age, which testify to sacrificial customs (Robinson 196). The people's prosperity, not to mention their very existence, depended upon Baal's generosity and the people's loyalty. Perhaps in the minds of some Israelites, the stern and invisible Yahweh of the wilderness seemed unsympathetic to their new agricultural endeavors. Jezebel's building a temple to Baal in Samaria may thus be the result of the people's predisposition to favor fertility gods.

For the Deuteronomic historian, however, Baal and all gods other than Yahweh are regarded as false and intolerable. The Bible's myriad references to "the living God" are meant to distinguish Yahweh from idols of wood and stone, which, teaches the Bible, cannot respond to human supplications.

As the Israelites come into contact with Baal, the Bible writer fears that they may incorporate foreign worship procedures into their own practices. Pure Yahweh ritual could be contaminated, from the Deuteronomist's point of view. Such corruption might take place rather innocently, given the benign meaning of the term *baal*. Any landowner could be considered a baal, and even Yahweh could conceivably be called by that term. In the minds of ordinary people, the distinctions between Baal and Yahweh might become blurred. Presumably, in the early days, some Israelites paid tributes or uttered prayers at local shrines to Baal. These offerings were made in exchange for the use of the land, in expressing thanks for an abundant harvest, or in an effort to avert the god's displeasure. It is probable that people participated in the cult of the local Baalim without thought that doing so abrogated the covenant involving Yahweh's exclusive demands for their loyalty (Peake 298). In other words, even if the ancient Hebrews occasionally paid tribute to Baal, they would still have regarded Yahweh as the uniting force among the twelve tribes, the God who had led them out of Egypt to freedom, the God to whom they owed their military prowess and their unique identity.

In worshiping a single, incorporeal God, the Israelites were indeed alone. The monotheism of Abraham's descendants was an unparalleled theology at the time. In the millennium before the birth of Christ, a mélange of gods and goddesses populated the countryside shrines and "high places" throughout the region. Israel's neighbors, such as Moab, Edom, and Egypt, supported a swarm of divinities. Most important to the Jezebel story is Phoenicia with its pantheon of gods, including El, the father supreme whom the Greeks identified with Kronos. El was originally the mightiest, but he had such powers that the people rarely dared to call upon him. Later subordinated to his son Baal, the two sometimes seemed fused into a single being. Baal was a beloved deity and gradually emerged as the most enduring and important god. He was assisted by his forceful sister, Anat. She killed Baal's perennial enemy, Mot, and plowed his body into the ground, thus allowing Baal to dominate (Trible, "Odd Couple" 168). Finally there was Astarte, the consort. She was the primary goddess, called the "lady of the sea," who advised her husband and symbolized the fruitful earth. The upright stone pillar referred to in the Bible is a symbol of the male divinity, and the term *sacred pole* (אשרה) refers to the female deity and is translated either as "Asherah" or as "sacred pole" in English Bibles. The Phoenician goddess Astarte should be identified with Asherah in the Hebrew Scriptures as the female consort of Baal. Additionally, there were lesser gods, including Melkaart (the city god of Tyre), Eshmun (the city god of Sidon), Dagon, Hadad, Adonis, Sydyk, Onca, Tanith, Tanata, and others.

It is possible that Jezebel felt like something of a missionary when she went as a young bride from cosmopolitan, coastal Phoenicia to what she might regard as the less civilized hinterland of Israel. Fostering good relations between the two countries was a political necessity, so Ahab continued his father's custom of tolerance for outside religions. Jezebel would eagerly embrace this tendency toward pluralism. Perhaps she would even believe that encouraging Canaanite religious cults and discouraging Yahwehism with its "many seemingly uncouth idiosyncrasies" (Frost 507) would be her greatest contribution to the culture of her adopted Israel.

The ancient Hebrews were attracted to Phoenician fertility deities. As the former wanderers became settlers, they faced a new dilemma: what to do about recognizing the host of foreign gods already in the land. Yet with the arrival of Jezebel, the problem escalated. No longer was Israel only plagued by the question of whether to acknowledge the validity of other gods. Now the issue was whether their status should be elevated as high as Yahweh's. Could Israel's ideal of a single God be sustained through threats by outside enemies, as well as by internal forces operating inside King Ahab's palace? Ahab tolerates Baal worship in Samaria for his political ends. While there is no doubt that Yahweh remains the paramount God of Ahab and his people, subordinating the monotheistic principle to political expedience gives rise to the harsh protest by Elijah (Robinson 196).

Jezebel is personally blamed by Elijah and by many scholars for attempting to force Baal worship on loyal, Yahweh-loving Israelites. Take, for example, the judgment of Chaim Potok:

> Jezebel was that rare breed of pagan—a fervent missionizer for her god. . . . Jezebel regarded with contempt the austerity and simplicity of imageless Yahweh worship. It was her intent to convert the court of the king to the cult of her god. The rest of the land, she believed, would soon follow, and Baal and his consort Astarte would reign supreme in Israel. (123)

The Hebrew Scriptures do not go as far as Potok to interpret Jezebel's motives, yet his pronouncements do seem in keeping with the Deuteronomist's intentions and sentiments. It is certainly true that Jezebel is Baal's champion in Israel. Owing to the natural popular appeal of fertility gods and to Jezebel's commanding presence among the Israelites, it is not inconceivable that some people, including the king, are influenced by Jezebel's presence among them.

Whether Jezebel is the primary corruptive influence in Israel or a convenient scapegoat for the Deuteronomic historian's anger over the country's apostasy, it is probable that the queen has a strong and sincere reverence for Baal. He epitomizes vigor and youth. He brandishes a club with one hand and hurls a thunderbolt with the other. His strivings for divine supremacy reflect the turmoil taking place among the god's human counterparts (Frost 514). Jezebel would probably understand Baal's power struggles and also identify with his other characteristics.

Jezebel's religious actions are a direct affront to monotheism and represent a monumental national crisis. She is an intelligent and plucky queen who demands acceptance for her deities and who seeks tolerance for companions to Yahweh. It is Jezebel's strength that leads to trouble. She seems to desire that her deities have a share of the people's allegiance. She organizes and supports guilds for hundreds of prophets of Baal and Asherah; 1 Kings 18.19 says that there are "prophets of Baal four hundred and fifty, and the prophets of Asherah four hundred, that eat at Jezebel's table." This is a truly impressive number of religious authorities to have on hand. The phrase about prophets sitting at Jezebel's table may be best understood as "chaplains attached to the queen's household" (Robinson 208). Perhaps the number is inflated and symbolic, but it underscores the Deuteronomist's assertion that Jezebel is personally involved in subsidizing her gods and encouraging Israel to enter what the queen may view as the mainstream of Canaanite religion. Furthermore, whenever possible, Jezebel destroys as many prophets of Yahweh as she can (1 Kings 18.4). Her efforts are aggressively territorial; she does not merely passively accept what her king permits her to have. Here Jezebel becomes the bad girl of the Bible, for her actions have dire religious consequences. She becomes the antagonist representing Baal and company, and Elijah emerges as the protagonist representing God.

In the Hebrew Scriptures, Baal worship is connected to more extensive condemnation of male and female gods. Jezebel is particularly associated with goddesses. Together Baal and Asherah comprise the male and female aspects of the great god of Canaan. So Jezebel's threat is not just to monotheism in general but also to the Father-God representing masculine authority. Exponents of the jealous, male Yahweh therefore are hostile to Jezebel because they are universally antagonistic to goddesses. In the Hebrew Bible, Yahweh has characteristics traditionally associated with the masculine *and* the feminine, but he takes over the female reproductive role unto himself and has no need of the goddess. A society in which the metaphor for life's eternal mystery is a father will structure itself differently from one in which the metaphor for the universe is a mother.

Monotheism must ultimately move beyond concepts of male and female distinctions. Yet there is surprising evidence that in ancient times Yahweh was thought to have a female consort who "became absorbed into the male deity . . . by a process of treating the female divinity as a hypostasis of the male rather than as having independent status" (Ackroyd 249). While the evidence is not highly publicized, it is possible that a community identifying itself as Jewish followers of God also worshiped a goddess in fifth-century BCE Egypt. Papyrus texts from Elephantine in southern Egypt (near modern Aswan) provide information about a group calling itself "the Jewish force," presumably a military border-patrol unit in place for approximately a century. In spite of the geographical distance between Elephantine and Jerusalem, this Diaspora outpost maintained close ties to temple officials in the homeland. Ackroyd points out that this southern Jewish community

claiming and being accorded recognition by Jerusalem, included among the objects of its reverence not only Yahweh (the name appears in a form *ya'u* [Yahu]) . . . , but also other deities entitled Anath-bethel, Anth-Ya'u, Ishum-bethel and Herem-bethel. . . . The interpretation of these titles or names is not entirely straightforward; but one point is clear, namely that a title or name Anath-bethel can only denote a female divinity. Ishum-bethel and Herem-bethel have been understood as alternative titles of Yahweh. . . . Anath-Ya'u would appear to be the consort of Ya'u. (248)

A second piece of evidence that Jews may have, long ago, worshiped a female, as well as a male, version of Yahweh has also been found. Fragmentary material excavated in the Sinai at a site called Kuntillet 'Ajrud includes texts that are forthright in their acceptance of dual deities. The material states: "may you be blessed by Yahweh, our protector, and by his Asherah" (Ackroyd 249). The Judeo-Christian value of a single God is absolute, and locating ancient polytheistic variations is equivalent to finding a skeleton in the biblical closet. The very idea is repugnant to many people. Yet Ackroyd concludes that the "evidence of these texts points clearly to the existence in ancient Judah of such apparently aberrant beliefs and practices" (251). The goddess had her followers among the Jews.

Like Baal, the goddess is associated with the earth and planting. Just as the human woman gives birth and nourishment to her young, who are needed to perpetuate the species, so mother earth gives birth to vegetation that is needed to sustain human life. This brings Joseph Campbell to conclude that "woman magic and earth magic are the same" (167), for the female anatomy is synonymous with the universe (plate 2). When crafting tangible symbols of the creative life force, the image concocted is naturally female. Along the Fertile Crescent's Tigris and Euphrates Rivers, in the Nile Valley, and down the banks of the Ganges where early agriculture thrived, the goddess predominated. In these regions, hundreds of female figurines representing goddesses have been found by archaeologists, while comparatively few male representations have surfaced. The goddess was known by many names: Ishtar to the Babylonians, Kali to the Indians, Aphrodite to the Greeks, Ostara to the Saxons, Nut to the Egyptians. She also had many roles to play for her loving people: virgin, bride, mother, prostitute, sorceress. She had more phases than the moon, calling both its light and dark sides her own. Animal figures, such as bulls and goats, sometimes personified masculine authority, but the goddess overshadowed them.

In Phoenicia, the great mother and fertility goddess was Astarte. She was the regent of the stars and the queen of heaven. She gave life and was the source of woman's fecundity. Her images take many forms. Often she appears as a naked female with long hair, sometimes braided, and with her two hands placed on her breasts. Sometimes she is portrayed as a mother, seated and nursing an infant. She sits on a throne flanked by two sphinxes and holds a bowl under her pierced breasts. (This is almost certainly a miracle statue; at the appropriate moment in the ceremony, milk would flow from a hollow in the head through the holes in her breasts to be captured in the bowl.) Occasionally the goddess is robed and holds a dove at her breast or strikes a commanding pose with one hand raised.

Into the planting culture of the goddess, Hebrew invaders came with their animal hunting and herding. Animal-based civilizations emphasized killing rather than planting, so different types of deities emerged. An animal that is killed remains dead forever, but a plant benefits from pruning and regenerates itself annually after a winter's dormancy. Replacing the female goddess who was a giver and nurturer of life, masculine warrior gods appeared. These fearful gods existed amid flashes of lightening and peals of thunder. Fighting was more prevalent in animal-based civilization than in planting societies because the nomads had to conquer the territory they invaded. In the Hebrew Scriptures, Joshua and Judges reveal how Canaan is overrun in a Bronze Age version of a divinely sanctioned blitzkrieg. The land of Mother Goddess succumbs; male-oriented theology gains control and dubs the female deities "the abominations of the nations" (2 Kings 21.2). As a later representative of the goddess, Jezebel is to be used as propaganda against her own sex.

In the period of time presented in 1 and 2 Kings, the people shift back and forth in their allegiance to various gods and goddesses. Elijah complains about the people's wavering: "How long halt ye between two opinions?" (1 Kings 18.21). Jezebel's deities are never accepted by the Deuteronomist. The historian of Kings discredits Jezebel because she is an embodiment of the female deity. Monarchs who worship on the mountaintops, places commonly associated with alien goddesses, are blasted in scriptures. Campbell points to the long-term repercussions of the Hebraic attitude toward the goddess:

> there was a very strong accent against the Goddess in the Hebrew, which you do not find in the Indo-European mythologies. Here you have Zeus *marrying* the Goddess, and then the two play together. So it's an extreme case that we have in the Bible, and our own Western subjugation of the female is a function of biblical thinking. (171–72)

A male deity carries with him a profound psychological effect on the nature of the society in which he is worshiped.

Some of the oldest civilizations had a dominant goddess, and the male was hardly present at all. Then the reverse appeared in the culture of the ancient Israelites. Finally, a third possibility surfaced, as in India, where there was more equal interplay between the sexes, for deities of both genders mixed in a freer and more balanced way. It follows then that, when the personification of the divine is a masculine father figure, a different set of symbols and messages governing civilization will result than if the metaphor of the divine message is feminine.

Conflict with the Prophet

Jezebel, representing the Canaanite goddess, must predictably collide with Elijah, representing the Israelite God. No genuine tug of war can exist without someone formidable on each end of the rope. In early conflicts with Jezebel, Elijah tilts his black beard toward heaven to praise God, and when that beard has grizzled, he lifts it to curse the queen. The Elijah Cycle (1 Kings 17.1–2 Kings 1.18) is a series of popular stories about the prophet as he fulfills the word of God. Bloodshed and idolatry incite the indignation of Elijah, the authoritative zealot for Yahweh. There is little attempt in the Bible to develop Jezebel as a character for her own sake; rather, she is introduced as an evil foil for God's preferred prophets and leaders. The Deuteronomist, dedicated to polarized thinking, develops the contrasts between Elijah and Jezebel. He is male, and she is female; he is from the arid desert, and she is from the moist seacoast; he is Israel's native son, and she is a foreign daughter; he stands for the pious religious establishment, and she ranks among the royal degenerates. Most important, of course, he epitomizes good and is venerated; she embodies evil and is hated.

The Midrash, a group of Jewish biblical commentaries begun early in the history of the people and continuing through the Middle Ages, is likely to brand as a "Jezebel" anyone who is the foe of any holy man, not just Elijah. For example, when referencing the prophet Hilkiah, who lived several generations after Jezebel, the queen's name is invoked: "The fact is that since Jezebel was massacring the prophets, [Hilkiah] came, cohabited by day, and fled" (Midrash Rabbah 577). Jezebel is remembered as a source of evil even after her death and Elijah's passing.

The first time that Elijah's name is mentioned in the Bible, the prophet proclaims that "there shall not be dew nor rain these years, but according to my word" (1 Kings 17.1). This protracted, destructive drought is hard for a people to forget. It is testified to in Tyrian annals, and Menander of Ephesus records it in his ledger about the reign of King Ethbaal of Tyre (Ellis 194). During the drought, death is written on the land. The earth is baked like a hard, dry brick. Fruits on orchard trees shrivel and drop to the ground. Seeds lay unsprouted in the earth. Cattle become lean and die. All the while, Jezebel remains a votary of Baal, believing him to be the god who causes life-giving rain to replenish the earth. Elijah's purpose is to prove to her, to Ahab, and to all Israel that Yahweh is really the supreme ruler of nature and the sender of rain. In his fight against idol worship, Elijah has all the tireless, unremitting fervor of a jingoist. Convinced of Yahweh's superiority, Elijah predicts, during his first meeting with Ahab, a Yahweh-inspired drought. This is a direct affront to Baal as water giver. Elijah is "not only a thorough-going theocrat but a kind of Cromwellian democrat also, believing that the worship of any other god than Yahweh, whether as substitute or subordinate, was religious treason worthy of death" (Clarke 227). This cantankerous prophet naturally clashes with Jezebel, and he launches repeated attacks on the queen because she is a representative of Baal and Asherah.

The extent to which King Ahab shares responsibility for Baal worship in Israel is debatable. Jezebel usually gets most of the blame because it is she who was raised with idols, but the biblical account points to Ahab's complicity. Perhaps Ahab is following the lead of Solomon, who builds sanctuaries in Jerusalem where his Egyptian, Moabite, Ammonite, Edomite, Sidonian, and Hittite women and their entourages can freely worship their own gods. Like Solomon, who in his old age worships in the manner of his foreign women, Ahab may also be influenced to turn his heart toward Jezebel's gods. Though it is plausible that Solomon himself occasionally worships at alien shrines, he never promotes such worship among the people of Israel, and neither does Ahab. The king's household includes prophets of Yahweh, and it is questionable whether Ahab's liberal religious policy would include the persecution of Yahweh acolytes on the scale suggested by the Deuteronomic historian.

Perhaps the text of Josephus (c. 37–105 CE) can shed some light on the guilt of Ahab and Jezebel. *Jewish Antiquities,* his history glorifying the Jewish people, forms the most important nonbiblical annals containing information about Jewish history, culture, and religion during a three-hundred-year period just prior to and just after the birth of Christ (Metzger and Coogan 383).

According to Josephus, Jezebel was the great-aunt of Dido, the founder of Carthage in 814 BCE. The legendary Aeneas was said to have met Dido on his journey from Troy to Rome. *The Interpreter's Bible* (3: 144) concludes that "this house of Ithobal [Jezebel's father, Ethbaal] certainly bred masterful women, for of them three close kinswomen, Jezebel, Athaliah, and Dido, were born to rule." What is never in doubt is that, if Jezebel were an Israelite follower of Yahweh or a convert to monotheism, her tenacity in affirming her convictions would make her a saint instead of a sinner. Instead, she must inevitably clash with 1–2 Kings' supreme representative of monotheism, Elijah.

Josephus sheds more light on the royal couple and how they lead Israel astray:

> Now Achab, the king of Israel, dwelt in Samaria and exercised the royal power for twenty-two years; in no way did he make a new departure from the kings before him except, indeed, to invent even worse courses in his surpassing wickedness, while closely imitating all their misdeeds and their outrageous behaviour to God and, in particular, emulating the lawlessness of Jeroboam. For he too worshipped the heifers which Jeroboam had made and, in addition, constructed other unheard of objects of worship. And he took to wife the daughter of Ithobalos, the king of Tyre and Sidon, whose name was Jezabele, and from her learned to worship her native gods. Now this woman, who was a creature both forceful and bold, went to such lengths of licentiousness and madness that she built a temple to the Tyrian god whom they call Belias, and planted a grove of all sorts of trees; she also appointed priests and false prophets to this god. And the king himself had many such men about him, and in folly and wickedness surpassed all the kings before him. (5: 743)

Immediately after this passage, Josephus launches into his discussion of Elijah.

Hundreds of tales have been told about Elijah, who is portrayed as a megahero, ranking second only to Moses among all the revered ones of Israel. The Deuteronomist clearly approves of Elijah and looks to individuals of such stature to provide spiritual guidance for a troubled people. Elijah's name means "Yah[weh] is my God." Though Elijah never actually claims to be a Jewish prophet, he certainly behaves like one from the beginning of the Kings narrative. The narrative of the drought, predicted by Elijah at the outset of 1 Kings 17, is interrupted so that the remainder of the chapter can establish his special relationship to God. The compilers of Kings pin upon Elijah the whole future of the Chosen People and give his story extended treatment, though many details that might be of interest are omitted. For example, Elijah seems to come out of nowhere; there is no exposition about his early life. He suddenly appears and dominates several chapters of Kings abounding in marvels.

Miracles are immediately associated with Elijah in chapter 17, and the forces of nature—presumably under God's command—take care of Elijah's physical needs. Reminiscent of the manna and quails divinely furnished to the children of Israel at the time of the Exodus wanderings, ravens give Elijah bread and meat to eat in the morning at the Wadi Cherith. Here God abruptly tells Elijah to hide himself (leading to scholarly speculation that a proper introduction to the Elijah story has been lost). The wadi is probably outside Ahab's jurisdiction; and in chapter 18.10, Obadiah, who is in charge of Ahab's palace, informs Elijah that the king has been attempting during the three years of drought to apprehend the prophet: "As the LORD thy God liveth, there is no nation or kingdom, whither my lord [Ahab] hath not sent to seek thee." While Ahab seeks Elijah, the prophet is working more wonders, as chapter 17 indicates.

Food is again miraculously supplied when Elijah encounters a widow and her son from Zarephath, a town on the Phoenician coast, about seven miles south of Sidon and definitely outside ancient Israel. Elijah's association with the widow of Zarephath is an especially poignant episode detailing a generous-hearted, poor woman who heeds God's command to help a stranger. Elijah feeds the widow, her son, and himself from a seemingly inexhaustible supply of food found in a small jar of meal and jug of oil. The increase-of-food miracle is intended to enhance Elijah's reputation as a wonder worker.

Immediately after Elijah's miracle feeds the widow and her son, the boy falls ill, presumably as punishment for some unspecified sin: "his sickness was so sore, that there was no breath left in him" (1 Kings 17.17). The lad is carried to an upstairs room, an anomaly for the abode of an otherwise destitute widow. A large, two-story house is a narrative necessity, however, to ensure that the Semitic customs of hospitality are observed while not casting doubt on the woman's virtue and modesty while Elijah is under her roof. Though the boy's malady is serious, the Hebrew phrase describing it stops just short of indicating that he is dead. To cure the child, Elijah exerts his magical personal contact; he "stretched himself upon the child three times, and cried unto the Lord" (17.21). God heeds Elijah's plea for aid and the child is revived. The widow, a resident of Jezebel's homeland of Phoenicia, is then convinced that Elijah speaks God's true message. Clearly, the writer means to communicate that God is all-powerful and Elijah is God's worthy servant.

Elijah's sojourn with the widow of Zarephath is an episode belonging to both the miracle and the persecution traditions associated with the prophet, for he works wonders while Ahab seeks him abroad unto death. There is yet another convincing theory for why the story of the Phoenician widow is included in the middle of the account of Elijah and the drought. Here the Deuteronomist uses Jezebel's own people, the Phoenicians, against her. The widow of Zarephath is intended as a foil, a kind and gentle counterpart to harsh Queen Jezebel. The widow acknowledges Elijah and his God. She and her son, obedient and helpful to Elijah, are sustained by the Lord's providence and the prophet's intervention. On the other hand, Jezebel and her two sons must perish in order to fulfill the word of the Lord as spoken by the same prophet (Smelik 242).

Though the widow believes in Elijah's power, the prophet is not always recognized by authority figures in Israel; yet Elijah finds valuable, albeit clandestine, support from at least one follower. Elijah has an ally inside Ahab's own palace. It is Obadiah "who was over the household" but who "feared the Lord greatly" (1 Kings 18.3). The text says that "when Jezebel cut off the prophets of the Lord," "Obadiah took a hundred prophets, and hid them fifty in a cave, and fed them with bread and water" (18.4). These one hundred men are not likely to be full-fledged prophets with status equal to Elijah's but rather are his loyal helpers or disciples. Israel possesses abundant caves, Carmel alone having approximately two thousand, so Obadiah could easily locate hiding places for those among God's faithful who fear Jezebel.

A story from Midrash Rabbah 111 uses the Obadiah incident to explain another event in the life of Ahab:

> The generation of Ahab were idolaters, and yet when they went out to war they were victorious. And why? Because there were no informers amongst them; therefore when they went out to war they were victorious. The proof is this: When Jezebel sought to kill all the prophets of God what did Obadiah do? He hid them in caves . . . ; and there was not a man to tell Ahab, Thus and thus did Obadiah do.

Also in the Talmud, R. Isaac states that God rewards Obadiah's action by giving him the gift of prophecy. "Let Obadiah, who has lived with two wicked persons [Ahab and Jezebel] and yet has not taken example by their deeds, come and prophesy" (*Talmud*, Sanhedrin 39b).

Folktales even praise the wife of Obadiah because she may have supported his brave actions against Ahab and Jezebel. For example:

> When the Holy and Blessed One wished to create Eve, He saw that from her the Generation of the Flood would come forth and the Generation of the Division of Tongues, with all those who would cause her children to sin. But a second time He saw again from her would come forth Sarah, Rebekah, Rachel, and Leah. And He saw that from her would come forth Jezebel, who would induce the prophets of Baal to sin, but then again He saw that from her would come forth the wife of Obadiah, who would sustain the prophets. (Bin Gorion 177)

Another story indicates that, after Obadiah's death, his widow faces creditors and wonders what would become of the couple's "holy children" if they have to grow up in the House of Ahab and Jezebel. The prophet Elisha advises the widow about how to obtain oil to sell to pay her debts:

> "Yet maybe," she said to [Elisha], "they will say in the house of Ahab: 'The money belongs to us.'" But he told her: "He who closed up the mouths of the dogs in Egypt will close the mouth of the house of Ahab." Then she said: "Maybe a heave offering and a tithe have to be paid from it (to the Temple)?" Said he to her: "Your husband sustained the prophets only with bread and water; this does not require heave offering or tithe!" (Bin Gorion 179)

After the three-year-long drought described in Kings, Obadiah must help his master, Ahab, in finding green pastures. Obadiah serves as a protector of the prophets and is always deferential to Elijah, yet his duties as the governor of Ahab's household also imply a distinct religious moderation. Obadiah's job requires him to act as something of a prime minister (Yadin 127), yet he takes direct action proving his loyalty to God in the cave episode. While going through the land to search out fodder for Ahab's horses and mules, Elijah meets Obadiah, who falls on his face before the great prophet. Obadiah fears that Ahab will kill his palace master upon learning that Obadiah knows Elijah's whereabouts. To prevent his own untimely death, Obadiah pleads that Elijah not force him to tell Ahab where the prophet is: "And it will come to pass, as soon as I am gone from thee, that the spirit of the LORD will carry thee whither I know not; and so when I come and tell Ahab, and he cannot find thee, he will slay me; but I thy servant fear the LORD from my youth" (1 Kings 18.12). Obadiah's fear that Ahab will kill him reflects a substantial change in administrative court policy. Here it appears that royal caprice carries as much weight as law, so Obadiah understandably desires reassurance that the elusive Elijah will remain nearby. After obtaining a pledge that the prophet will not vanish, Obadiah tells Ahab where he can find Elijah, and the king goes out to meet the prophet.

The three-year drought forces Ahab to survey all springs and brooks around Samaria and look for grassy places to pasture his animals lest they die of thirst. Such a sustained period of no precipitation would surely have destroyed all plant and animal life. The Gospel writer Luke later hints at the purely symbolic significance of that length of time and says that Elijah's drought lasted not three but three and one-half years, significant because it is exactly half the sabbatical period. In other biblical stories from both the Hebrew Scriptures and the New Testament, three and one-half years is depicted as a critical length of time because it is precisely the number of days and months that must elapse before the end of the world (Daniel 12.7; Revelation 12.14).

One of the most moving of all biblical stories about the conflict between Jezebel and Elijah involves this extended drought, which Elijah predicts as soon as he is introduced in the narrative at 1 Kings 17.1. Acting as God's spokesman, Elijah claims to be in control of the forces of nature: "there shall not be dew nor rain these years, but according to my word." Exactly how long the drought lasts is uncertain. A drought that starts when (1) the spring rains of one year do not materialize, continues when (2) the subsequent autumn storms fail (the Jewish new year begins in September or October), and ends (3) after autumn following another new year could be reckoned as lasting for three years, although the actual lapsed rainless period is only eighteen months (Ellis 194). When it is finally time for the rains to recommence, Elijah strikes an unusual pose and indicates intense concentration as he prays on the top of Mount Carmel: "and he bowed himself down upon the earth, and put his face between his knees" (1 Kings 18.42).

In Elijah's day, the best opportunity to eliminate the religious pluralism that Jezebel represents coincides with this serious drought. When Ahab and his father, Omri, allow the people to worship other gods, it is considered as serious a sin as if the kings are themselves idolaters. These royal rapscallions are held responsible for the country's apostasy, and so Elijah must protest Israel's proclivity toward the Baal cult, end Jezebel's persecution of Yahweh's prophets, and demonstrate that God is supreme. In the third year of the drought, God is ready to end the misery and commands Elijah to meet with the king. Ahab's greeting to the prophet demonstrates the gravity of their rift when he asks of Elijah, "Is it thou, thou troubler of Israel?" (1 Kings 18.17). In the next verse, Elijah bravely gives an ad hominem retort that it is Ahab who troubles Israel because he has forsaken God's commandments to worship no other and has instead followed the Baals.

The prophet quickly proposes a solution in the form of a contest between Baal and Yahweh, a kind of "god-off" at Mount Carmel to see who has the puissance to conclude the extended and deadly drought. Carmel may have been selected as the scene for the battle because it had long been a center for Baal worship, as indicated in a reference to Carmel, called the "Sacred Cape," in Egyptian chronicles (Ellis 194). Another theory is that Elijah picks the mountain because his associates are already there hiding in caves selected by and therefore known to Obadiah. Carmel is not a single mountain peak but rather at least a ten-mile limestone ridge rising as much as eighteen hundred feet above sea level from the coastal plain of Phoenicia. Its proximity to the ocean makes it an ideal location to challenge Baal's dominion over water and rain; in addition, its closeness to Jezebel's homeland makes it doubly effective as the place to throw down the gauntlet before the queen and her gods. Another view, however, is that Jezebel's influence could not possibly extend so far northwest beyond Samaria, and the contest at Carmel is just an attempt by a fanatic Yahwehist to rid the Carmel area of its local shrine.

Whatever the motivation for choosing Carmel, at the contest's conclusion Israelites who have been liberal enough not to see any incompatibility in their simultaneous devotion both to Yahweh and to the nature cult of Baal will be shown which god is more potent. Elijah and all the prophets of Baal and Asherah are to assemble on the mountain. The situation is made more dramatic because Elijah alone represents God, while Baal has hundreds of prophets brought into Israel by Jezebel to serve her foreign gods. Elijah, greatly outnumbered, will prove that God is the most stalwart of deities. On Carmel two sacrificial bulls are hacked into pieces and laid on two separate wooden pyres. Fires underneath the bulls are not lit. Instead, Jezebel's prophets call upon Baal, and Elijah calls upon God, "and the God that answereth by fire, let him be God" (1 Kings 18.24).

Divine lighting of a holy altar fire is a metaphor in other Bible stories as well, showing God's strong approval of human actions. The Carmel fire thus links Elijah to earlier heroes. In Leviticus 9.23–24, for example, Moses and Aaron exit the tent of meeting and bless the assembled masses, "and the glory of the LORD appeared to all the people. Fire came out from the LORD and consumed the burnt offering and the fat on the altar; and when all the people saw it, they shouted and fell on their faces." Furthermore, after Satan encourages David to conduct a census, always a perilous undertaking since God's promise to Abraham in Genesis 13.16 that the Israelites would be too numerous to count, a plague is visited upon the land, and God sends an angel to destroy Jerusalem. In this troubled time, David erects an altar to God and calls upon him; God answers him "with fire from heaven on the altar of burnt offering" (1 Chronicles 21.26). So proposing that the God of Elijah show himself through fire at Carmel is not without precedent and is a tie that binds generations of Israelite leaders.

Everyone consents to Elijah's proposal of a contest on Mount Carmel. Baal's prophets are shown in Kings to go to extreme lengths to conjure up their god's power. Jezebel, Our Lady of the Golden Bull, is absent from the all-male event, but her cavalcade of prophets makes a prodigious effort on her behalf. We can imagine them howling, roaring, leaping over and around the altar, and practically frothing at the mouth before a silent Baal. Their conduct on the mountain is one of the best sources available for showing the nature of Baal worship. From morning until noon, they beg an unhearing Baal to heed their pleas. They "danced in halting wise about the altar which was made" (1 Kings 18.26, in the JPS version,) and they "limped about the altar" (in the NRSV rendition), both translations indicating a ritualistic, corybantic-style dance. At noon Elijah mocks the dervishes with an example of some of the Bible's most blistering sarcasm: "Cry aloud; for [Baal] is a god; either he is musing, or he is gone aside, or he is in a journey, or preadventure he sleepeth, and must be awakened" (1 Kings 18.27). "Going aside" may be a euphemism for urinating and points to the unseemly character of a god who must attend to bodily functions, thereby heightening the contrast between the baseness of Baal and the greatness of Yahweh. Awakening a god was a custom in Egypt, where during the second millennium there was a daily ritual to rouse the god to his duties. Furthermore, in Jezebel's homeland of Tyre during the age of Hiram (Solomon's contemporary), there was a rite performed every spring to awaken deities who slept through the winter (Gray 398). So Elijah's snide remarks about ending the slumber of Baal and the apathy that his sleep suggests are well grounded in the mythology of the day. Despite their best efforts, however, Baal's prophets cannot stir him.

During the long afternoon, Baal's prophets redouble their efforts, using large knives to cut themselves and allowing their blood to flow freely in their effort to attract Baal's attention. The bloodletting may be a substitute for actual human sacrifice or an attempt to establish a blood bond with Baal. Such self-mutilation may have been common among pagans but, once again, the practice unambiguously emphasizes the dissimilarity between the two religious traditions. For example, the Torah repudiates maiming the human body that is given by God. Leviticus 19.28 commands, "You shall not make any gashes in your flesh," and Deuteronomy 14.1 asserts, "You are children of the LORD your God. You must not lacerate yourselves." Throughout the day at Mount Carmel, Baal's prophets' sometimes solemn, sometimes wild supplications remain unanswered. The Deuteronomic historian declares Baal's silence in an emphatic, threefold stillness that symbolizes the superlative degree of muteness: "There was neither voice, nor any to answer, nor any that regarded" (1 Kings 18.29). Number symbolism continues as Elijah takes charge and begins his single entreaty to God. With twelve stones, representing the tribes of Israel, Elijah repairs an altar of the Lord on Carmel (18.30).

Elijah rebuilds the altar, digs a trench around it, chops wood, and places the bull's carved up carcass on the pyre. He commands that four jars of water, perhaps symbolizing the four directions from which Elijah solicits rain, be poured over the wood three separate times. Soaking the logs renders them more difficult to ignite, safeguards against fraud during the contest, and increases the contrast between his pyrotechnics and that of the Baalites. When the time arrives for the evening sacrifice, Elijah calls upon God only once. The fire is miraculously lit; the people accept Yahweh as the one and only supreme God; and Jezebel's prophets are removed to the Wadi Kishon for execution.

In the context of the day's sacrifice of bulls on Mount Carmel, this slaughter of Jezebel's prophets may appear to be part of the human sacrifice custom that is still occasionally performed in Yahweh country (though it is condemned firmly, as in Micah 6.7–8). The judgment at Wadi Kishon is an extreme one, representing the Deuteronomist's view of the life-and-death struggle between monotheism and polytheism. Though the Torah does permit capital punishment for some crimes, biblical sanction of the simultaneous execution of "the prophets of Baal four hundred and fifty, and the prophets of Asherah four hundred, that eat at Jezebel's table" (1 Kings 18.19) is notable, if not unprecedented, in its brutality. Another possibility, however, is that the elimination of Baal's numerous prophets may not have actually occurred until the time of Jehu's massacre of Baal's devotees in Samaria at 2 Kings 10.18–24 (Gray 386).

The emphasis on numbers continues to the end of the episode, when Elijah tells his servant to look out toward the ocean to see if storm clouds are gathering. Nothing promising appears, then:

> And it came to pass at the seventh time, that [the servant] said: "Behold, there ariseth a cloud of the sea, as small as a man's hand." And [Elijah] said: "Go up, say unto Ahab: Make ready thy chariot, and get thee down, that the rain stop thee not." (1 Kings 18.44)

Since the Genesis story, in which God created the universe in a week, seven has been the number symbolizing perfection and completeness. Elijah's miracle is now perfectly concluded.

The implications of God's victory at Carmel are significant. As a result, the people declare their allegiance to Yahweh, now proven to be the providential power of nature through demonstrations controlling fire and rain, while Jezebel's deities are vanquished. The "god-off" verifies to the people that Yahweh is not just a wilderness deity whose edicts are not germane in the settled, agricultural land of Canaan, that he is, on the contrary, firmly in control of the whole universe. Since he provides rain, he is sovereign over all agricultural endeavors. The Israelites have no need to make supplication to any foreign god for any reason (Robinson 213). The ancient conflict between herding culture and planting culture is now resolved in Yahweh's favor. There should be no further need of gods or goddesses to ensure that life-giving rain will fall and crops will grow. Jezebel and the female fertility deities she represents are obsolete. The unisexual nature of Yahweh is established. He is masculine but also productive, and he needs no female assistance in producing life. By controlling when the sun shines and when the rain falls, God's creative energy has dominion over the entire earth.

It is impossible for us to know exactly what happened when the sacrificial fire suddenly ignited on the Mount Carmel pyre and the rains began. Carmel's challenge to Baal conjures up memories of Moses' competition with Egyptian magicians in Exodus 7–8, though Elijah's opponents have none of the success sometimes enjoyed by pharaoh's officials. The altar fire may have resulted from a naturally occurring phenomenon, such as a bolt of lightening, which could strike, not unexpectedly, on a high place preceding a thunderstorm. Later novelists and dramatists interpret the events variously and offer explanations and theories about what really occurred, sometimes rejecting as violent invective Elijah's eminence at the Carmel competition. Perhaps the Deuteronomist exaggerates the story and deliberately creates a legend in keeping with the leitmotif of God's mysterious and magical power. With the consequences of the drought, the Deuteronomic historian certainly intends to tell a miracle story about punishment for defection to Jezebelian custom and Baal worship. Figuring out the specifics of what happened is less important than comprehending the consequences.

After the successful completion of the contest, Elijah tells Ahab to "eat and drink; for there is the sound of abundance of rain" (1 Kings 18.41). This command indicates that Ahab has been fasting during the proceedings. Prayer generally accompanies a fast, a solemn rite practiced by believers, and suggests Ahab's loyalty to God and hope that the forces of Elijah will be triumphant. The meal also implies a renewed communion among God, Elijah, and Ahab, even if the king's devotion is only going to be temporary.

To celebrate the victory, Elijah "girded up his loins, and ran before Ahab to the entrance of Jezreel" (18.46). In other words, in his enthusiasm to herald God's vanquishing of Baal, leonine Elijah runs ahead of Ahab's chariot to spread the wonderful news. Mount Carmel is approximately seventeen miles from Jezreel, so the story is testimony not only to the strength of Elijah's resolve but also to the miraculous fitness of his aging body.

The Queen's Transgressions
&∞

Flight from Jezebel

In the contest of chapter 18, Yahweh wins resoundingly. Because of this putative triumph, the next episode is curious. Its ironies invite the reader to consider carefully who has really been victorious at Carmel and raises more textual problems about proper chronology. At the beginning of chapter 19, Ahab has returned to Jezreel to tell Jezebel what she will regard as the disastrous news that her votaries have been slaughtered and that Elijah's God has won the day. Perhaps the confrontation at Carmel is deliberately planned and implemented behind Jezebel's back. It is possible that Elijah needs the queen's absence during the momentous demonstration of power, not because he fears her but because her husband does (Wiesel 49). Love for Israelite prophets never quickened in Jezebel's heart, but after Carmel it is entirely dormant, if not extinct. Now Jezebel becomes the personal persecutor and enemy of Elijah. The queen, never pliant or faint of heart, listens to Ahab's news, swears vengeance for the deaths of her prophets, and sends a message to Elijah: "So let the gods do [to me], and more also, if I make not thy life as the life of one of them by to-morrow about this time" (1 Kings 19.2). Jezebel's menacing words, directed to the prophet she never actually meets face to face in the Bible, also lead readers to recall how these two adversaries have killed each other's followers. They would probably not hesitate to kill again in the name of religion. In this unflattering respect, Jezebel and Elijah are simpatico. They are willing to eliminate anyone who gets in their way. In the Greek Septuagint, there is an additional phrase at this point in the scripture, emphasizing Jezebel's position as a direct adversary of the prophet. She says volcanically: "If you are Elijah, so I Jezebel."

Yet even without the Septuagint amplification, Elijah, previously so excited that he became a long-distance runner proclaiming Baal's overthrow, is now suddenly afraid of the queen's ability to carry out her death threat. When the events transpiring on Mount Carmel dazzle everyone else, Jezebel remains immutable. She understands that religious truth is intertwined with religious faith. Thus, so-called miracles are only acknowledged by people who are already predisposed to accept them. Nonbelievers may be temporarily impressed, but the effect will soon diminish and things will return to normal (Frost 509). But is not Jezebel's unfulfilled threat against Elijah an admission of her impotence? Had she dared to strike down the charismatic curmudgeon, surely she would have done so without first issuing a warning. Even with all her boldness, perhaps Jezebel cannot muster the audacity to eliminate Elijah, the victor of Carmel (Peake 311). Jezebel is not in a position to murder Elijah. If she were, she would attack first and ask questions later. She is, however, powerful enough to effect his immediate exile and turn the Carmel conquest to ashes.

No longer showing extreme chauvinism or patriotism, a cowering Elijah flees for his life, absconding into the wilderness a day's journey beyond Beersheba in the southern kingdom of Judah. Elijah's appearance at Beersheba is a strange occurrence, for the town is 130 miles south of Jezreel, an extremely long journey on foot. His destination indicates how far he is prepared to go to escape Jezebel's wrath, and the flight itself undermines the Carmel victory. If God is mighty enough to ignite the sacrificial fire on Mount Carmel, why does Elijah not have faith that God will protect the prophet now? Elijah vacillates concerning God's saving power. At the beginning of chapter 19, it is clear for the first time that Jezebel is the leading protagonist of Baal and the most resolute antagonist of Elijah. The conflict between Baal and Yahweh is mirrored in the clash between Jezebel and Elijah (Robinson 217), and Jezebel is in control at Jezreel. Elijah's action looks like cowardly trembling. Instead of standing as an unfaltering example of God's omnipotence, the incident on Carmel now appears to be no more than a momentary setback for Jezebel, whose iron resolve makes Elijah's determination appear flaccid by comparison.

A textual theory may help to explain Elijah's odd flight on the heels of his vindication at Mount Carmel. Elijah's glorious victory seems fleeting and momentary because he then runs to a distant destination. Actual events may be telescoped in the story as it has been preserved for us. Elijah's flight so far to the south could be part of the earlier narrative concerning tribulations of the prophet when he is characterized as a fugitive from Jezebel's wrath and must escape to the far north, as when he visits the widow of Zarephath in chapter 17 (Gray 407). The edited version of the text, as it has come down to us, may not place events in the correct order.

The compiler is not interested in reporting straightforward biography and may rearrange events to suit the pedantic purpose of the story. Suppose that, when the young queen first goes to Israel, her husband erects a sanctuary for Baal, at which she and other devotees of Phoenician gods may worship. Jezebel appeals to some people and uses her position as queen to gain for Baal a prominent place in their hearts. This ingratiation works well enough with ordinary citizens but causes extreme antagonism between the queen and God's prophet. Jezebel goes on the offensive and takes active measures against Elijah. A submissive Ahab, probably not wholly approving of his wife's actions, lacks her energy and cannot (or chooses not to) counter her moves. Elijah leaves the court and goes to Horeb to pray for guidance and formulate his plans against the queen. There he, temporarily at least, utterly despairs over Jezebel's relentless pursuit of idols. Reassured by a theophany at the site of God's original revelation to Moses, Elijah returns to Jezreel and predicts the drought to King Ahab. This scenario seems more plausible than the sequence of events in 1 Kings. Nevertheless, as the story about Elijah's flight beyond Beersheba appears after the Carmel incident, it suggests a moment of reckoning with Jezebel. In the version handed down to us, the prophet needs to reevaluate recent events he thought had demonstrated God's might. One does not admire Elijah as he runs for his life. His victory at Carmel begins to look like a failure because it only stimulates Jezebel's anger and encourages her to threaten the life of Yahweh's chief prophet.

Another possible explanation of Elijah's swift departure from Israel is that after the Carmel conquest he needs time to meditate upon the experience and commune with God in isolated silence. Never is the prophet intimidated by Jezebel; he just needs a vacation. The Deuteronomist would not be likely to concede that Jezebel is a worthy adversary. According to this interpretation, Elijah is not withdrawing from the queen herself. Though powerful, she is nonetheless only a woman and unworthy of being credited with the ability to strike terror in the heart of so great a man. Rather, Elijah is temporarily seeking spiritual refuge at Horeb and abandoning the lurid atmosphere of the court that is embodied in the person of Jezebel (Ziolkowski 8).

The journey into the wilderness does serve several purposes. First, it gives the Deuteronomist a brief opportunity to criticize Jezebel indirectly by showing her murderous nature. Second, it establishes God's continued favor toward the prophet, almost elevating the narrative to an Elijah hagiography. The story emphasizes Elijah's isolation, especially when he laments at 1 Kings 19.10, "I, even I only, am left," an obvious hyperbole indicating his feelings of solitary distress that, despite his best efforts, Jezebel refuses to acquiesce. Third, and mainly, though, the desert trip firmly links Elijah to Moses and Joshua and is a sort of sentimental journey to the birthplace of the nation and the source of ancestral faith. It is interesting to note that Queen Jezebel is the link between the two mountaintop experiences of Elijah: at Mount Carmel and at Mount Horeb.

Elijah's doubts in the desert are reminiscent of Moses' initial reluctance to undertake the job of leading the Israelites out of Egypt and his despair when the children of Israel lapse into apostasy at the golden calf episode. Moses has to be asked five times before he accepts God's sacred commission (Exodus 3–4). Moses' modesty and feelings of inadequacy are in sharp contrast to Elijah's confident, puffed-up image at the beginning of the drought narrative. But by chapter 19, verse 4, even Elijah wants out of the arrangement and asks for death in the wilderness. In requesting death, Elijah leaves the matter in God's hands. Suicide is rare in the Bible; King Saul and his armor bearer, Ahithophel, Zimri, and Judas Iscariot take their own lives, but for Elijah this is not an option. Determining life and death is exclusively within Yahweh's domain.

Elijah's pilgrimage beyond Beersheba recalls specific details of the Exodus (though Amos 5.5 denounces Beersheba as a pilgrimage destination and stresses the importance of one central shrine for worship). Just as God gives Moses and his people bread and water in the desert, an angel of the Lord miraculously provides Elijah with a cake to eat and a jar of water to drink. Fortified by the divinely provided food, Elijah "went in the strength of that meal forty days and forty nights unto Horeb the mount of God" (1 Kings 19.8). The number forty, a round number traditionally found in Semitic folktales and symbolizing a long time, is closely connected to the Israelites' wilderness wanderings and Moses' ascent of Mount Horeb, as well as to numerous other Bible stories. Horeb is the holiest of places, and though no one knows its exact location, Elijah could probably have walked there in under forty days. Since Jezebel has threatened the prophet personally, he is in danger. Nothing short of a pilgrimage to the mystical mountain can reinstate the prophet's power.

The cave where Elijah spends the night (19.9) suggests the same location where Moses beholds Yahweh's glory. Recalling Moses' theophany on Horeb when he hides in a cleft in the rock while God causes his goodness to pass by (Exodus 33.18–23), "the LORD passed by" Elijah too (1 Kings 19.11). Elijah experiences a wind, an earthquake, and a fire on the mountain, but God is not contained in any of them. Instead, God is "a still, small voice" (19.12) or "a sound of sheer silence," according to the NRSV. The quiet voice speaks loudly to Elijah and reveals future events to him. The purpose of the theophany is to instruct Elijah not just to expect the workings of God in extraordinary events, such as a storm that ends a long drought. Instead, Elijah receives a revelation. He should seek God's direction in the commonplace experiences of daily life (Gray 410). The experience on Horeb teaches a lesson to mercurial Elijah, whose preaching style would today be characterized as high voltage. God is not only a lightening-hurling, thunderbolt-clapping deity of spectacle but also a softer presence, a gentler whisper that is intelligible and accessible to humanity. In Joshua 5.13–15, another theophany occurs wherein Joshua meets a "commander of the army of the LORD." Always ready to battle for God, Joshua inquires what he should do to serve the commander. The reply is to perform a sacred task rather than to execute another conquest and plunder. Invoking the exact words to Moses in Exodus 3.5, Joshua is instructed in this theophany to remove his sandals because he stands on holy ground. When Joshua complies, he is linked to Moses of past greatness and to Elijah of future glory, for all three men have something about the nature of God revealed to them. So on the one hand, Elijah's flight beyond Beersheba decries his powerhouse image by making him appear frightened of Jezebel, a mere woman, but on the other hand, it also enhances his image as a man of God who is heir to the tradition of Moses and Joshua.

There is another puzzling legend about Elijah as he retires to the cave in 1 Kings 19. Rabbi M. Grunwald (128), writing from Vienna at the turn of the twentieth century, claims that Jezebel is about to outlaw circumcision in the northern kingdom, inspiring Elijah to seek refuge in the cave near Beersheba to pray for guidance. The verse at Kings 19.10 does allege that the people "have forsaken [God's] covenant." While this might be an allusion to circumcision, the biblical text makes no direct mention of the rite. Grunwald, however, staunchly maintains that, as punishment for the people's forgetting this obligatory sign of the covenant, ordained in the days of Abraham, God commands that no future circumcision take place unless Elijah is present. This may be either a commendation of Elijah for his zealousness or a measure instigated by God to protect Israel. For if Elijah is in every instance satisfied that the covenant is not being broken, then the country remains true to its unique character and is safe in its special relationship to God. Accordingly, the Talmud orders that a distinct seat or bench be reserved for Elijah at every circumcision and that the prophet be considered a revered guest every time an infant boy is initiated into the clan on the eighth day of his life. Elijah will be present, in spirit if not in body, at every circumcision.

Many Talmudic and medieval legends exist about Elijah, picturing him as a wise and kind leader. The fair-minded diplomat presented in these stories bears little resemblance to the fire-breathing opponent of Jezebel. For example, when Talmudic rabbis had a dispute, they often postponed further debate until Elijah could return to earth and settle the matter. Even today stories persist concerning the prophet's regular visits. Not only is a seat reserved for Elijah at every circumcision, a cup of wine is poured for him at every Passover meal. There are at least three possible reasons why the volatile foe of Jezebel in the Holy Scriptures is transformed into a benevolent hero of folktales. First, since technically Elijah does not die but is whisked off to heaven on a chariot of fire (2 Kings 2.11), he is a good candidate to return to earth whenever he is needed. Second, of all the Jewish prophets, Elijah is perhaps the most qualified to perform miracles, having accomplished so many in 1 and 2 Kings. Third, and most interesting, Elijah must make amends for his arrogance and self-aggrandizement. When he proclaims at 1 Kings 19.14, "I, even I only, am left," Elijah implies that he is the last remaining monotheist on the planet—an exaggeration then and now. To atone for this inflated view of his own self-importance and lack of confidence in the constancy of other believers, Elijah must bear witness to the Jewish people as they continue to practice their religion in every generation—at the circumcision of males brought into the fold, at the Passover seder, and at quarrels over religious issues (Telushkin 87–88).

Elijah dominates 1 Kings, and his story also spills into the early part of 2 Kings. But Elijah is not the only prophet with whom Jezebel must contend. While Elijah is on Mount Horeb "the still, small voice" of God tells Elijah how to pass the torch to the next generation of divinely commissioned leaders. Though Elijah's end does not take place until 2 Kings, and he will continue to play a prominent role until then, 1 Kings relates who Elijah's successor will be. The great prophet is to anoint Hazael as the king of Aram, Jehu as the king of Israel (in place of Jezebel's son), and Elisha as the prophet to replace the redoubtable Elijah.

Elisha's name is אלישׁע and means "God is salvation." He will fulfill two of God's demands of Elijah on Horeb, perhaps because the mountaintop theophany comes near the end of Elijah's life. Elijah does not exactly anoint Elisha but rather "cast[s] his mantle upon him" (1 Kings 19.19), and Elisha becomes Elijah's servant. The mantle, part of Elijah's personal apparel, comes into contact with the prophet's body and is thus intimately connected with him. Touching Elijah's clothing is a magical contact experience, an investiture that imbues Elisha with mystical qualities that rub off from the cloak onto him. Later stories of Jezebel bear out this interpretation, for in 2 Kings it is Elisha who will oppose the queen and oversee the biggest triumph over Jezebel—Jehu's revolt. The most significant victory over foreign worship does not come at Carmel at all, whatever kernel of historical truth the episode may or may not contain. Elijah's impact at Carmel has been greatly exaggerated, for if it were so important it would leave nothing for Elisha to accomplish. It is certain that the longest-lasting demonstration of Yahweh's power comes not during the time of Elijah but during the revolt of Jehu, won under the inspiration of Elisha, when Jezebel dies and the House of Ahab is dismantled.

So in 1 Kings, Jezebel, representative of false gods and goddesses, comes into conflict with the prophets of God. She is portrayed as a radical who demands an environment of religious pluralism, insists on the right to worship as she pleases, and perhaps wishes to impose her views on others. Her sincere devotion to her religious habits is obvious, and some blame her for trying to convert Yahweh-fearing Israelites to her cult. She is clearly a threat to male-oriented monotheism and patriarchal authority. Another interpretation is that the unforgivable sin that Jezebel commits is not tenaciously clinging to her native customs but failing to comprehend the doctrine of Israel's election as God's Chosen People. She perpetrates a single, fatal blunder as far as the Deuteronomist is concerned. She is introduced to the nation of Israel and is ideally situated to convert to Yahwehism and recognize Israel's unique role among the nations. Not only does she fail to do so, she also tries instead to remake Israel in the image of her Phoenician homeland. Had she been successful, Israel would have been forgotten long ago, another footnote in history associated with the departed grandeur of such places as Tyre, Babylon, and Carthage (Frost 515–16). The forces for Yahweh are working hard to preserve Israel's singular identity as God's favored nation. The compiler of the

Kings narrative may recognize that, if Israel were to undergo a religious mutation of the sort that Ahab and Jezebel wish, then the nation might continue to exist as one of numerous states along the Fertile Crescent, but as *Israel*—the covenant people of God created at the time of the Exodus and eternally bound to the deity in a unique partnership—the country would vanish from the earth (Frost 506). According to this view, Jezebel never comprehends that the living God is more creative, more reliable, and more enduring than her idols. While the queen possesses many admirable traits and deserves less condemnation than she receives, the compiler's final judgment against her is that she never accepts Israel's special role in world history.

The prophet-versus-potentate conflict originally flares in the fire of Mount Carmel as venerated Elijah strives to teach contempt for Jezebel and her gods. This struggle continues, but the campaign to make the queen a pejorative figure is not reflected only in discord over deities. The arena will soon expand to include the political, as well as the religious, scene. The setting will move from the mountain to the palace, where the lawlessness of Jezebel becomes the prime topic. Always at the heart of Israel's politics is its foundation in Mosaic law, and since the law is divinely ordained, religion and politics are inextricably bound. In the Naboth episode, the Deuteronomist plunges Jezebel further into sin. She violates the civil law of her adopted land, and Elijah returns to Jezreel to predict the manner of her death.

Skullduggery at the Palace

Jezebel's story now resumes but with a slightly different emphasis: all God's laws, not just those governing worship customs, are sacrosanct. The episode about Naboth's vineyard in 1 Kings 21 expands upon the ethical teachings of previous Jezebel tales. The conflict between the queen and Elijah in the drought story of 1 Kings 17–19 describes the necessity of observing the prime commandment to worship only Yahweh. As the narrative continues, the Naboth story reminds us that other laws must be obeyed as well. Everyone, from the highest to the lowest in the land, must follow the rules of conduct prescribed in the Torah. Not even the king and queen are above the laws of society.

The laws promulgated throughout the Torah dictate the religious obligations and practices of the people. From first to last, the laws indicate ethical monotheism. The religion of the Jews contains laws for how to behave toward God and toward one's fellow human beings. Ethical precepts for human interaction cover the gamut of human experience, especially duties regarding establishing justice, rendering mercy, and eschewing oppression. Jezebel deliberately defies these sacred standards in the Naboth episode, which serves as a polemic against the queen.

The story is simple. Naboth the Jezreelite owns a vineyard that adjoins Ahab's palace. The king covets the land and proffers a trade or an outright purchase, suggesting that he will either give Naboth a better piece of land or buy this one from him. Naboth declines all offers, as is his right. The Potentate of Pout, a dejected Ahab sulks and refuses to eat. Jezebel then tells her sullen, feckless husband that she will acquire the land for him. She brazenly arranges for bogus charges to be brought against Naboth so that he is executed; the crown then seizes the property. After Naboth's death, Elijah appears on the scene to condemn the House of Ahab for the treachery against one of the king's loyal subjects. Ahab repents for his misdeeds, but Jezebel does not.

It is possible that this story is the Deuteronomistic historian's revamping of an old tale in which Ahab shoulders full responsibility for Naboth's murder. The Deuteronomist, according to this theory, strongly opposes intermarriage and deliberately rewrites the plot so that Jezebel becomes the undisputed villain (Rofé 92). Changing the narrative suits the writer's theological contention that foreign women with alien customs cause Israel's fall. The imported queen is a convenient outlet for rage against the influence of outsiders.

There is no hard evidence indicating when in Ahab's reign the Naboth story occurs. Nevertheless, the narrative is best understood as a supplement to the monarch-prophet conflict begun at the Carmel contest. The Deuteronomist believes that the Naboth tale illustrates the continuation of adverse consequences resulting from Omri's legacy—the hope of synthesizing Canaanite and Israelite traditions through the marriage of his son Ahab to Jezebel. It is possible that the vineyard event actually occurred before the drought and contest at Carmel (Yadin 127). This arrangement is unlikely because, at the end of chapter 21, when Elijah suddenly appears on the scene to debunk Jezebel's scheme to steal the vineyard, he and Ahab seem to be reenacting an old enmity. Elijah does not directly mention any former royal indiscretions, but his verbal exchange with Ahab suggests past collisions between crown and prophet. It does seem plausible, however, that the Naboth episode should precede the new prophet Elisha's investiture by Elijah, an act that anticipates Elijah's immediate demise (Gray 435).

The Naboth incident begins with a man-to-man proposition. Ahab's offer appears fair, even generous. He does not demand, command, or exploit his position as king. Instead, as one citizen to another, Ahab says, "Give me thy vineyard, that I may have it for a garden of herbs, because it is near unto my house; and I will give thee for it a better vineyard than it; or, if it seem good to thee, I will give thee the worth of it in money" (1 Kings 21.2). Naboth declines the king's offer, not because it is unreasonable or unjust or because he is a stubborn man but because God's law says he should. Specifically, Naboth responds by invoking the name of

Yahweh, "The LORD forbid it me, that I should give the inheritance of my fathers unto thee" (21.3). The vineyard is a family plot, and Israelite law and custom dictate that it remain in the family. It is a sacred trust.

Ahab's action is prohibited many times in the Hebrew Scriptures. Deuteronomy 19.14 states, "Thou shalt not remove thy neighbour's landmark, which they of old time have set, in thine inheritance which thou shalt inherit, in the land that the LORD thy God giveth thee to possess it." Additionally, Numbers 27.7–11, Jeremiah 32.6–9, and Ruth 4.9 give examples of situations similar to Naboth's and underscore the rightness of his decision. Deuteronomy 23.25 mentions a vineyard specifically, outlines what rights the general citizenry have concerning the fruit, and warns against coveting another person's possessions: "When thou comest into thy neighbour's vineyard, then thou mayest eat grapes until thou have enough at thine own pleasure; but thou shalt not put any in thy vessel." In other words, Ahab should not be greedy concerning his neighbor's belongings or presume upon his neighbor's goodwill to the point of stealing from him. One of the best known of the Ten Commandments admonishes people not to covet anything belonging to a neighbor (Exodus 20.17). The Bible is not suggesting that it is wrong merely to desire for oneself what someone else has obtained. Coveting is unique in the Decalogue. The lone commandment pertaining to thoughts rather than actions, coveting is sinful because it leads to misdeeds. A misdeed occurs when an individual craves with an intention of dispossessing ownership of a neighbor's tangible or intangible goods. Ahab and his wife clearly covet Naboth's property.

Ahab asks the vineyard keeper to forfeit his patrimony. Naboth's status in the community is linked to his heritage, and no other parcel of earth or sum of money can confer upon him the same connection to his ancestors. It is possible that his deceased family members are buried on the plot (Robinson 236). Selling the land would thus be a disgraceful act of betrayal to family honor, and Naboth has no intention of breaking faith with his kinsfolk. The king and his loyal subject have therefore reached a stalemate. As an Israelite, Ahab should understand that his wish for the herb (sometimes translated as "vegetable") garden cannot take priority over Naboth's legal and moral obligations to retain the land. It is doubtful that Ahab is purblind to Israelite law and custom concerning inheritances. Ahab also knows that he is not an autocrat, as Jezebel's father Ethbaal may have been. The Israelite king should accept and respect Naboth's decision, even though it bitterly disappoints and frustrates him; he is a king who undoubtedly would prefer to have his own way.

It would not be shameful or impious to sell the vineyard during times of serious hardship. During the three years of drought in chapter 18, for example, Naboth could have sold his land in order to secure desperately needed money for food without staining the family name. In Jewish tradition, saving a life is always deemed more important than following the letter of the law. Yet while the prolonged drought ravaged the land and destroyed food supplies, Naboth apparently clung tenaciously to his property, however useful the profit from selling it would have been at the time. If Naboth steadfastly resisted surrendering his land during the famine, he would be unwilling to release it once the danger had passed. Though the Deuteronomist may expect Ahab to understand Naboth's position, the queen's response is another matter.

The compiler of Kings believes that Jezebel, as a foreigner, does not have proper regard for Hebraic law. Therefore, in this episode, she asserts her personal will and whim, flouting the law to get what she wants. Ironically, she may also be ignoring customs from her native land. Archaeological evidence indicates a Phoenician tradition similar to the Hebrew. Late Bronze Age cuneiform tablets unearthed at Ugarit, north of Tyre and Sidon, contain many property deeds stipulating family succession to the land in perpetuity (Andersen 49). This finding suggests a general Canaanite adherence to the principles Naboth struggles to uphold in defiance of royal wishes, for the Ugarit tablets emphasize inherited power and privilege. Jezebel's father, Ethbaal, was not king at Ugarit, but the city-state was certainly part of the Phoenician coastal settlement. Practices at Ugarit hint at Phoenician customs, but the cities were independent and may have had their own unique traditions.

The Naboth story is often read as a sketch contrasting Israelite and Tyrian court life. Jezebel is traditionally viewed as a Phoenician aristocrat who believes in the divine right of kings and their authority to do as they please, a notion also treasured in European history. Jezebel, according to this interpretation, supposes that the king is the king, not to be denied by any of his lowly subjects. She has steel in her soul and is obdurate in supporting Ahab's desire to obtain the vineyard. The only monarchy she reveres is one that recognizes no law except that of despotic omnipotence. When Naboth's obstinate determination not to yield to the king thwarts the royal desire for a garden, Naboth puts his life in jeopardy, for Jezebel cannot tolerate such insolence. Throughout the entire episode, Jezebel stands out as the leading conspirator; but as monarch, Ahab cannot be released from responsibility, even if he does not know the details of her nefarious plot to kill Naboth and confiscate his land. Perhaps the king of Tyre considered himself to be above the law, and Jezebel had grown up with this model of monarchical privilege in which the king is less subject to the law than are ordinary community members. Yet some historians argue that sovereigns throughout the ancient Near East generally upheld their nation's legal precepts, casting doubt on the theory that Ethbaal could ignore the law in Tyre and Sidon (Ackroyd 256). It is more natural to assume that kings, in Israel and elsewhere, were mere mortals who were not always thrilled to accept the confines of the rules that they claimed to safeguard for the general public. Jezebel's role in the story may be intended by the writer to show that Ahab's behavior is the result of unwholesome, alien influence. The king does not argue with his queen.

Though Ahab initially accepts Naboth's decision not to part with the vineyard, the king is greatly upset. Why would Ahab want the vineyard so badly? His palace would have been on high ground with lovely views of surrounding gardens, fruit orchards, and nearby Mounts Herman and Gilboa. Perhaps the Jordan River was even visible from a top-floor window. Why can't the king content himself with another location for his herb garden when fertile ground is all around? Why does he behave like a spoiled child who is disciplined by a scolding parent? After the interview with Naboth, Ahab returns to the palace at Jezreel, "sullen and displeased . . . and he laid him down upon his bed, and turned away his face, and would eat no bread" (1 Kings 21.4). Perhaps Ahab's disappointment stems from his knowledge that Naboth is legally and religiously correct. Respect for Yahweh should cause the king to acquiesce to Naboth, if the king is still a believer. Ahab knows he should not abuse royal authority, and his conduct is certainly unbecoming of God's anointed leader. This is not the first time that the Bible has characterized the sovereign as moody and brooding. Before the Naboth episode opens, at the end of chapter 20, a similar portrait of Ahab is drawn.

Chapter 20 is a bit of a detour devoted to Ahab's successful battles, and the queen is absent throughout, perhaps because she does not wish to concern herself with military matters. The first forty-three verses of chapter 20 are probably composed by someone other than the Deuteronomist, a different editor who is favorably disposed to the king. Elijah and Elisha disappear temporarily and are replaced by prophets who support Ahab as he fights King Ben-hadad of Aram. At verse 35, however, there is an abrupt shift in tone as the Deuteronomist apparently returns to rebuke Ahab. The king must pay for his bad judgment in not obeying the word of God; instead of killing the enemy king as commanded, Ahab releases Ben-hadad. One could argue that Ahab is demonstrating the admirable trait of mercy in sparing Ben-hadad, but other Bible stories also censure Israelite kings (notably Saul in 1 Samuel 15) for similar offenses. An anonymous prophet foretells that disobedient Ahab will be forced to forfeit his own life and that of his people. Foreshadowing Ahab's sour reaction to Naboth's refusal to sell the vineyard, Ahab responds to the unknown prophet's criticism by going home "resentful and sullen" (1 Kings 20.43). He is condemned for what looks like a magnanimous act toward Ben-hadad, and the episode shows that Ahab and God are not communicating well. Ahab becomes melancholy.

The king's somber mood turns bitter in chapter 21 when Naboth becomes an obstacle to the king's desires. Powerful Ahab now thinks of himself as an underdog. This is the point where Jezebel reenters the narrative. She sees her unhappy husband and asks the cause of his gloom. When she realizes that Naboth is the culprit, she immediately undertakes to rectify what she regards as a ridiculous situation. She rebukes Ahab and in Lady Macbeth style scoffs at his lack of manhood in not being able to take decisive action and put a commoner in his proper place: "Dost thou now govern the kingdom of Israel? arise, and eat bread, and let thy heart be merry; I will give thee the vineyard of Naboth the Jezreelite" (1 Kings 21.7). Perhaps Jezebel is outraged and repulsed by Ahab's whining impotence and regards him as a poltroon with annoying scruples. Perhaps she welcomes an opportunity to flex her own royal muscles and instruct Ahab on how to command authority and respect from his subjects. Whatever her motivation, she embarks upon a dangerous plot that wins her husband the vineyard but also increases the hatred of the Deuteronomic historian.

Though the Bible never intimates how Ahab feels about the way his wife takes over, Wiesel is convinced that Ahab must resent Jezebel's interference. Ahab often leaves home to fight battles and tend to his affairs. At these times, Wiesel contends (51), Ahab reverts to the faith of his people, but as soon as he returns to Jezebel, all his good intentions to reform vanish. When the queen reappears in the Naboth episode of chapter 21, after an absence during the military narrative of chapter 20, she seizes control of the domestic situation. There is much debate about what Ahab knows of Jezebel's plot to defame and murder Naboth. Whether or not he is cognizant of specific details, Ahab certainly does know that she is going to take action because she tells him so in 21.7. He gives tacit approval by not attempting to dissuade her from proceeding. His silence suggests acquiescence. Ahab must suspect that something sinister will have to be contrived to relieve the recalcitrant Naboth of his land, but the vexed king imposes no limits on Jezebel and never tries to prevent her from carrying out whatever scheme she might devise.

The first thing that Jezebel does is write letters, using Ahab's name and seal. When the technology was developed for transforming papyrus into parchment on which to write, a scarab seal was typically used to secure rolled up documents, thus ensuring that they remained unopened until delivered to the intended addressee (Harden 215). The king would have a unique seal, as would the queen. A seal of unknown provenance but dating from the ninth or eighth century BCE, a scaraboid made of gray opal, has been donated to the Israel Department of Antiquities. Though it cannot be traced directly to Jezebel, it certainly seems worthy of royalty. Its inscription is יזבל, Hebrew for Jezebel, but not the spelling איזבל preserved in the scriptures. It is possible, of course, that more than one spelling was used during her lifetime. Though no one can establish definitively that this seal belonged to Queen Jezebel (Avigad 275), it is an excellent example of the type used in the region. The point of the biblical story, however, is that Jezebel affixes *Ahab's* seal to the letters she sends in her effort to frame Naboth: "So she wrote letters in Ahab's name, and sealed them with his seal, and sent the letters unto the elders and to the nobles that were in his city, and that dwelt with Naboth" (1 Kings 21.8). It seems unlikely that Jezebel could obtain access to the king's seal without his knowledge and approval, but the Bible is silent on the degree of Ahab's complicity in the details of the plot against Naboth. Jezebel is careful not to overstep the boundaries of established royal prerogative; she seems to know her place and observes royal conventions (Trible, "Exegesis" 11). She writes, but she does so in the name of Ahab. She uses a seal, but not her own. Thus begins Jezebel's elaborate ruse against innocent Naboth, the king's seal lending symbolic authority to sanction the queen's actions. While the Deuteronomist suggests that Jezebel has no respect for Hebrew law, she seems able to comprehend and use it for her own selfish purposes.

Jezebel attaches the king's seal because she is bright enough to realize that in Israel she cannot simply move against Naboth in the high-handed, violent manner that might be acceptable in dictatorships. Even tyrants often prefer not to violate the law blatantly if it is possible to manipulate it for their own ends. For example, when foreign King Ahasuerus is angry with Queen Vashti for not appearing before him as ordered, he immediately consults the sages acquainted with the country's laws to discover how he might legally rid himself of his queen (Esther 1.10–22). Ahasuerus wishes to give a semblance of legal credibility to the punishment his humiliation and rage compel him to inflict upon Vashti. In like manner, Jezebel needs to cloak her actions in the guise of Hebraic law, making her perfidy in killing Naboth and confiscating his land appear to be morally and legally correct. Therefore, she goes to the trouble of arranging a public trial with trumped-up charges and false witnesses against her opponent. The monarch does not have absolute power of life and death over the people. Subjects can only be brought to trial and executed for cause. Otherwise, Jezebel might not bother to concoct so elaborate and risky a scheme, involving so many accomplices.

Letters were usually written by a scribe or amanuensis. Jezebel apparently dispenses with a middleman for this correspondence to avoid exposure of her plot. She prefers instead to communicate directly with the elders and nobles (or freemen). Jezebel sends the letters in Ahab's name to officials who offer no resistance in carrying out the royal wishes. They never question monarchal authority, consult the king, or protest that they cannot cooperate in the ruse. The elders are possibly family heads who form a sort of town council. Israelite nobles were usually wealthy and powerful people of high birth (Ellis 196). The idea that Jezebel knows she can rely on these men indicates the extent of the royal hold on them. Perhaps they have followed the king and queen's lead in sinister deeds on previous occasions, for Jezebel seems confident that they will not reveal the diabolical secret.

The letters outline the entire plot against Naboth. The instructions to the nobles state: "Proclaim a fast, and set Naboth at the head of the people; and set two men, base fellows, before him, and let them bear witness against him, saying: Thou didst curse God and the king. And then carry him out, and stone him, that he die" (1 Kings 21.9). The elders are to find some pretext for proclaiming a public fast. This in itself is suspicious and perhaps points to the Deuteronomist's manipulation of facts for the sake of getting the story told; one would expect that only King Ahab has the authority to declare a fast day. In Jonah, however—a book beset by textual problems concerning the chronology of events—the people of Nineveh proclaim a fast before the king does, though he later declares that no person or animal throughout the city shall taste food. In the Kings rendition, leading Jezreelites apparently also wield the same sort of power as the Ninevites. Perhaps they could declare that the entire city has erred against God and needs to do penance. A fast would be a way to atone for the sin and to prevent divine punishment of their offense. In an emotionally charged situation like this, it would not be difficult to convince the citizenry that one individual, Naboth, is the potential cause of general misfortune because of an infraction during the fast. Naboth is to be treated as the leader of the people during the fast, seated at a place of honor. Bestowing distinction upon Naboth would help to conceal that a plot is brewing against him and to ensure that later charges will carry more weight. One cannot help but admire the psychological astuteness of Jezebel's strategy. She compliments and elevates the very man who will soon be the victim of her machinations. Queen Esther's treatment of Haman is similar (Esther 7), though Jezebel's elevation of Naboth is more public. It is even possible that conferring such honor on Naboth will inflame the jealousy of the people and make them more anxious to kill him when they hear the false testimony stating that he has marred the fast's sanctity.

Two "base fellows" ("scoundrels" in the NRSV translation), whose corrupt testimony can be obtained for a bribe, are planted near Naboth. The Hebrew for "base fellows" is literally "sons of Beliyyaal," בְנֵי־בְלִיַּעַל, meaning "sons without worth." These two rogues are also suborners who will later perjure themselves in the trial by bearing false witness against the vineyard owner. The fact that there are two of them is important because in Hebraic law a single witness does not suffice. "At the mouth of two witnesses, or three witnesses, shall he that is to die be put to death; at the mouth of one witness he shall not be put to death" (Deuteronomy 17.6; also at 19.15). Jezebel's show trial is going to have no procedural flaws. Acting alone or on behalf of her husband, Jezebel cannot appear to move arbitrarily against a member of the Israelite community. Her motive is evil and her actions malfeasant, but all has the appearance of propriety. Naboth will be tried and condemned according to Israel's established customs concerning due process, but the high degree of local lawlessness and corruption is evident.

The specific charge against Naboth is that he curses God and King Ahab at the fast and within earshot of the two witnesses. This crime is a rebellion against God and a repudiation of Israelite society's organization. The Hebrew actually says that Naboth blesses (ברך) God, a euphemism typical of biblical stories. That the name of God would be profaned so outrages the Deuteronomist that he cannot even write the word *curse*. Instead, the opposite term, *bless*, is recorded in Hebrew, the author being confident that readers will understand the antonymous meaning and the true nature of the infraction. A similar circumstance exists in Psalms 10.3 and in the Book of Job. Appalled at the calamities that have befallen an innocent man, Job's wife advises her husband, "Curse God, and die" (Job 2.9). Here again the Hebrew text actually uses the verb *bless*, but it is translated as *curse* or *blaspheme* to make matters clear to modern readers.

Blasphemy is a capital offense, and the penalty against Naboth is death by stoning. "Then they carried him forth out of the city, and stoned him with stones, that he died" (1 Kings 21.13). At the conclusion of the stoning, Naboth's body will be mangled, mutilated, and bloody. Since he is innocent, all his abused limbs and body parts deserve retribution. Poetic justice demands that similar fates befall the guilty queen and king, a notion not lost on the Deuteronomic historian. Elijah will soon predict a mode of death for the monarchs, one befitting the crime they committed against the wronged Naboth.

For the present, however, Ahab is free to claim the vineyard. The text's assumption is that the property of men condemned to die escheats automatically to the crown. By walking through the property, Ahab can lay claim to it, as in Genesis 13.17. That Jezebel has knowledge of this Israelite custom explains her malicious strategy. Otherwise, she would need to deal with Naboth's survivors, who would probably possess the same attitude toward the land as their kinsman. The text of Josephus summarizes the matter:

> Thus, as a result of the queen's letter, Naboth was accused of having blasphemed both God and Achab, and was stoned to death by the people. When Jezabele heard of this, she went in to the king and bade him take possession of Naboth's vineyard without paying for it. (5: 765)

When Ahab claims the vineyard, the letter of the law has been observed but the spirit destroyed. God's purpose in giving the Torah to the people of Moses is to ensure their righteous behavior; the law is supposed to help secure a just and compassionate world. Jezebel perverts the law and makes it an instrument for fulfilling human greed. She contaminates the moral infrastructure of society.

While Jezebel's plot is clever, it is also risky. It seems implausible that she could carry out such an elaborate fraud without being discovered. Perhaps she could have achieved the same end if she had merely produced forged papers indicating that Naboth had agreed to sell his vineyard and later reneged (Andersen 53). This strategy would have had advantages. It would have been rooted in the fact, probably well known at court, that Ahab had approached Naboth with a generous offer for the land. It would also have reduced the number of accomplices. Instead of requiring all the elders and nobles to proclaim the fast and hiring the two mercenaries to perjure themselves against Naboth, a single loyal scribe could have been induced to assist the queen. Documentation showing Naboth breaking faith with the king would have been legal grounds for royal seizure of the vineyard. If Jezebel had chosen this alternative ruse, much unpleasantness might have been avoided, but the Deuteronomist has no intention of avoiding unpleasantness. The writer wishes to explain the fall of the House of Ahab by making the evil foreign queen the clear culprit. The worse Jezebel looks, the better. A prophet will be needed to pronounce against Jezebel and Ahab the judgment that the Deuteronomist knows they deserve.

God calls upon Elijah, the fire-breathing Tishbite, who now reappears on the scene after being absent since commissioning Elisha. If Jezebel's concept of kinghood were allowed to triumph, Israel would be profoundly changed for the worse. Elijah's job is to ensure that the truly guilty are punished and that Israel's role, to be a moral and spiritual light unto the nations, is reestablished. It is up to Elijah to be the conscience of Israel, the champion of social justice, and the oracle of divine retribution. God tells Elijah what to do: "Arise, go down to meet Ahab king of Israel, who dwelleth in Samaria; behold, he is in the vineyard of Naboth" (1 Kings 21.17). It is interesting to note that the word *dwelleth* is inserted into the English translation (though the Hebrew text simply states that Ahab is in Samaria בשמרון) to clear up the contradiction arising from the verse about the king being in Naboth's vineyard, which is located in Jezreel and not in Samaria.

The prophet is the mouthpiece, but the next words, a rhetorical question, come to Ahab directly from God via the venom of the Deuteronomist: "Hast thou killed, and also taken possession?" (1 Kings 21.19). After Abel's murder, God poses a similar rhetorical question to Cain, "What hast thou done?" (Genesis 4.10). The omniscient deity already knows full well that Cain has murdered his brother, and the Deuteronomist knows that Ahab's indirect action during Jezebel's plot leaves the king just as guilty as the queen. Elijah is to go into the Jezreel vineyard where he will find Ahab enjoying his new acquisition (plate 3). There the encounter will take place. In a setting appropriate to the occasion, on the property that he has stolen, Ahab will hear God's judgment. Even before Elijah speaks, his demeanor suggests he has not come in friendship, for Ahab says, "Hast thou found me, O mine enemy?" (1 Kings 21.20).

God directs Elijah's speech: "Thus saith the LORD: In the place where dogs licked the blood of Naboth shall dogs lick thy blood, even thine . . . because thou hast given thyself over to do that which is evil in the sight of the LORD" (21.19–20). Though Elijah's prophecies against Ahab will not be fulfilled until 1 Kings 22.38, at the end of the Naboth episode, the fierce prophet is reintroduced as the organ for Yahweh's condemnation. God cannot tolerate what his anointed king has allowed to happen, so now God will be the vindicator who clears the dead Naboth's name and cleanses Israel of royal guilt. The mention of blood is an indication of divine justice, for Naboth's body, cut and bloody after the stoning, is to be avenged by dogs licking the blood of Ahab. Dogs were the scavengers of eastern communities, living on scraps and refuse. God indicts Ahab for three apodictic infringements against the Ten Commandments: coveting, bearing false witness, and murdering. Divine judgment prescribes that Ahab's crime and punishment be parallel. Ahab's death will mirror Naboth's. The victim's spilled blood will be avenged by more blood gushing from the perpetrator.

The Deuteronomist's application of the Torah's talion rules becomes evident in the outcome of the Naboth episode (Carmichael 113). The lex talionis, or law of retaliation, is first given to Israel by Moses just after the Decalogue. If a fight among men causes a pregnant woman to miscarry, then her husband is to receive a financial settlement. Yet if any more harm comes from the incident, "then thou shalt give life for life, eye for eye, tooth for tooth, hand for hand, foot for foot, burning for burning, wound for wound, stripe for stripe" (Exodus 21.23–25). Similar phrasing is seen again at Leviticus 24.19–20: "And if a man maim his neighbour; as he hath done, so shall it be done to him: breach for breach, eye for eye, tooth for tooth"; and at Deuteronomy 19.21: "And thine eye shall not pity: life for life, eye for eye, tooth for tooth, hand for hand, foot for foot." Injuries to life and limb are to be met with similar punishments. Yet few biblical passages are as misunderstood as the talion laws. "Life for life" is intended as a restrictive measure that designates the only situation in which capitol punishment is appropriate. Rather than being a warrant for unbridled lack of restraint, the talion laws pose limits on the revenge that society may take against criminals. Talion laws seek to end the continuing escalation of violence.

The talion laws are also implemented with regard to the setting for Ahab's punishment. God's curse will fall upon the couple in Jezreel rather than in Samaria, the capital of Israel. Poetic justice demands that Naboth's blood be avenged in the same locale where he was unfairly convicted and murdered. Even though Samaria is the religious, commercial, and judicial center of the northern kingdom, it is not the scene of the crime against Naboth. Therefore, it cannot be the place where dogs will lick the blood shed by the guilty ones.

God's condemnation of Ahab does not end with pronouncements about his doom in blood revenge in Jezreel. The feisty prophet Elijah continues to voice God's plans for future revenge against the House of Ahab:

> Behold, I will bring evil upon thee, and will utterly sweep thee away, and will cut off from Ahab every man child, and him that is shut up and him that is left at large in Israel. And I will make thy house like the house of Jeroboam the son of Nebat, and like the house of Baasa the son of Ahijah, for the provocation wherewith thou hast provoked Me, and hast made Israel to sin. And of Jezebel also spoke the LORD, saying: The dogs shall eat Jezebel in the moat of Jezreel. Him that dieth of Ahab in the city the dogs shall eat; and him that dieth in the field shall the fowls of the air eat.
> (1 Kings 21.21–24)

These verses end the record of Ahab and Elijah's meeting. The lines repeat the earlier formulaic censure of Jeroboam at 14.1–11 and Baasa at 16.1–4, which may have been known axiomatically throughout the land by the time Elijah restates them here. Jezebel's demise is not reported until 2 Kings, and the last sentence of Elijah's prophecy of doom is actually fulfilled at 2 Kings 9.25–26. Maledictions against Jezebel stem from the Deuteronomist's objections to her vigorous influence over Ahab and to convictions that a foreign woman is a demonstrated source of skullduggery and venality for the king.

Overcome by Elijah's dire predictions, Ahab repents. The Deuteronomist allows the king to express regret and receive forgiveness. Yet no such opportunity is granted to Queen Jezebel, who is not even permitted to reply. The Bible says that Ahab wears the traditional garb of mourning, torn clothing and sackcloth. He also fasts, a custom usually marking a period of prayer and petition. The Talmud (Taanith 25b) contends that Ahab's fast begins at the ninth hour (equal to 3:00 P.M., the traditional time for a king to dine) on the day that Elijah informs Ahab of his impending doom. Furthermore, the Bible notes that Ahab "went softly" (1 Kings 21.27), as if to suggest that treading lightly would not attract God's attention and would provide the deity with time to cool off.

Despite the thundering words uttered through Elijah, God is now impressed with Ahab's piety and humility. God forgives Ahab "because he humbleth himself before Me" (21.29). Ahab's sons and not the king himself will have to pay the price for the sin against Naboth, for the Lord says: "I will not bring the evil in his days; but in his son's days will I bring the evil upon his house" (21.29). This repeats the pattern found in the stories of several other biblical reigns, including Kings Solomon and Hezekiah. In effect, with Ahab's repentance, the full weight of the punishment is postponed, transferred to succeeding generations.

The word for "repent" in Hebrew is תשובה, which also means "return." Ahab's repentance signals not only his remorse but also his return to the faith of his people. With the Naboth story, the Deuteronomist shows what is at stake if the Canaanization of Israel is allowed to continue. The first profoundly negative impact is that foreign gods will be favored over Yahweh. The episode with Elijah at Mount Carmel presents Jezebel's attempt to cause Israel to break faith with God. The Carmel contest shows that religious purity is vulnerable to outside influences, epitomized by Jezebel. The incident with Naboth is a continuation of the same theme. The vineyard tale presents the assumption that Israel's legal code, given to the people by God through Moses and essential to their identity as the Chosen People, is susceptible to damage from hostile outside forces, embodied by Jezebel. Taken together the Carmel and Naboth stories demonstrate why some biblical sources (notably in 1 Samuel) are uncomfortable with the concept of an earthly, corruptible king. A human monarch, such as Ahab, is susceptible to an evil influence, such as Jezebel. The monarch can go astray, failing to maintain faith in Israel's religious and legal establishments. Only through the intervention of an extraordinarily spirited prophet like Elijah is royal repentance likely.

The debate over whether to establish a monarchy begins in Judges when the people ask their successful hero, Gideon, to be their sovereign. In an act often interpreted as the greatest glory of Gideon's career, he refuses: "I will not rule over you, neither shall my son rule over you; the LORD shall rule over you" (Judges 8.23). Clearly, the writer is wary of anyone other than God governing the people. This theme continues into the story of Saul, Israel's first king. Some editors express disquietude about the concept of monarchy. Who besides God is good and strong enough to protect the people from their enemies and to rule according to divine law? Ahab is not the first or the last Israelite ruler to disappoint the Lord, but his story is one of the most poignant. Because of the specificity of narratives, such as Jezebel's finagling of Naboth's vineyard, the reader sees how easily a mortal sovereign can travel down the wrong path.

Years before Ahab ascends to the throne, the reign of King David marks the monarchy's zenith. It is interesting to note that David is guilty of crimes almost identical to those of Ahab and Jezebel. David covets and murders. Jehu believes Jezebel is a whore, though there is no story in the Bible that shows her infidelity.

David, on the other hand, is a proven adulterer. So great is his lust for Bathsheba that the king is willing to deceive and kill her husband, Uriah the Hittite. David's plot against Uriah in 2 Samuel is every bit as devious as Jezebel's plot to slay Naboth in 1 Kings. When Bathsheba becomes pregnant with David's child, the king calls Uriah home from war. Hoping to fool Uriah into believing that he has fathered David and Bathsheba's child, David encourages Uriah to go home and sleep with Bathsheba. Earnest Uriah, loyal to his comrades in arms, refuses the comfort of a bed and his wife while his cohorts are still on the battlefield. After David's first underhanded attempts to elicit Uriah's cooperation fail, the monarch takes more drastic steps. He orders Joab to have Uriah killed in battle, thus making David guilty of murder.

There is clearly a double standard here. David repents, is punished for his sins, and is ultimately absolved of guilt. He continues a long and successful public reign, though his personal life, as the prophet Nathan predicts, is beset with problems that are the penalty for immorality. Just as Jezebel plots to kill Naboth, so David orders the death of a loyal subject and innocent man. Both rulers covet possessions not belonging to them (a vineyard and a woman), and both scheme to dispose of their opponents (Naboth and Uriah). David is forgiven, however, keeps the lady he acquires through wrongdoing, and makes her his legal wife. Ahab and Jezebel do not have the opportunity to restore their honor, despite Ahab's repentance. What is the difference between these two similar cases? The Deuteronomist exonerates David because he remains loyal to monotheism. David may become angry at Yahweh, as when Bathsheba's first child dies, but he always believes in God and worships no other. Therefore, David does not endanger the existing patriarchal power structure buttressed by monotheism. Jezebel, on the other hand, remains a serious threat to the establishment. She is female and foreign, and she never adopts the religious and legal precepts so dear to the heart of the Deuteronomist.

Jezebel's ability to carry out her plot against Naboth suggests that she might serve as an unofficial co-regent with her husband, at least on some issues. She certainly is capable of swaying behavior at court, and she continues to do so even after her husband's death and the ascension of her sons to the throne. In the Naboth case, the Deuteronomist shows that Jezebel's leadership subverts the law. She is the source of the scheme, but it is also apparent that Ahab never truly learns how to cultivate his own garden, as Voltaire suggests people should do. Ahab acquiesces and acts like a henpecked husband.

If the Deuteronomist is recording the truth in the Naboth case, Jezebel's actions are indefensible. Her political machinations cause nothing but trouble. She flouts the law of the land, not in some sort of righteous protest because the law is immoral but because it is moral. She causes her husband to be sucked down into a bottomless morass. She deceives, connives, arranges for false evidence in court, and kills to achieve her avaricious ends. Though the story uses an omniscient observer to relate the narrative, it is impossible to know whether it departs from what actually happened. Is the Naboth incident fact, or is it slander against the queen?

If Jezebel is able to orchestrate a judicial murder while following the letter of Hebrew law, she is indeed a remarkably astute woman, well ahead of her time. She is also lucky. To involve so many elders, nobles, and perjurers and to trust them not to expose her hostile plan stretches readers' credulity. The Mount Carmel episode requires that readers believe in divine miracles, but perhaps it is easier to demand that readers have religious faith in marvels than to insist that they have confidence in the trustworthiness of men engaged in unlawful conduct. It would be easy for any one of Jezebel's accomplices to tattle to Elijah. If Jezebel is innocent, if her name is just being used by the ethnocentric and sexist Deuteronomist to teach lessons about the evil influences of foreign pagan women, then the queen is much maligned.

The hatred of the biblical chronicler is obvious, and for this reason alone Jezebel's case deserves a second hearing. The accusations made are not always convincing. Evidence against Jezebel is hearsay. Declaring her guilty is problematic, for there are places in the story where a tug on the imagination is needed to believe that the queen could successfully implement such an elaborate and diabolical conspiracy for such a paltry payoff as an herb garden. This is, nonetheless, exactly what we are supposed to believe. We are asked to forget that Ahab's secure position as king is never in doubt, that his continued authority as monarch is in no way tied to the outcome of his property dispute with Naboth. We must accept that though Jezebel has lived in Israel for many years and is smart enough to lay such complicated schemes, she does not comprehend that she and Ahab are not above the law of the land. There is clearly much venom on the lips of her accuser. The Deuteronomist shows Jezebel to be a believer in false gods in the Mount Carmel episode. Though this should be sufficient condemnation, the Naboth chapter compounds the queen's crimes. She now breaks not only God's religious laws but society's code of moral conduct as well. She is not found guilty by an earthly trial but by the heavenly decree of Yahweh. At the conclusion of the Naboth episode, Jezebel stands convicted of being a heretic and a felon, an outlaw for all time.

Plate 1. *Eve*, Lucas Cranach the
Elder, oil on panel. Charles H.
and Mary F. S. Worcester Collection, 1935.295, The Art Institute
of Chicago. Photograph © 1997,
The Art Institute of Chicago. All
Rights Reserved.

Plate 2. *Early Goddess,* from *Emblemata Nova,* by Michael Maier (1618).
By permission, Archives & Special Collections, Columbia University
Health Sciences Library, Columbia University.

Plate 3. *Jezebel and Ahab Met by Elijah,* Frederick Leighton, oil on canvas. By permission, Scarborough Borough Council: Department of Tourism and Amenities, and The Bridgeman Art Library International

Plate 4. Ivory plaque, woman at the window (restored), c. eighth century BCE, from the Nabu Temple, Khorsabad (Iraq). Courtesy of the Oriental Institute of the University of Chicago.

Plate 5. "Jezebel is killed by horses and eaten by dogs" and "Athalia is slain by horses," from the Amiens Picture Bible, Latin Ms. 108, fol 125v. By permission, Bibliothèque Municipale d'Amiens.

Plate 6. *The Death of Jezebel,* Luca Giordano, oil on canvas. By permission, Whitfield Fine Art Limited, London.

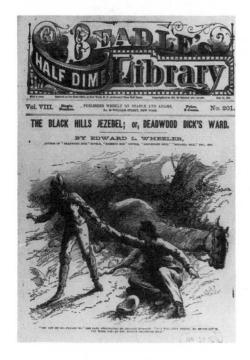

Plate 7. Cover illustration, from *Jezebel*, by Denise Robins (rev. ed.), Bath: Chivers, 1977. By permission, Chivers Press Limited.

Plate 8. Cover illustration, from *The Black Hills Jezebel; or, Deadwood Dick's Ward*, by Edward L. Wheeler, Beadle's and Adam's Half Dime Library 8:201, New York: Beadle, 1881.

Plate 9. "'Hear me!' Jezebel Cried," illustration by Corwin K. Linson, from *Jezebel: A Romance in the Days When Ahab Was King of Israel,* by Lafayette McLaws, Boston: Lothrop, 1902.

Plate 10. Bette Davis and Henry Fonda, in *Jezebel* (1938).
Warner Brothers Archive. By permission, Wisconsin Center for
Film and Theater Research, State Historical Society, University
of Wisconsin–Madison.

3

Last Gasp of the Goddess

෨෬

"Now get you to my lady's chamber,
and tell her, let her paint an inch
thick, to this favor she must come."

—William Shakespeare, *Hamlet*

AFTER THE INCIDENT OF NABOTH AND THE VINEYARD, THE HOUSE OF AHAB
begins to crumble. Every royal person connected to Ahab and Jezebel is overthrown and dies. Some are killed in battle; one dies accidentally; and others are assassinated, bringing the predictions of Elijah the prophet to fruition. The story of the fall of Jezebel and her family is told in 1 Kings 22 through 2 Kings 11. The queen survives some fifteen years after her husband's death and always seems to exert power at court; her children, both in Israel and in Judah, follow their mother's lead in religious matters. In the end, Jezebel's execution is brutal. Thrown off her balcony on the order of rebel leader Jehu, her body is left for the vultures to peck and dogs to eat. Jezebel's demise is intended to rid Israel of her impure influence. When the queen dies, the goddess she represents is supposed to die along with her in a dramatic final gasp.

Jezebel's end is embedded in stories about all the other primary and ancillary players in the saga. Twelve chapters in the Bible relate the following pared-down chronology of the demise of the dynasty. It begins when Ahab is fatally wounded by a stray arrow during battle. The prophecy of the king's death is fulfilled, and Jezebel's son Ahaziah rules in the northern kingdom of Israel. After a brief but wicked reign, Ahaziah falls from an upper window and perishes. Jezebel's second son, Jehoram (sometimes spelled Joram in the biblical text), ascends to the throne. Then her old enemy Elijah ascends into heaven on a chariot of fire. King Jehoram rules for twelve years until the 842 BCE insurrection of Jehu, who is anointed king under the auspices of Elisha while Jehoram is still on the throne. Shortly after Jehoram is killed by Jehu, the rebel also commands that palace eunuchs assassinate the queen. Next, Jezebel's friends and relatives are put to death. Ahab is said to have seventy sons in Samaria; all are eliminated at the time of the insurrection. During this purge, even Ahab's priests are executed. Jehu reigns but is not careful to obey all God's laws, so he too dies. Finally comes the story of Athaliah, Jezebel's villainous daughter. Athaliah becomes queen in the southern kingdom of Judah after her son dies by Jehu's hand. Like her mother, Athaliah causes trouble and is executed. In the end, order is restored in the land. Jehoiada the priest makes a covenant with the Lord, the new king, and the people and stipulates that they should all be people of God. The temple to Baal is destroyed in Judah, and a king loyal to Yahweh reigns at last. It takes a long time to accomplish, but the influence of Jezebel finally disappears.

Death to the King

The first royal person to die is King Ahab in the prediction and fulfillment story at 1 Kings 22, the original source of which is probably the lost "Acts of Ahab." Israel has enjoyed three years of peace stemming from the treaty ending the war with Aram at 20.34 and Ahab's generous treatment of Ben-hadad. Forming an alliance with King Jehoshaphat of Judah by marrying his daughter, Athaliah, to Jehoshaphat's son (2 Kings 8.18), Ahab marches with Jehoshaphat to Ramoth-gilead to take the town, which they believe is properly theirs. King Solomon had established administrative officials at Ramoth-gilead, according to 1 Kings 4.13. At some unknown date, the Aramians captured the Israelite city, so the two Israelite kings—Ahab and Jehoshaphat—now join forces to reclaim it.

At Jehoshaphat's request, King Ahab seeks divine sanction of the upcoming battle for Ramoth-gilead. Jehoshaphat is a more orthodox king who remembers to inquire about God's will, while Ahab has to be reminded. Ahab consults his four hundred court prophets and is repeatedly assured of victory, though this great number of holy men is likely an exaggeration intended to parallel the number of Baal's prophets in the Carmel story. The point is that, when meditating upon what will be his final military expedition, the one that will cost him his life, Ahab still acts in a way that demonstrates some belief in God. The four hundred visionaries now consulted are probably followers of Yahweh but heavily involved in court politics and tainted by the Baal cult of Jezebel. King Jehoshaphat, skeptical about propaganda flowing from the mouths of these particular men, requests that other holy viziers also be sought. Jehoshaphat is right to doubt the legitimacy of Ahab's court cronies' predictions. The four hundred turn out to be false prophets who tell Ahab what he wants to hear.

At this point in the story enters Micaiah, a true prophet. In earlier episodes with Elijah, the antipathy is between the Deuteronomist's view of the one true God (advocated by Elijah) and the Baals (advocated by Jezebel). Here the clash is between true and false prophets of Yahweh, so Jezebel is rightly dropped from the narrative. These prophets of Ahab must surely be honest men who believe they speak the Lord's words, yet they are so devoted to Ahab that they are completely confident of his victory and blind to the truth. Even Micaiah, who realizes their statements are wrong, believes that, since the men are prophets, they really are uttering ideas transmitted to them by God. The Deuteronomist explains the situation by showing that God deliberately reveals incorrect information to the court prophets. Micaiah is the only divinely inspired speaker of the truth.

Micaiah bluntly relates his vision of the Ramoth-gilead fight: "I saw all Israel scattered upon the mountains, as sheep that have no shepherd" (1 Kings 22.17). A shepherdless flock is an image well understood in the culture of these ancient people, showing them to be especially weak and vulnerable. This simile is an effective literary artifice used to suggest Israel's defeat and Ahab's demise on the battlefield. It also reveals a philosophy wherein God is responsible for all occurrences under heaven, benevolent and destructive. How does Micaiah explain the favorable proclamations of the court prophets? He attests that the Lord has placed "a lying spirit" in their mouths (22.23), another supernatural personification of the divine personality. Micaiah's prediction is a warning of total annihilation. It indicates that God is still in complete charge of events. Even the mendacity of Ahab's prophets is ordained by God. Nothing can alter the divinely prescribed outcome of the battle at Ramoth-gilead. A furious Ahab imprisons Micaiah, and the two kings proceed against their foe.

Ahab's previous military prowess is evidence of his stoutheartedness. At Ramoth-gilead, a more complex view of Ahab's valor is offered. Perhaps Micaiah's warning has frightened Ahab, for the king disguises himself and fights incognito during the Ramoth-gilead skirmish. Clothed in the paraphernalia of his office, Ahab would certainly have been an easy target. When Aramian captains see Jehoshaphat in royal robes, they mistake him for Ahab and attack, but the king of Judah cries out, perhaps proclaiming his true identity in an effort to save his own life. Meanwhile, an enemy bowman shoots a random arrow that fatally strikes Ahab in a gap between his upper and lower armor. Though the archer is not aiming at anyone in particular, the fact that he hits the king in the abdomen is intended to indicate that God has guided the arrow. Ahab's disguise and attempt to control fate cannot alter divinely prescribed destiny.

Though Ahab appears cowardly when he disguises himself in battle, he dies well. His men prop him up in his chariot until evening, preventing Israelite soldiers from realizing that the king is dying and from losing heart, as they surely would do if they were to discover that their leader has fallen. An alternative interpretation (Gray 455) is that Ahab's body must remain in ranks because it would be impossible to turn around a single chariot surrounded by many others in the pitch of battle. Thus Ahab dies, though his injury might have been successfully treated if he had been moved behind battle lines, and God's authority to determine man's fate is again asserted. During the day, Ahab's blood flows from his wound and collects on the floor of the chariot. We have a vivid picture of a seriously ailing king whose very presence still inspires his men to continue the fray. Even in his death, Ahab is responsible for the good morale of his soldiers.

When the battle is over, the host offers up הרנע, which can be properly translated as a "song," "shout," or "call for help." It is termed "a cry" in the JPS Bible and "a shout" in the NRSV. Glad that the bloody contest is concluded, the men celebrate and "cry": "Every man to his city, and every man to his country" (1 Kings 22.36). The Talmud responds to the first translation—a "song" that is sung at the end of the Ramoth-gilead conflict. Tractate Sanhedrin 39b expresses concern that there is happiness at the wicked Ahab's death:

> And there went out the song throughout the host [I Kings XXII, 36 with reference to Ahab's death at Ramoth in Gilead]: R. Ahab b. Hanian said: [It is the song referred to in the verse.] When the wicked perish there is song [thus] when Ahab b. Omri perished there was "song." But does the Holy One, blessed be He, rejoice over the downfall of the wicked? . . . The Holy One, blessed be He, does not rejoice in the downfall of the wicked.

Following the song, cry, or shout, all the men gratefully return home.

King Ahab is also taken home to Samaria, his capital, for burial. There the stains in his chariot are cleaned with water: "And they washed the chariot by the pool of Samaria; and the dogs licked up his blood; the harlots also washed themselves there; according unto the word of the LORD which He spoke" (1 Kings 22.38). The Talmud maintains, "This was in clear fulfillment of two visions, one of Micaiah, the other of Elijah" (*Talmud*, Sanhedrin, 39b). Dogs lapping up the bloody water fulfills only part of Elijah's prophecy because the retribution is set in Samaria and not in Jezreel as Elijah predicts. Sanhedrin 39b also contains the Talmud's description of the harlots that Jezebel has painted on Ahab's chariot so that he may look at them and become sexually aroused. The Talmud explains that it is those chariot drawings that are being scrubbed after Ahab's death, hence the biblical reference to harlots washing themselves. Another way to elucidate the harlots is that the word is a gloss on *dogs,* a term sometimes applied to male prostitutes (Ellis 197). Whatever the reason for the whores' presence, they are deliberately introduced to debase the king's memory. The story of Ahab concludes with the chronicler's formulaic obituary in verses 39–40. Ahab sleeps with his ancestors, and his wicked son Ahaziah ascends to the throne and rules briefly in the 850s BCE.

The End of Sons and Prophet

Denouncing Jezebel and Ahab's son Ahaziah is one of the last things that the prophet Elijah does before his own exit. Judgment on Ahaziah comes as soon as he begins his two-year reign:

> And he did that which was evil in the sight of the LORD, and walked in the way of his father, and in the way of his mother, and in the way of Jeroboam the son of Nebat, wherein he made Israel to sin. And he served Baal, and worshipped him, and provoked the LORD, the God of Israel, according to all that his father had done.
> (1 Kings 22.53–54)

There ends 1 Kings, with an introductory formula commencing the story of Ahaziah.

The tale continues in 2 Kings. Foreshadowing his mother's being thrown out of her balcony window, Ahaziah accidentally falls through the trellis of his upper room in the Samaria palace at 2 Kings 1.2. Tumbling Humpty-Dumpty style to his death is symbolically appropriate, for Ahaziah indeed has a great fall. His descent is quite rapid. A tragic hero traditionally falls from a high position, and Ahaziah's death makes the metaphor literal.

Ahaziah's death is also significant because it stands as a foil to the story about the widow of Zarephath and her son (Smelik 241). Elijah resurrects the poor, anonymous woman's son in the roof chamber of her home, her strong belief in God being a critical element in saving the boy's life. Like the woman in 1 Kings 17.8–24, Jezebel is also a widow of Sidon when her son becomes ill. In the story of Ahaziah, Elijah comes again to the scene, but not to help the young man. Instead, Elijah ominously predicts that, because of the king's faithlessness, Ahaziah will not recover from his wounds. The contrasts in the stories make it clear that the two Sidonian widows have diametrically opposite convictions concerning Yahweh. Allegiance to Elijah and his God saves the Zarephath woman's child in his upper room, while worship of Baal causes dowager queen Jezebel's son to die from injuries sustained in his fall from the window. The mother of the Zarephath boy places her trust in God's prophet; the mother of the Israelite king wants to murder prophets of the Lord.

After he takes his tumble but before his death, the young King Ahaziah sends messengers to call upon Baal-zebub, lord of the flies. Baal-zebub was Baal's oracle at the northern city of Ekron, the Philistine settlement closest to Samaria. Flies were considered a pestilence in Israel because they spread epidemics, and this Ekron deity was often associated with Greece's Zeus Apomuios (Zeus, the averter of flies) who possessed the ability to eliminate the pests. Ahaziah asks the pagan Baal-zebub for predictions about whether the injuries are fatal.

An angel of God knows of Ahaziah's sinful plan to consult a false prophet. The angel tells Elijah the Tishbite to intercept the king's emissaries and say, "Is it because there is no God in Israel, that ye go to inquire of Baal-zebub the god of Ekron?" (2 Kings 1.3). Elijah declares that Ahaziah will surely die, never rising again from his sickbed. Consequently, Ahaziah deploys "a captain of fifty with his fifty" (1.9), probably to capture or kill the monarchy's old enemy Elijah. In a replay of the Carmel miracle, a fire swoops down from heaven and annihilates Ahaziah's blameless emissaries. The chapter concludes with the death of Jezebel's first son, according to Elijah's word.

The next time the prophet appears, it is for his own final scene. Jezebel is not mentioned in this episode, but it is clear that Elijah's earthly end is the opposite of the queen's own and her elder son's literal falls from grace. A beautiful folktale illustrates the end of God's zealot, Elijah. In a whirlwind, he flies up to heaven on "a chariot of fire, and horses of fire" (2.11), without actually dying first. God is described as a whirlwind in the Book of Job, and the only person in Jewish tradition other than Elijah who departs for heaven without having to die is Enoch in Genesis 5.24. The reader seeking a rational explanation for Elijah's spectacular ascendancy may think of the whirlwind as a huge dust devil, the type adjoining a sirocco. Fire could also be associated with a sirocco's heat, and the visible upward spiral of a desert dust storm may be analogous to galloping horses pulling a chariot (Gray 475). With this sensational image, the author artfully manufactures a legendary, supernatural conclusion to Elijah's mission on earth. The manner of Elijah's passing, his being magically transported into the realm of God, befits this prophet, a figure always described in mythical and historical proportions. Elijah is himself something of a whirlwind; his prophecy is searing fire. Throughout his life, strong gusts and scorching fire seem to travel alongside him. They typify his temperament, even during his theophany at Horeb. Ironically, there is one strange similarity common to the passing of Jezebel and that of Elijah: neither person has a burial plot. Both simply disappear from the earth—Jezebel ignobly, Elijah resplendently. The symbolism of their ends demonstrates the heights that the writer's poetic imagination may scale—the terrestrial and the celestial.

The glory of Elijah's passing is not tainted by mention of the queen who has hounded Yahweh's prophets and sought their deaths for many years in Israel. At the beginning of 2 Kings 3, however, Jezebel is referred to once again. Her second son, Jehoram, is now king, and the chronicler is displeased with Jehoram's performance. Amazingly, Jezebel is not held directly responsible for this son's sinfulness:

> And [Jehoram] did that which was evil in the sight of the LORD; but not like his father, and like his mother; for he put away the pillar of Baal that his father made. Nevertheless he cleaved unto the sins of Jeroboam the son of Nebat, wherewith he made Israel to sin. (3.2–3)

We are explicitly told that Jehoram's apostasy is different from his parents', for he actively opposes Baal worship. Jezebel's first son, Ahaziah, dies a mere two years after becoming king, but her second son, Jehoram, rules for twelve years. Jehoram is inept in his own way, however: he does not win the battle for Moab and is wounded in the fray. In 2 Kings 9, he returns to Jezreel to recuperate and confront Jezebel, who is still an imposing presence though reduced to the status of queen mother.

Jehoram and Jezebel now face two worthy adversaries in Elisha and Jehu, and the conflict between regent and religious zealot continues. With Elijah's exit, Elisha assumes the role of chief prophet in the land. Several miracle stories relating Elisha's special power and relationship to God prepare the reader for this younger prophet's prominent role in the fall of the House of Ahab. But Elisha only indirectly foments Jehu's revolt against the monarchy. Fulfilling the last of the Mount Horeb dictates to Elijah, Elisha now assigns an associate to anoint Jehu, instead of Jehoram, as sovereign. Jehu is the tenth king of Israel and begins a dynasty lasting more than one hundred years. It does seem highly unusual that Elisha himself does not personally oversee this momentous occasion, yet Jehu is the only king of the northern kingdom to be officially anointed. In fact, stories of his consecration are told twice, perhaps resulting from different sources. After Jehu becomes king, no prophet is mentioned again in connection with his rebellion, perhaps because the redactor is dismayed at the way Jehu's reign ends in sinfulness (2 Kings 10.31). Despite his shortcomings, Jehu (יהוא) can be roughly translated as "Yahweh is God," implying a salient contrast between this newly anointed king and Jezebel's reigning son. Jehu's investiture takes place in an "inner chamber" (9.2) to build suspense and to ensure secrecy concerning the exact auspicious moment when Jehu will begin his dramatic coup d'état, lest soldiers loyal to Jehoram have time to prepare a defense against the onslaught.

Jehu's anointing ceremony is set at Ramoth-gilead, where he is encamped and fighting the Aramians. King Ahab perished and Jehoram is later wounded at Ramoth-gilead, underscoring the irony of the location for God's newly chosen leader to begin his uprising against Jezebel's monarchy. Elisha's assistant now voices God's decree to Jehu:

> And thou shalt smite the house of Ahab thy master, that I may avenge the blood of My servants the prophets, and the blood of all the servants of the LORD, at the hand of Jezebel. For the whole house of Ahab shall perish; and I will cut off from Ahab every man-child, and him that is shut up and him that is left at large in Israel. (9.7–8)

God remembers that Obadiah was able to save only one hundred prophets when Jezebel determined to murder them, and now the deity will take revenge. After more general maledictions, the manner of the queen's death, originally foretold by Elijah, is cited again by this new prophet: "And the dogs shall eat Jezebel in the portion of Jezreel, and there shall be none to bury her" (9.10). Jehu's garrison is apparently concerned about the erratic behavior of the young prophet, who is viewed by one loyal soldier as "this mad fellow" (9.11). When Jehu's rebels hear the news of his anointing, they hastily improvise a throne, blow the ceremonial horn, and hail him as king. The revolution begins.

The drama of the situation escalates as the tale of Jehu's revolt unfolds in a three-tier structure. He swears his resurgents to secrecy so that news of the impending insurrection will not reach Jezreel before Jehu can ride there in his chariot. The Deuteronomist reports that, in his haste to start the uprising, Jehu drives בשגעון, which literally means "in madness" (as in the well-known Yiddish word *meshugge*) and is translated as "furiously" in the JPS Bible and as "like a maniac" in the NRSV. It is the same root used to describe the young prophet, the "mad fellow" at verse 11. In the town are the two reigning kings of Israel and Judah, Jehoram and Ahaziah (Jezebel's son and grandson), plus the dowager queen herself. Twice sentinels in Jezreel see Jehu approaching. Jehoram sends out messengers to inquire about Jehu's intentions. Both times the palace men ask, "Is it peace?" (2 Kings 9.17–19), and Jehu rhetorically replies, "What have you to do with peace?" (9.18–19). The question that King Jehoram has his couriers ask indicates that until the last moment he is seeking intelligence about the battle ensuing at Ramoth-gilead, unaware that treason is brewing much closer to home.

Instead of dispatching messengers again, Jehoram and Ahaziah themselves ride out to meet Jehu when the scenario is laid out a third time. The pace of the narrative is as rapid as Jehu's horses. The three leaders' chariots converge at the plot of land where Naboth's vineyard had been, and Jehoram apprehensively poses the critical question, "Is it peace, Jehu?" (9.22). The author's urgent tone is reflected in Jehu's response, which is one of the most serious condemnations of Jezebel yet uttered in the Bible. It goes beyond any of the direct accusations heretofore leveled against the queen. Until this moment, Jehoram and Ahaziah anticipate that

Jehu has important news from the front, but they never suspect that he intends any military hostility against them. There is no room for doubt when Jehu now replies, "What peace, so long as the harlotries of thy mother Jezebel and her witchcrafts are so many?" (9.22). The Deuteronomist has previously blamed Jezebel for being an idol worshiper and murderer, but now she is also deemed a whore and a witch.

Jehoram tries to flee instead of standing his ground and fighting for his own and his mother's honor. Jehu shoots an arrow that hits Jehoram between the shoulders, and the king of Israel dies. Remembering Elijah's oracle about Ahab's children paying for their father's sinfulness, Jehu orders his aide, Bidkar, to dump Jehoram's body on Naboth's property—a prime example of poetic justice. Ahaziah also tries to escape but is fatally shot by Jehu's arrow and taken to Jerusalem for burial. Following the ignominious deaths of the two kings, Jehu's rampage continues as he rides into Jezreel for the denouement, the execution of Queen Jezebel.

The Painted Queen

One of the most significant things about the life of Jezebel is the way she faces her death. Her bravery during her last moments on earth eclipses all else. The text says that she learns about the approach of Jehu and prepares to meet him: "And when Jehu was come to Jezreel, Jezebel heard of it; and she painted her eyes, and attired her head, and looked out at the window" (2 Kings 9.30). These three elements—applying makeup to the eyes, fixing the hair, and peering out of the window—are all fascinating details that reveal the queen's character. Since Jezebel has been informed that Jehu is on his way, she probably also knows that Jehoram and Ahaziah are dead. If she realizes that Jehu is already a double regicide, surely she comprehends that he will not hesitate to kill her too. Yet in the last moments of her life, she does not panic or attempt to flee. Instead, she calmly adorns herself and confronts her foe. She wears a kind of mask, almost war paint, as she takes control of her emotions and faces her final battle. As the Apocrypha's Judith prepares to meet her foe, Holofernes, she adorns her body in a style similar to Jezebel's. Judith dresses in festive clothes, combs her hair, and dons a tiara "to entice the eyes of all the men who might see her" (Judith 10.4). Yet Judith's primping is praised as a clever strategy to defeat an enemy of God. The Latin version of the tale even asserts that Judith is endowed with supernatural beauty because her motive is pure. Jezebel, on the other hand, is condemned for similar behavior because her motive is judged to be evil.

The first phase of Jezebel's primping involves eye makeup and has been responsible for the queen's being labeled a "painted hussy" down through the ages. The Hebrew says that she בפוך עיניה, literally "put [or treated] her eyes with antimony."

Stibium, or antimony, is a black powder used by Near Eastern women to darken the eyebrows and the area above and below the eyelids. Outlining the eyes makes them appear larger and more lustrous. In modern times, a lovely group of insects containing luminescent "eyes" in the center of their wings has been named the Jezebel butterfly in honor of the queen. Through the ages, Jezebel's body decoration has been partly responsible for her sinister image as a trollop.

Ancient Egyptians probably began the custom of marking around the eyes with dark paint to enhance womanly pulchritude, as illustrated by Cleopatra (who lived after Jezebel, 69–30 BCE), by Nefertiti (wife of Akhenaton, who ruled from 1379 to 1362 BCE), and even by Nefertiti's son-in-law King Tutankhamen (who ruled from 1361 to 1352 BCE). Furthermore, Leonidas and his Spartan soldiers at Thermopylae followed the ritual of beautifying their bodies before battle. Hardly effeminate, the men thought they might die in the fray and wanted to look their best. Then when they began their next life, they would possess handsome bodies (*Interpreter's Bible* 3: 236). The practice of applying cosmetics, including eye shadow and eyeliner, is still widespread today. Many women would not leave home without "fixing their faces," and books containing the beauty secrets of celebrities are often bestsellers. Raquel Welch, Victoria Principal, Jane Fonda, and others with credentials far more humble than a Phoenician-born queen's eagerly share their techniques for increasing sex appeal. Yet there is clearly a double standard where condemnation of Jezebel's makeup is concerned.

The Bible is characteristically silent concerning Jezebel's motivation for darkly shading her eyes. Since antimony makes the eyes more brilliant and sensuous, one possible reason for applying the cosmetic is to seduce a man. Today many women, of course, wear makeup when they are engaged in everyday activities and not at all interested in attracting the opposite sex. In literature of the ancient Near East, however, Jezebel's action is consistent with women who are preparing themselves for lovemaking (Parker 68). Jezebel's purpose is, according to this interpretation, to seduce Jehu, evidence of a foolish grandmother's vanity and arrogance. Jezebel is probably fifty years old when she is assassinated, certainly well past her nubile prime. Some insist that Jezebel believes she can save her own life by joining Jehu's harem as he becomes Israel's new king.

The Deuteronomist intends that negative connotations be implied by Jezebel's actions, for other biblical passages give unfavorable reports on the custom of applying eye paint or batting the eyes flirtatiously. As early as the story of Joseph in Egypt, Potiphar's wife expresses her wanton sexual desire through her eyes: "And it came to pass after these things, that [Joseph's] master's wife cast her eyes upon Joseph; and she said: 'Lie with me'" (Genesis 39.7). Isaiah shows a relationship between women's lust and lifting their eyes to behold the object of their sexual appetite. God will smite the daughters of Jerusalem who "walk with stretched-forth necks and wanton eyes" (Isaiah 3.16). The futility of attempting to cover up evil with surface adornments is found in one verse that even seems to parallel Jezebel's end. Jeremiah 4.30 contains a harsh reproof of a reviled strumpet and compares rejecting her to the way Jerusalem will be rebuffed if the people do not repent:

> And thou, that art spoiled, what doest thou,
> That thou clothest thyself with scarlet,
> That thou deckest thee with ornaments of gold,
> That thou enlargest thine eyes with paint?
> In vain dost thou make thyself fair;
> Thy lovers despise thee, they seek thy life.

The prophet Ezekiel is equally appalled at how the citizens of Jerusalem and Samaria are seduced into pagan worship practices. He chastises God's people for lusting after false gods, "for whom thou didst wash thyself, paint thine eyes, and deck thyself with ornaments" (Ezekiel 23.40). Finally, the writer of Proverbs 6.24–26 has advice for young men who may otherwise succumb to womanly wiles, especially the wiles of foreigners, such as Jezebel:

> To keep thee from the evil woman,
> From the smoothness of the alien
> tongue.
> Lust not after her beauty in thy
> heart;
> Neither let her captivate thee with
> her eyelids.

In all three of these biblical passages, the eyes are connected to seduction, and wearing makeup is often shown as a precursor to pagan worship.

After all the books of the Bible are canonized, writers of sacred literature continue to show a connection between a woman's unlawful fornication and her eyes. For example, in the Apocrypha's Ecclesiasticus, Jesus Ben Sira writes that an adulterous wife reveals herself through her eyes. The way a woman holds and decorates her eyes is implied in Ben Sira's distich to be the primary tool of seduction: "The haughty stare betrays an unchaste wife; her eyelids give her away" (Ecclesiasticus 26.9). The next verses reveal distrust for a headstrong daughter whose eyes reveal her lack of scruples: "Be on guard against her impudent eye, and do not be surprised if she sins against you" (Ecclesiasticus 26.10–11). Thus in biblical and postbiblical literature, male writers use a woman's eyes against her. The eyes are portrayed as the primary tool for a wayward woman, such as Jezebel, to reveal her sinful nature.

Jezebel's second action is to brush her hair, literally "make good or beautiful her head," ותיטב את־ראשה. It is difficult to find evidence of the coiffure as an instrument of seduction in ancient literature of the Mediterranean region (Parker 68), yet this form of primping is always a part of the masculine and feminine toilette. Good grooming naturally includes attempts to arrange the hair in a flattering style, regardless of whether seduction is on a person's mind. In the Spartans' beauty preparations prior to battle, they also combed their hair. Jezebel's carefully fixing her hair and eyes before appearing at her window to receive Jehu has led some to believe that her purpose is to entice him sexually.

Though Jezebel is probably cognizant of the deaths of the kings of Israel and Judah, the traditional interpretation of the story asks us to believe that she rapidly calculates how best to save her own skin. Jezebel, so loyal to her husband that she had been willing to murder Naboth in order to make Ahab stop pouting and fulfill his slightest whim, is now immediately able to do a fidelity flip-flop. Without further thought concerning her dead family members, she hopes to ingratiate herself to the usurper of her heritage. If Jehu is the man of the day, she will be his woman. Showing no apparent compunction, she instantly switches her allegiance to the murderer of her son and grandson. Thus Jezebel meets Jehu as she does Naboth, an underhanded and resourceful manipulator, still the mastermind of court intrigue.

It is true that Jezebel is a calm and fast thinker, for sitting down to complete her toilette indicates that she quickly forms a decision about how to behave as Jehu's chariot of death charges into Jezreel. Yet this sexist interpretation of her applying makeup in an attempt to seduce Jehu vilifies the queen to the point that she is even incapable of feeling human love for her immediate family. It further suggests that women can only obtain power through feminine, sexual tricks, that Jezebel is happy to use her aging body to curry favor with the new king, and that she believes she has the opportunity to lure him into her bed. If she can become part of his harem, she can save her own life. Her subsequent death is then merely an abrupt frustration of her latest political ruse.

It is conceivable, though unlikely, that Jezebel could persuade Jehu to allow her to be a concubine or wife. If the queen were to wed him, Jehu's political claim to the throne might, perhaps, be greater. In several cases in 1 and 2 Samuel, for example, having the king's woman is tantamount to possessing the king's royal authority. In such stories, the women are not dealt with as individuals. The writer is interested in women mainly as symbols of masculine dominance. In the Jezebel narrative, Jehu chooses to assert dominance by killing the painted queen not by marrying her.

A more reasonable interpretation of Jezebel's primping is that she holds no illusions about her fate. She knows the grave nature of the forthcoming encounter with Jehu and desires to go out boldly, like the regent she is. In Shakespeare's *Antony and Cleopatra*, the Egyptian queen prepares for death in a similar manner. Cleopatra longs to follow her lover Antony into the grave. She is suspicious of Caesar's sweet promises to take her to Rome, her distrust of Caesar mirroring Jezebel's wariness of the approaching Jehu. Just before committing suicide, Cleopatra bids her attendants to dress her in the royal robes she wore when she first met Antony: "Show me, my women, like a queen: go fetch / My best attires. . . . Bring our crown and all" (5.2).

Jezebel dresses royally not in any hope of beguiling her would-be assassin but because she is proud and wishes to die with dignity. She is not attempting to stay alive by becoming Jehu's new lover, a futile plan given the political realities in Israel at the time. As long as the queen lives, she is a threat to the new dynasty that Jehu is establishing. He is unlikely to be attracted to her under these circumstances; but whether he is or not, the political benefit of her death far outweighs the advantage of keeping her alive. Jezebel, as long as she is alive, is definitely a person around whom loyalists to the House of Ahab could rally. After spending her entire life in palaces, Jezebel must understand this concept.

It is also implausible that the queen is seeking mercy from the rebel claimant to her husband and sons' throne. All that Jezebel has left in life now is the way she faces her death, and she is determined to exit with courage and grace, looking her queenly best. Her conduct is heroic. Cool and composed, Jezebel adorns her face and arranges her hair before she proceeds to the upper window to meet certain death.

Jezebel at the Window

Appearing at the balcony window is the third part of Jezebel's preparation to meet her attacker. The Bible does not specify whether Jezebel looks through a lattice-covered opening or through a wide-open space. Given the privacy observed by harem women in keeping themselves away from the peering eyes of men not their husbands, it may be that Jehu has never before seen the queen's face (Gray 550). Now her behavior indicates that she indeed wishes him to see her. In Egypt a royal audience was often granted while the monarch posed on an upper-chamber parapet, and Jezebel's posture there on the height may signal no more than that. While Jezebel's appearance at the window seems like an innocuous gesture, the perch-like setting implies volumes about the queen's nature. Jezebel is in control here, taking time to prink and to choose the location where Jehu will first view her. From her second-story vantage point, she is literally and figuratively gazing down imperiously upon a hostile visitor.

The Deuteronomist may have another image in mind, however, one that is far less flattering to the queen. The wording of Jezebel's death in 2 Kings 9 shares many commonalities with the conclusion of the Song of Deborah, when Israel's enemy Sisera dies. His mother, at home by her window, has not yet heard the news of her son's death. The poem concludes with a stern warning not just to this mother at her window but also to anyone who stands between Israel and its God:

> Through the window she looked forth, and peered,
> The mother of Sisera, through the lattice:
> "Why is his chariot so long in coming?
> Why tarry the wheels of his chariots?"
> . . . .
> So perish all Thine enemies, O Lord;
> But they that love Him be as the sun when he goeth forth in his might.
> (Judges 5.28, 31)

Each woman, Sisera's mother and Jezebel, is a Baal worshiper who receives news concerning the death of her son. Like Sisera, Jehu also is a chariot driver. The moral tag at Judges 5.31 definitely prefigures the sentiments of the Deuteronomist concerning the fate that all idol worshipers deserve. The sentiment could just as easily be applied to Jezebel.

Jezebel at her window also provides an allusion to an architectural design motif that may well be familiar to the Deuteronomist and that is associated with alien goddess worship. In the Bronze Age, an image of a woman at a window was carved on ivory plaques (unearthed recently in several cities, including Samaria, Nimrud, Arslan-Tash, and Khorsabad). Carved between the ninth and seventh centuries BCE, the ivories are fine examples of Phoenician craftsmanship and show a smiling woman behind a recessed casement frame (plate 4). Elaborate columns intimate that the lady is poised behind a balcony balustrade, and her elaborately arranged hair and jeweled headdress hint at the goddess Astarte. It is possible that these ivory carvings were once housed in Phoenician temples (Robertson 316). Jezebel's being thrown out of the window thus symbolizes the vanquishing of the goddess that the painted queen represents to the Deuteronomist.

Jezebel at the window conjures up images of the marzeah (מרזח), which was a social and religious institution for property-owning families who worshiped specific pagan deities. The people met regularly, perhaps monthly, to revel for days at a time with abundant food and drink. The celebrations included sacral sexual orgies as part of the ritual (Beach 94). The region's excavated ivories are icons of the marzeah and help explain biblical references to it. The prophet Amos's oracle to the northern kingdom blasts the opulent self-indulgence of those "That lie upon beds of ivory, / And stretch themselves upon their couches" (Amos 6.4). Pieces of ivory furniture used as festal couches during the marzeah have been discovered. Motifs carved into the ivories were often significant religious symbols and included the picture of the woman at the window. The Phoenicians who produced the ivories probably intended that they be used in ceremonies marking life-and-death moments of the royal family. The special coronation moment, when royal power was transmitted from one generation to another, or the sad moment of a monarch's funeral may have been fitting occasions for bringing out the marzeah couches with their ivory inlays. The reader cannot help but recall the reference to the ivory house that Ahab builds at 1 Kings 22.39, proof of his wealth and power and perhaps suggestive of his worship practices, unacceptable to the Deuteronomist. Later in Amos, those who are secure in such luxury will be the first ones God sends into exile. When Jezebel appears at the window and is thrown down, it is as if the goddess of pagan festivals is being presented and rejected by the Jews (Ackroyd 258). The Kings writer discredits Jezebel, the goddess, and the idol worship they represent. Jehu's last obstacle to the crown is now eliminated.

The lady at the window also appears in nonbiblical literature of Canaan. For instance, in Canaanite mythology, the god Mot (death) enters Baal's palace through a window that the god has been encouraged not to build (Christensen 402). In a tale told by Ovid, a queen who is handsome, vain, and cruel glares down from her palace window at an approaching funeral procession meandering through the streets of Salamis (Robertson 317). This certainly echoes the vision of Jezebel at the window and mocks her lack of a proper funeral. At the opposite end of the ritual spectrum, the scene at the window calls to mind a royal bride's ritual preparation for her wedding. The female goddess appears at the window just before the lady's union with the king (Parker 70). If Jezebel does, in fact, hope to be joined to Jehu in marriage, this is the way she should first be seen by her husband-to-be.

When Jezebel looks out her balcony window, hair and eyes freshly made up for the occasion, she hurls an astonishing sentence to Jehu, waiting below. In Hebrew it is השלום זמרי הרג אדניו, the translation of which is debated. The version most often cited is found in the JPS Bible: "Is it peace, thou Zimri, thy master's murderer?" (2 Kings 9.31). The word שלום can mean "hello," "goodbye," and "peace," but it can also denote general well-being. The less frequently used alternative translation, "Is all well, Zimri . . . ," is accurate though less acceptable.

If this second version is employed, "Is all well . . . ," a politically unaware Jezebel may not be so much concerned with the dire peace or war situation as with whether Jehu's day is shaping up normally or irregularly. On the other hand, she may realize that she is in great danger and apprehensively articulates her frantic hope that all will turn out well. It seems unlikely that Jezebel would suddenly become so lacking in astuteness, but the translation of השלום as "Is all well?" does have several precedents in the Bible. Earlier in the story, for example, when Jehoram dispatches his men to investigate the progress of the battle at Ramoth-gilead, they inquire in some translations, "Is all well?" This Hebrew is the same as that now translated as "Is it peace" as Jehu's charging chariot screeches to a halt beneath Jezebel's palace window. Furthermore, in 2 Samuel 18.32, King David asks if his son Absalom is still alive following the young man's failed attempt to usurp his father's throne. David has ordered that no harm come to his rebel heir and inquires, "Is it well with the young man Absalom?" Again, השלום is used. Later in 2 Samuel, the treacherous Joab ironically asks Amasa, "Is it well with you, my brother?" (20.9). The Hebrew השלום is used to convey the thought, and Amasa, captain of the resurgent forces under Absalom, now forfeits his life. Joab stabs Amasa in the belly to repay the treason against King David and to show that all is not well for traitors.

Moving to Jezebel's death scene, if the popular JPS translation of השלום ("Is it peace . . .") is accepted as accurate, then the queen's words are laced with bitter irony. She snidely taunts Jehu and harbors no illusions that he hastens to the Jezreel palace in peace. Jezebel boldly faces certain death when she appears at the window and peers at the young upstart waiting below. When all the power is in his hands, she mocks the rebel claimant to her dead husband's throne. Jehu comes as an assassin, and she contemptuously reproaches him.

The queen's jeering welcome to Jehu is further evidenced by her allusion to Zimri, another throne usurper mentioned in 1 Kings 16.15–20. Zimri killed Elah and others in the House of Baasa, just as Jehu now destroys Jehoram and members of the royal family, but Zimri ruled a mere seven days. Jezebel's father-in-law, Omri, quickly overthrew Zimri, who was not able to muster the support of God or the people of Israel. Zimri apparently never obtained the full support of Israel's military, as he would need and expect to do if his rebellion were to succeed. Historically, Zimri was also a chariot commander, so the comparison to Jehu is quite effective. For Jezebel to see the parallel and compare Jehu to Zimri is thus to ridicule Jehu and to warn him indirectly that his reign will last no longer than a week. Zimri's coup was unsuccessful, the symbolic number of seven days not necessarily meant to be taken literally but clearly showing an ephemeral reign and a divine displeasure with the ruler. The Bible indicates that Zimri is evil, as wicked as Jeroboam, who causes Israel to sin.

Jezebel's greeting at the window implies that she comprehends Jehu's violent intentions and has no hope of receiving mercy from him. She believes that the inevitable result of Jehu's treason against the House of Ahab will be that he will lose power as quickly as Zimri had. If Jehu lacks confidence in any way, the insult that Jezebel hurls out of the window will cause the new leader momentary doubt. She sees Jehu as an illegitimate usurper who will perish soon after seizing the crown, just as Zimri lost control and committed suicide at Tirzah approximately forty-five years earlier. Her words "Is it peace, thou Zimri, thy master's murderer?" thus evoke in the reader the same admiration for her that one feels for John Webster's defiant heroine when she declares, "I am Duchess of Malfi still!" (4.2). In the face of dire tribulation, when death is a foregone conclusion, Jezebel is still queen of Israel. She has the wherewithal to remain composed. Her remark to Jehu is a sarcastic and imperious invective. Despite her obvious faults, one cannot help but admire Jezebel's sangfroid at the end of her life. She remains proud and determined to cut an imposing figure as she leans out of her second-story window, literally and figuratively above her attacker.

Evidence of the interpretation that Jezebel's window "welcome" to Jehu is a marriage proposal and not an open taunt is based on an alternative translation of the passage "Is it peace, thou Zimri, thy master's murderer?" The name *Zimri* may be a variant of an archaic word derived from the root זמר (zmr) and appearing in ancient Ugaritic, Amorite, and Hebrew personal names. It is also theorized that the same root has its etymology in an antiquated noun meaning "strength" or "protection" (Parker 72). Far from being a malediction, Jezebel's sentence to Jehu is thus a flattering expression of her admiration for his greatness. He has proven himself in battle as being a better man than either Jehoram or Ahaziah, so pragmatic Jezebel wishes to unite with him and share his glory. The queen's words to Jehu could thus be translated as "Is all well, strong one, who has killed his master?"

An alternative interpretation is that the root for Zimri is used epigraphically in Leviticus 25.3–4 and in Isaiah 5.6 as a verbal reflex meaning "to prune a vineyard" (Olyan 206). Jehu is, according to this view, metaphorically pruning God's vineyard or taking care of God's business by righting the wrong committed in the Naboth incident. Readers would no doubt recall Jezebel's deliberate miscarriage of justice in the episode in which Naboth refuses to sell or trade his vineyard to the royal couple. Now Jehu is the pruner, the one who cuts down the rotten branches of the House of Ahab. He removes the ill effects of the legal shenanigans perpetrated by the queen and restores order in the garden. It is a powerful image.

Jezebel at her window provides a logical, ritualistic way for the redactor of Kings to conclude her story, for he blames her more than anyone else for idol worship in Israel. Though the writer has access to historically accurate stories about the reign of King Ahab, the episode of Jezebel's last-minute primping before appearing at the window has the earmarks of fictional invention for dramatic effect (Robertson 318). It evokes the motif of a funeral procession of a rejected lover, the mourners moving through the streets and causing the lady to look down from her balcony. The Deuteronomist hopes to recapture that motif of the rejected lover and apply it to Jezebel's death and the end of goddess influence in Israel.

Jehu looks up at Jezebel's window and cries, "'Who is on my side? who?' And there looked out to him two or three officers. And he said: 'Throw her down'" (2 Kings 9.32). Although the JPS translation indicates that the people in Jezebel's rooftop room who declare themselves to be aligned with Jehu are "officers," the Hebrew word is סריסים, which clearly means eunuchs. The NRSV corrects this translation error. It is somehow ironic and satisfying that those who betray so interesting a queen are themselves something less than the most robust examples of manhood. Gory details follow concerning the manner of Jezebel's death and are intended by the Deuteronomist to be an example of poetic justice. According to the redactor, Jezebel gets what she deserves, and Elijah's prophecy is fulfilled.

When the eunuchs toss Jezebel out of her upper-floor window, "some of her blood was sprinkled on the wall, and on the horses; and she was trodden under foot" (9.33). The blood of Naboth, visible after his stoning, is now repaid with the blood of the one who is responsible for the innocent man's death. During biblical times, ritual sacrifices performed at centers of Jewish worship included the blood of animals sanctified and offered to God. Blood courses through our veins and keeps us alive, therefore becoming a symbol of life. Ironically, since blood is shed in battle, it can also be a symbol of death. In Jezebel's murder, a sort of counter-sacrifice, an unholy offering, is implied by the Deuteronomist as her blood streaks down the palace facade and retaliation for Naboth's murder is achieved. To add to the insult of regicide, Jehu deliberately leaves Jezebel's body unburied on the street where she lands. He goes in to eat and drink, to rest and regain strength from the day's work, and to celebrate his victory.

After Jehu refreshes himself, he orders Jezebel's burial: "Look now after this cursed woman, and bury her; for she is a king's daughter" (9.34). The queen has indeed received a kind of curse; she has lost God's blessing because of her actions against monotheism. Why does Jehu relent and attempt to have Jezebel buried? Perhaps it is because he is now royalty himself and feels a personal interest in how the bodies of dead monarchs are handled, so he decides to treat her remains with respect. It may also be that he realizes she has faced her end with dignity and wishes to pay homage to her courage. Perhaps now that he has won, he realizes that he can afford to be decent and that he may gain the love of the people by being magnanimous. Yet his gesture comes too late. Jezebel's body has already been trampled by horses and eaten by animals, and Jehu's officers "found no more of her than the skull, and the feet, and the palms of her hands" (9.35).

Jezebel's death scene is an excellent example of the Bible's application of talion laws. When Jehu rides into Jezreel to kill the queen, a great deal of attention is paid to her body parts. When interment is finally ordered, nothing but a few odd bones—skull, feet, palms—can be located. Dogs eat her body. It is possible that, in preparing to meet Jehu at the window, the queen had just rubbed her face, feet, and hands with henna, a reddish dye often used in cosmetics of the day. The natural scent of henna serves as an animal repellent (Loewenthal 21) and could explain why those particular body parts are not consumed by dogs. Furthermore, the Talmud suggests that the one good thing Jezebel did during her reign was to use her hands and feet while fulfilling the commandment of dancing with a gladdened heart before a bride. Ergo, God did not allow those body parts to be devoured by dogs. Traditionally, the fate of the queen's mutilated remains is inexorably linked to Naboth's mangled corpse. The talion law demanding life for life has literally been fulfilled. Today more people remember Jezebel's name than Naboth's and Jehu's, despite the fact that Jehu speaks the intended moral of the story:

> This is the word of the Lord, which He spoke by His servant Elijah the Tishbite, saying: In the portion of Jezreel shall the dogs eat the flesh of Jezebel; and the carcass of Jezebel shall be as dung upon the face of the field in the portion of Jezreel; so that they shall not say: This is Jezebel. (2 Kings 9.36–37)

Actually, 1 Kings 21.23 predicts that the dogs will consume Jezebel's body בחל, in the "moat of Jezreel" (JPS translation) and "within the bounds" of Jezreel (NRSV translation). Moving to the 2 Kings description of where the event actually occurs, the Hebrew word is spelled one consonant differently, בחלק, which means "plot of ground." In other words, the two texts indicate a slight difference of opinion about where the retribution against Jezebel occurs. Since it is important that Elijah's prophecy be carried out exactly, this small point matters. It is appropriate for the dogs to devour Jezebel "within the bounds" of Jezreel, for therein lies Naboth's vineyard.

When the death of Ahab is reported in 1 Kings 21, dogs (הכלבים) lick his blood. Now when Jezebel's decomposing body is left in the Jezreel streets, dogs again appear on the scene to consume the corpse, which is an intentional insult to the memories of both monarchs, for in the Middle East, dogs were not the pampered pets of today's Western nations (plates 5 and 6). Dogs were thought to be dirty animals in biblical times. They were the scroungers and refuse eaters of Israelite society, and both *The Iliad* (book 24) and *The Odyssey* (book 3) indicate that Homer's Greece also regarded dogs as animals assigned to chewing the rotting corpses of cursed people. Yet there is an even more disturbing, albeit highly improbable, interpretation of the biblical "dogs." A homonym for the Hebrew word for "dog" means "servant" and is used in biblical days to denote a temple functionary who attends to religious rituals. In the Mount Carmel contest,

Jezebel's priests serving Baal ritually cut themselves during their ecstatic danc-ing around the altar. Perhaps, then, the dogs that lick Ahab's blood and eat Jezebel's body are really Baal's temple servants who consume raw flesh as part of their religious ritual (Margalith 230). The moral of the story then becomes a warn-ing to those who condone Baal worship practices, including the blood rituals, that they may become victims of those pagan customs.

In *Jewish Antiquities,* Josephus's report on the death scene of Jezebel also includes the dogs, though he omits the specific reference to Zimri and makes some other minor alterations:

> Now as Jehu entered Jezarela, Jezabela, who had adorned herself and was standing on the tower, cried, "A fine servant, who has killed his master!" But he looked up at her and asked who she was, and commanded her to come down to him; finally he ordered the eunuchs to throw her from the tower. And, behold, as she fell, the wall was splattered with her blood, and she was trampled by the horses, and so died. After these happenings, Jehu came to the palace with his friends, and refreshed himself after his ride with food and other things. He also ordered the servants who had sent Jezabela to her death to bury her, out of respect for her lineage, for she came of a line of kings. But the men who had been ordered to bury her found nothing more of her body than the extremities alone; all the rest had been devoured by dogs. When Jehu heard this, he marveled at the prophecy of Elijah, for he had foretold that she would perish in this manner at Jezarela. (6: 67)

The Aftermath of Jezebel's Death

Jehu, whom Josephus reports as marveling at Elijah's words, knows how to cloak his brutal actions in religious piety. After he assassinates Jezebel, he continues his bloody coup d'état against the rest of her family. Though it is traditional to destroy any potential male rival who could threaten the new king's succession and initi-ate a lengthy blood feud, the horror of Jehu's rampage extends across two coun-tries, Israel and Judah, even though no one offers resistance. The purge begins with the murders of Ahab's "seventy sons" (2 Kings 10.1), though the large num-ber need not be taken literally. Perhaps the figure seventy includes grandsons or other royals. It may be a conventional figure used to denote all male members of the king's household. The number is also found in the literature of other cultures of the day; for example, Ugaritic mythology ascribes seventy divine progeny to the god El (Frost 511). There is biblical precedent too. Seventy, a symbolic, round number, is mentioned in Judges 8.30, which discusses the seventy sons of Gideon; and Genesis 46.27 says that a total of seventy persons accompany Jacob into Egypt. The point is that Jehu plans to exterminate the whole House of Ahab and Jezebel.

Even friends and religious leaders of the former king are eliminated as Jehu wipes the political slate completely clean: "So Jehu smote all that remained of the House of Ahab in Jezreel, and all his great men, and his familiar friends, and his priests, until there was left him none remaining" (2 Kings 10.11). The slaughter continues as Jehu travels to Samaria, for the coup could not be considered finished without the taking of Ahab's capital. Along the way, Jehu meets and executes forty-two relatives of former King Ahaziah of Judah, people who are in Israel for a visit. Forty-two may be another symbolic number, and it seems highly implausible that Ahaziah's kin would journey to Samaria at this time, unaware of his death and the revolution that foments throughout the area. Perhaps this incident is not reported in its correct chronological sequence, or perhaps it is purely a fictitious addition inserted for impact (Gray 556). In the NRSV, these folks are on their way home. By translating the Hebrew in this way, their presence in Israel is more understandable. Whatever the timing of their sojourn, the massacre of the forty-two is cruel. Yet Jehu is not killing indiscriminately; he executes those with direct connection to power.

The story cannot end here, for there remains alive one more threat to Yahwehism: Athaliah, called the daughter of Ahab—and presumably Jezebel (2 Kings 8.18; 2 Chronicles 21.6)—and also called the daughter of Omri (2 Kings 8.26; 2 Chronicles 22.2). These statements are not necessarily contradictory, for as Ahab's father and founder of the dynasty, Omri may rightfully in common usage be termed Athaliah's father when he is actually her grandfather. Some scholars, working with extrabiblical sources to pinpoint dates, believe it more likely that Jezebel and Athaliah are sisters-in-law rather than mother and daughter (MacCallum 12). Whoever Athaliah's parents might be, she is considered another personification of evil, and her image is closely linked with Jezebel's. In 2 Chronicles 24.7, Athaliah is called "that wicked woman," and there is a noticeable family resemblance in the personalities of Athaliah and Jezebel. They seem to be kindred spirits, and the closeness between Jezebel's royal court in Jezreel and Athaliah's court in Jerusalem suggests a high degree of mutual sympathy and goodwill between the women.

In the seventh year of her reign, Athaliah is killed in an insurrection commanded by Yahweh priest Jehoiada. The only legitimate heir to the throne of Judah has been hidden from Athaliah for six years in the House of the Lord, recalling the story of Moses being concealed in the bulrushes. That child, Joash, is now made king so that the people will have a new leader after they kill Queen Athaliah. The citizens swear allegiance to God and tear down the temple to Baal. The formal conclusion to the episode is typical of the Deuteronomic historian, but the double reference to Athaliah's death at two different points in the story suggests more than one source. The second mention reveals the writer's special pleasure in her demise: "So all the people of the land rejoiced, and the city was quiet; and they slew Athaliah with the sword at the king's house" (2 Kings 11.20). The town is hushed because if any subjects still support the queen they have either been permanently silenced or lack the courage to protest. Athaliah's role in the narrative is to be Jezebel's incarnate in Judah. Athaliah's death signals that the work begun by Jehu in the northern kingdom is now completed in the south.

Exactly who is this man Jehu, the egotist whose successful purge against the House of Ahab extends into the southern kingdom? Jehu is the son of Jehoshaphat (no relation to the king of Judah by the same name) and also the founder of Israel's fifth dynasty, lasting from 843 to 743 BCE. The prophets Amos and Hosea refer to the unconscionable atrocities that Jehu commits. God says, "I will visit the blood of Jezreel upon the house of Jehu, and will cause to cease the kingdom of the house of Israel" (Hosea 1.4). The whole episode of his revolution seems like a bad dream, its depravity practically unparalleled in the Hebrew Scriptures. Jehu dies in the twenty-eighth year of his reign because he does not follow the letter of Hebrew law, just as his predecessor, Jezebel, had not done. His obituary reads, "But Jehu took no heed to walk in the law of the LORD, the God of Israel, with all his heart; he departed not from the sins of Jehroboam [Jeroboam, King of Judah], wherewith he made Israel to sin" (2 Kings 10.31). The specific charge against the king is that he allows golden calf worship to continue in his land, probably for reasons of political expediency. So Jehu is a complex figure—an anointed king, a regicide, and a tolerator of one form of idol worship. He also seems to have traits in common with Jezebel, for he willingly disposes of anyone who gets in his way. In fact, he possesses some of the very same qualities for which Jezebel is notorious, especially her notion that "might makes right" (Parker 73). Why then are the people expected to accept Jehu as their sovereign and reject Jezebel and her family?

The answer lies in the fact that in 1–2 Kings Jehu is presented as Yahweh's instrument for destroying the Baal worship that permeates the House of Ahab. When Jehu murders two kings and a queen, he is performing God's sacred task. God may want the result, but it should be noted that there is never a divine command for such a bloodthirsty method of reaching the goal. Jehu's success story is a result of the Deuteronomist's theology, and no trace of revulsion on the part of the chronicler can be detected in the narrative of Jezebel's assassination. Ahab, on the other hand, incurs the historian's animosity because of his marriage to an idol worshiper and her subsequent influence in the land of Israel and Judah. As Jehu makes his dramatic ride into Jezreel, he comes to avenge religious wrongs done during Jezebel's lifetime, for the reign of Ahab and Jezebel stands as a monolith of sin in the redactor's eyes. Despite Jehu's shortcomings, which cause his downfall, God rewards him by permitting his dynasty to rule for five generations. Furthermore, Jehu restores peace, or well-being, in Israel after his insurrection. Peace, so much discussed as Jehu draws near to Jezreel, will be restored to Israel by this violent man. Gradually readers are made aware of how badly Israel needs a peaceful monarchy (Coe 131). During Jezebel's reign, Baal worship increases, the law is manipulated so that an innocent man dies, and tranquility seems remote. Yet the redactor of the Kings stories is not satisfied with justifying Jehu's revolt solely on the grounds of ethnocentric disgust for a foreign woman and her customs. Jehu's insurrection is supported by higher theological reasoning. Yahweh rejects anointed kings when they elevate themselves above God's will and divinely sanctioned prophets. Jehu's greatest achievement is ridding the land of a monarchy deemed foul and unworthy of God's special protection and love. Jehu's most important contribution is that he "destroyed Baal out of Israel" (2 Kings 10.26) and is God's instrument in the realization of historical events.

The good reputation of the House of Ahab and Jezebel is destroyed, root and branch, by the dramatic story of Jehu's revolt. The entire dynasty is rejected by God, and Jezebel is cast as a major contributor to the downfall. Yet however much the biblical narrative seeks to vilify the queen, it is difficult for us to discount all the evidence of her courage and dignity in the face of death. One interpretation of the meeting with Jehu is that Jezebel dies heroically by donning regal garb before meeting certain doom; another is that she exhibits baseness by applying kohl to her eyes and trying to seduce her opponent. One thing is certain. Through the ages, Jezebel has been reviled. It may be that she has been judged for all time without the possibility of an appeal. People who cannot accept religious and cultural pluralism would only condemn the queen. The miracle stories connected to Elijah and Elisha may leave some skeptics wondering what really happened in the conflict with Jezebel. Perhaps historical accuracy is sacrificed for the sake of dramatic storytelling. Furthermore, close examination of all the evidence against the queen suggests that some of it is implausible. For example, the Naboth plot is foolhardy and therefore in doubt because Jezebel elicits help from an indefinite number of people, any one of whom could easily have betrayed her scheme to become a religious hero or to fulfill personal ambition. The episode of Jehu's revolt is fast paced and exciting, but some details also stretch a reader's credulity. On many occasions, it seems possible that the writer's moral purpose far outweighs his sense of historical accuracy.

The Bible imputes to Jezebel acts of idolatry, legal duplicity, and murder. She is said to worship false gods, threaten to kill the prophets of Yahweh, stage a sham trial with perjured testimony, murder an innocent man, and exert unwholesome foreign influence over her husband and the entire royal family. For all this deceptiveness and wickedness, she is utterly destroyed. Part of the price she pays seems to be not only immediate condemnation by the Deuteronomist but eternal reproof by succeeding generations of readers, who use her name as a resounding symbol of evil. She is the vulgar painted floozy, the manipulative woman who will stop at nothing to get what she wants.

Through it all, Jezebel remains an intriguing figure. She is certainly a threat to patriarchal prerogative and monotheism, and so the biblical writer must defame her. Jezebel is feared because she is a foreigner, a woman, an advocate of another religion, an intelligent and fast-thinking leader. Why is she damned through the ages? She is sentenced by a religious tribunal loyal to a single, masculine deity. Since the revolution against Jezebel's family is conducted in the name of God, she faces a type of ancient inquisition. The result is a foregone conclusion. With Jezebel's death, the biblical writer hopes to destroy alien worship customs and bring about the last gasp of the goddess. Jezebel's final act at the balcony offers much insight into her personality, however. She tidies her face and hair then stands at her window to taunt God's conquering hero, King Jehu, representing traditional masculine authority and religious authenticity. For having the audacity to insult male-dominated society and to suggest that minority worship beliefs be permitted to exist alongside the established state religion, she is destroyed. But she goes out splendidly, every inch a queen. Whatever her character flaws, she remains true to herself. Jehu's 2 Kings 9.34 peroration calling for her burial says volumes about how Jezebel should be remembered: "she is a king's daughter." We are now witnesses in a case that posterity seems to have judged against a fascinating woman.

Part Two
The Eternal Jezebel

4

Prose Adaptations of the Jezebel Story

૭ᘐ

At every word a reputation dies.

—Alexander Pope,
"Rape of the Lock"

I N 1993 SENATORS JESSE HELMS AND EDWARD "TED" KENNEDY DEBATED whether foreigners with AIDS should be granted residency in the United States. As the political discussion became a heated shouting match, archconservative Helms of North Carolina bellowed, "Let me adjust my hearing aid. It could not accommodate the decibels of the Senator from Massachusetts. I can't match him in decibels or Jezebels" (Helms 24).

Ad hominem attacks are a time-honored, if unscrupulous, part of political wrangling, but this one is especially interesting. The assonance and parallelism of "decibels and Jezebels" formed a clever quip, which no doubt drew knowing smiles from those who heard it and demonstrated the enduring power of the name Jezebel. At the time of Helms's remark, Ted Kennedy's political career had survived a series of scandals dating all the way back to his cheating at Harvard, his campaign worker's death at Chappaquiddick, his divorce, his alcoholism, and his long-standing reputation as a womanizer. By 1993 Kennedy had remarried and reformed, and the thought of a tamer Kennedy was gaining acceptance with Americans. It was therefore a good time for Helms to remind people of his adversary's inglorious past by associating Kennedy with ivory palaces and fallen women. By besmirching the newly reworked Kennedy image and recalling visions of promiscuity and misuse of power, Helms trivialized and deflected attention from the issue at hand, humanitarian assistance to foreigners with AIDS. No one would need an explanation of the Jezebel allusion; everyone would get the point.

The Eternal Jezebel
ⓢⓢ

What better person than Jezebel could Helms have selected to assist in his jab against Kennedy? The queen of ancient Israel remains the perfect choice. The archetypal power of Jezebel's name stretches across the millennia with long, incorporeal fingers and sullies the reputations of those unlucky enough to be linked to her in prose retellings of her story. Whether prose writers relate their themes directly (through sermons) or indirectly (through novels), they frequently return to the image of Jezebel. The Deuteronomist may have hoped to effect the last gasp of the goddess, but she surfaces again and again in the literature of every generation.

Religious Tractates and Sermons

As it is today with Jezebel references, so it has been for millennia. Two thousand years before Jesse Helms, the first biblical commentators portray the queen as evil. In addition to the writings of the immediate postbiblical period, notably the Talmud, some of the prose from the earliest Church Fathers casts Jezebel as a wanton woman. For example, St. Ephraem Syrus (c. 306–378), born in Nisibis, wrote passionately about biblical subjects and won respect for his scholarship and lyrical style. His *Nisibene Hymns* compares Jezebel to Sheol, the Hebrew Scriptures' term for the place of departed spirits (corresponding somewhat to the New Testament's hell). Ephraem Syrus states, "Jezebel was the true Sheol, who devoured the just" (qtd. in Ziolkowski 8). Next, St. Ambrose (c. 339–397) was a Roman churchman who fought for the integrity of religion at the imperial court. He resisted the empress-regent Justina and well understood the conflict between monarch and prophet. Eloquent St. Jerome (c. 342–420) produced the Vulgate, a Latin version of the Bible, and composed biblical commentaries and fiery invectives. In one of his many works, Jerome uses the Latin word *hortus* (meaning "garden") to assert that Jezebel's selfish motivation for killing Naboth is to create a pleasure garden for herself and Ahab. Jerome contends that the land they acquire is Sodom's vineyard (Ziolkowski 9), a playground for sexual impropriety.

Medieval noblewomen were particularly vulnerable to comparisons to Jezebel, for the rich and famous were certain to draw fire from the pious poor. One medieval writer says:

> In her ruthlessness of character, her lust for power, her unshrinking and resolute activity, her remorseless brushing aside of anything and everything that interfered with the carrying out of her designs, [Jezebel] was the veritable prototype of Catherine de Medici. (qtd. in Ziolkowski 16–17)

Catherine (1519–1589) was the great-granddaughter of Florentine Lorenzo the

Magnificent. When she married Henri II of France, the Medici family influence began to spread throughout Europe. Though she encouraged the arts, like many of her highly cultured ancestors, in politics Catherine was dishonest and ruthless. In the Protestant-Catholic religious wars, she originally supported the Protestant Huguenots against the Catholic Guise faction, but she later switched sides. Catherine was largely responsible for the St. Bartholomew's Day Massacre of 1572, in which thousands of French Protestants were murdered. It is probably this incident that caused her to be compared to the Jezebel of the Naboth episode, since both women were held accountable for slaughtering the innocent.

About the same time, in 1531, forty-year-old English King Henry VIII wrote of an incident when Anne Boleyn, at the time his undisputed ladylove but not yet his queen, was compared to Jezebel:

> The Friar warned me, "A King who is besotted with his own Jezebel, a woman who is bringing about his ruin and that of the Church, I say unto you as Elijah said unto Ahab, 'The dogs shall lick your blood.'" He expected me to stand out guiltily but I continued to sit calmly in the royal box. ("Henry VIII")

In 1532 the Nun of Kent, Elizabeth Barton, a woman prone to visions and opposed to the royal divorce, foresaw Henry's adultery as leading to Christ's second crucifixion. The nun, who would be arrested in 1533, had a mystical experience in which she predicted that Anne Boleyn would become a Jezebel and be eaten by the dogs (Fraser 205). When Anne failed to produce a male heir and Henry's ardor for her cooled, Anne was put on trial and beheaded. Interestingly, she and Catherine de Medici shared the same fate in one respect: they were both seen by many of their contemporaries as dangerously evil women who had the power to influence political events. They were both Jezebels.

Jezebel's name often appears in sermons. It is hardly surprising that religious discourses would include lectures denouncing evil women. Most church and synagogue sermons are not recorded for posterity, however, so it is impossible to know exactly how frequently Jezebel has been maligned from the pulpit. Yet some prominent examples of sermons have been preserved, especially when the sermonizer hates a particularly powerful or controversial woman. In such situations, the detested contemporary woman is likely to be called a Jezebel.

In Madrid the Jesuit sermon "Oratio ad Milites," delivered to Spain's Armada fighters, terms Queen Elizabeth I the "second Jezebel" (Griffin vii). In fact, in the Roman Catholic–Protestant struggles of the sixteenth century, any woman on the opposing side is considered a Jezebel. For example, when King Edward VI died in 1553 and was succeeded by his staunchly Catholic half-sister Mary Tudor, name-calling began in earnest. In his pamphlet *The First Blast of the Trumpet against the*

The Eternal Jezebel

Monstrous Regiment of Women (1558), Protestant Reformation leader John Knox produced a bombast against Catholic Mary of Guise, then regent of Scotland on behalf of her juvenile daughter, Mary, Queen of Scots. Knox (c. 1514–1572) had been raised a Catholic and perhaps even entered the priesthood, but as a young man he was swept up by the Protestant movement and became one of the six chaplains to England's Edward VI. When Mary Tudor ascended to the throne, Knox avoided the fate of out-of-favor zealots by fleeing to Lutheran Germany, where he perfected his dissent. Later he returned home to become the autocrat of the Reformation in Scotland and a leading fashioner of Protestant propaganda.

Reformer Knox considered Mary and other female leaders to be the Jezebels of his day and was not afraid to say so. Knox believed that "Female Government" was against nature, reason, right, and law. The opening sentence of the preface for *The First Blast of the Trumpet* uses the name Jezebel to call forth ancient memories of past wicked female rulers and to lament that more clergymen are not speaking against current women monarchs, Protestant or Catholic, because the queens are again exiling God's true prophets:

> Wonder it is, that amongst so many pregnant wittes as the Ile of Great Britany hath produced, so many godlie and zealous preachers as England did sometime nourishe, and amongst so many learned, and men of grave judgement, as this day by Jesabel are exiled, none is found so stowte of courage, so faithfull to God, nor loving to thair native countrie, that they dare admonishe the inhabitantes of that Ile, how abominable before God is the Empire or Rule of a wicked woman, yea, of a traiteiresse and bastard. (365)

Knox's plea did not go unanswered. His colleague, Christopher Goodman, in a work entitled "How Superior Powers Ought to be Obeyd of Their Subjects," echoes Knox's sentiments against Queen Mary, referring to her as an idolater and bastard. A woodcut produced at the time shows Goodman and Knox blowing their trumpets in front of the queens of England and Scotland.

The First Blast of the Trumpet makes numerous references to Jezebel and her daughter, Athaliah, directly comparing them to Mary of Guise and her daughter, Mary, Queen of Scots. People who support the current monarch especially dishearten Knox. He believes that the evil spirit of the two ancient queens could be found in his day:

> But in these of our ages, we finde crueltie, falshed, pride, covetousnes, deceit, and oppression. In them we also finde the spirit of Jesabel and Athalia; under them we finde the simple people oppressed, the true religion extinguished, and the blood of Christes membres most cruellie shed. (404)

Knox concludes that the "cursed Jesabel of England, with the pestilent and detestable generation of Papistes, make no litle bragge and boast, that they have triumphed" (418).

Misogynistic Knox, fearing female rulers in general, was particularly offended by Catholic women monarchs. When Mary of Guise died in 1560, Knox soon had to contend with young Mary. The Scottish Parliament passed the "Confession of Faith," declaring the pope to have no authority in Scotland and prohibiting the celebration of mass. Having taken refuge in France, young Mary was first wed to that country's boy king, Francis II, eldest son of Catherine de Medici. When Francis died and Mary returned to Scotland, she immediately began to hold mass illegally and regularly at Holyrood Chapel in Edinburgh. Protestants, threatened by Mary's actions, were convinced that she had the power and influence to return Catholicism to the country. Knox preached against Mary relentlessly and successfully, often at nearby St. Giles, showing his uncompromising antipathy toward the queen. When she was forced to abdicate in 1567, Parliament reconfirmed its previous regulations against the Catholic religion. Knox's single-minded fanaticism was in some ways similar to the high-voltage rodomontade of the prophet Elijah. Like Elijah, the biblical foe of Jezebel, Knox was never bashful about condemning his queen because her religious beliefs were different from his own. The Jezebel connection was a natural one for Knox to espouse, for he would stop at nothing to damage Mary's reputation, his sermons often possessing the sting of a Portuguese man-of-war. Queen Jezebel and Queen Mary were both heretics in his view, apostate women whose high positions made them extremely dangerous.

About the same time, across the Atlantic Ocean, another woman was enduring the Jezebel comparison. Anne Hutchinson (1591–1643) was born the daughter of a Lincolnshire, England, clergyman. She and her husband emigrated to Boston, Massachusetts, in 1634, where she frequently lectured and condemned local clergy for being more devoted to the principle of grace through good works than to the New Testament's hallmark doctrine of justification by faith. Hutchinson's censure of the clergymen resulted in bitter controversy that divided the Massachusetts Bay Colony. She was placed on trial for heresy and sedition; she was then banished from the colony "for traducing the ministers and their ministry" (Benet 488). Perceived of as a threat to men already in power, Hutchinson was inevitably compared to Jezebel, and in fact was often referred to in writings of the day as the "American Jezebel." Her crime was to be a woman who criticized the establishment's religion and who attempted to introduce reforms. Like the Israelite queen, Hutchinson possessed religious notions unpopular with male authority figures of her day. Those opposing a public role for women and unable to accept theology contradicting their own believed Hutchinson deserved such epithets as "disobedient Eve" and "Jezebel woman." Name-calling was intended to keep all women in their traditional place and to discourage them from venturing into the public realm and meddling in church affairs.

Clergyman had a field day with women like Hutchinson. One example is the leading English poet and churchman of the early seventeenth century, John Donne (c. 1572–1631). Like Knox, Donne was raised a Roman Catholic, an alien religion in the Protestant England of his time. In his twenties, Donne's faith was shaken and he converted to the Church of England, being ordained in 1615, advancing to the position of chaplain to James I, and finally becoming dean of St. Paul's in 1621. His sermons, more than one hundred sixty of which are extant, were polemics against the Catholics and contained masterful prose, marked by its tendency toward combustibility and showing "all the symptoms of fever" (Fausset 278). They helped earn him a place as one of the most renowned preachers of his era "by silhouetting in darkest horror all the unresolved conflicts of his soul" (Baugh 613). In one of his better-known sermons, Donne discusses Jezebel's errant preoccupation with the physical body at the expense of the immortal soul. The flavor of Donne's baroquely eloquent prose style and explosive heat are evident when he recalls that "Jezebel had painted and perfumed this body" but she died anyway because "nothing in temporal things is permanent" (Donne 573). Therefore, one should look forward to the Resurrection; adorning the body is futile vanity.

The Rev. Isaac Williams was another clergyman who turned his attention to Jezebel. Born in 1802 near Aberystwyth, Wales, he wrote religious poetry, as did his predecessor John Donne. Williams was a fellow at Trinity College, Oxford, and is best remembered for his sermons, especially Tract 80 entitled "Reserve in Religious Teaching." A work that includes Williams's examination and evaluation of Jezebel's life, *Female Characters of Holy Scripture: In a Series of Sermons,* was published posthumously in 1873, eight years after the parson's death. Its purpose, as stated in the preface, is to provide women with the special guidance they require, the most appropriate place to seek such instruction being the Holy Scriptures. Williams's sermon "Wickedness in Power" begins with the familiar quote from 1 Kings 21.25: "But there was none like unto Ahab, who did give himself over to do that which was evil in the sight of the Lord, whom Jezebel his wife stirred up." Concerned with the culpability of women in general, Williams poses a disturbing question: If Ahab is the most depraved of all Israelite kings and his evilness results because he is spurred into action by Jezebel, then how much more depraved must she be? He cites the first woman, Eve, with responsibility for succumbing to the powerful influence of evil, through which the forces of darkness are able to control man. Displaying the sexism of his era, Williams maintains that Jezebel is yet another example of "women who have seemed as if they themselves were more fully and directly under the influence of evil spirits, and were used by them as instruments to seduce and confirm in guilt more hesitating minds" (169). In other words, women are spiritually weaker than men. Since women are less able to resist temptation, they are to blame for the Fall of man, who would perhaps be able to avoid sin if he could only eschew woman. Williams goes so far as to compare Jezebel to the Antichrist.

Williams believes Jezebel to be among history's wickedest characters. Her special sin occurs because of her knowledge and awareness of Yahweh. She does not act in ignorance but deliberately rejects the one true God. She has an opportunity to live among the Israelites, to learn from them, and to accept their deity. Considering the abuse of this privileged position, the Rev. Williams is appalled that, in her final moments of life, Jezebel utters words about peace ("Is it peace, thou Zimri" [2 Kings 9.31]). Williams finds that Jezebel is "full of the wisdom of the serpent, suggesting peace; the whoredom and witchcraft of one who herself had little to do with peace. As the evil spirits confessed Christ, so her last words speak of peace" (173).

What moral lessons can be learned from the Jezebel story? Williams believes the tale teaches that the will of God is stronger than the volition of human beings. Jehu finally orders a burial for Jezebel not because he is a compassionate man but because doing so is the will of God. Furthermore, the story persuades us of God's forbearance. Though the Lord must have been angry with Jezebel from the beginning, divine benevolence results in the postponement of her punishment. God exhibits heavenly tolerance in the face of extreme provocation. Such patience is what Elijah has to learn at Mount Horeb, and the rest of humanity should emulate this sublime model of restraint. Jezebel's misdeeds are, Williams asserts, primarily sins against God. Atrocities that Jezebel perpetrates against the prophets and people are not motivated by her hatred of them as individuals or as a group; instead, the evil queen's desire for vengeance against the ancient Jews is "because they belonged to Him" (176). From the Jezebel story, one can see what happens to those who oppose God.

A political-religious speech that sounds remarkably like a sermon is *Jezebel: Speech of the Rev. Hugh M'Neile, at Market Drayton, Salop, December 19, 1839.* The minister M'Neile is speaking at a Protestant meeting, held in a schoolroom on a Thursday evening, for the purpose of "considering the best means of arresting the encroachments of the Papacy" (1). It is another anti-Catholic diatribe in which he declares "Romish doctrines" to be repugnant to God, blasphemous, and dangerous. M'Neile maintains that he has been falsely accused of comparing Queen Victoria to Jezebel: "But though there be no more resemblance between Jezebel and our most gracious Queen than there is between me and Hercules, yet the resemblance between Jezebel and Popery, I may say, with Fluellen, in Shakespeare, is 'as like as my fingers are to my toes'" (4). The comparison is appropriate, he concludes, because Jezebel bowed down to graven images—and so do Catholics. Likenesses of Mary, the mother of Christ, found in Catholic churches, encourage idol worship, in M'Neile's view, for modern Catholics kneel before her statue. "We find Popery, I say, introducing into the Christian Church precisely the parallel of what Jezebel introduced into the Jewish Church" (13). Thus, Popery is equal to "that woman Jezebel," and "the character of Jezebel, the name of Jezebel, and the end of Jezebel, belong to the Papal system" (14).

The Rev. M'Neile expresses relief because a Catholic "woman Jezebel" cannot be on the throne of England or married to the sovereign. Yet he fears that Papists have infiltrated the government at all levels. He lists the names of Catholic officials possessing political power—Mr. Wyse, Mr. O'Ferrall, Mr. Sheil, and Mr. O'Connell—and warns his audience not to listen as they bluster away in the Treasury, the Privy Council, and the Parliament. The preacher M'Neile is also alarmed that tax money is used to support Catholic schools. He recalls that Jezebel fed idolatrous prophets at her table, thus comparing the British government's paying for schools that train Catholic priests to Jezebel's support of false prophets. If the Catholic Church continues to gain strength in the government, he asserts, then the wrath of God will fall against the country. Jezebel must be rooted out because "no Government can keep the reins of Government—no, not for a month, without pledging itself to national Protestantism in Church and State" (26).

As generations pass, sermon writers continue to rely on references to Jezebel. In the twentieth century, Robert G. Lee is an excellent example of those who rail against the biblical queen. The Rev. Lee graduated from Furman University, Greenville, South Carolina, and was ordained in 1910. He was president of the Southern Baptist Convention; a pastor in Charleston, New Orleans, and Memphis; and conducted revivals throughout the United States. One particular sermon, "Pay-Day—Someday," published in 1957, was delivered more than six hundred times. It is thirty-two amazing pages of over-the-top attacks against Jezebel and all women. Purple prose abounds:

> Hear [Jezebel's] derisive laugh as it rings out in the palace like the shrill cackle of a wild fowl that has returned to its nest and has found a serpent therein! With her tongue, sharp as a razor, she prods Ahab as an ox driver prods with sharp goad the ox which does not want to press his neck into the yoke, or as one whips with a rawhide a stubborn mule. With profuse and harsh laughter this old gay and gaudy

guinea of Satan derided this king of hers for a cowardly buffoon and sordid jester. What hornet-like sting in her sarcasm! What wolf-mouth fierceness in her every reproach! What tiger-fang cruelty in her expressed displeasure! What fury in the shrieking of her rebuke! What bitterness in the teasing taunts she hurled at him for his scrupulous timidity! Her bosom with anger was heaving! Her eyes were flashing with rage under the surge of hot anger that swept over her. (9)

Lee insists that with bejeweled fingers Jezebel tickles Ahab and promises that she will acquire Naboth's vineyard. Extrapolating from the case of Jezebel, the minister conjectures that throughout history women have had an evil influence on men—Lucrezia Borgia, Catherine de Medici, Delilah, Bathsheba, Herodias, Drusilla, Potiphar's wife, Zeresh (wife of Haman), Job's wife, Kitty O'Shea, Cleopatra. According to the pastor, it is women who have caused most of the world's ills:

Take the stirring crimes of any age, and at the bottom . . . the world almost invariably finds a woman. Only God Almighty knows the full story of the foul plots hatched by women. But we know enough to say that some of the foulest plots that have been hatched out of Satan's incubator were hatched out of eggs placed therein by women's hands. (12)

All these Jezebels who have come to bad ends have gotten what they deserve. The women who served Christ comprise the only exceptions in the Rev. Lee's misogynistic tirade; these are the only good women he acknowledges.

The anti-Jezebel–antiwoman thesis is also developed in Francis Frangipane's 1989 work entitled *The Three Battlegrounds,* which the author claims is about "spiritual warfare" (iv). It contains four sermons directly involving Jezebel, whose spirit caused millions of Israelites to turn to Baal. Frangipane believes that, while the Jezebel spirit has no gender, it "is more attracted to the uniqueness of the female psyche" (98). Today Jezebel targets women who are embittered against men and who desire to manipulate and control others. Women who attend church hoping to seduce the pastor have been sucked in by the Jezebel spirit. The entertainment industry is riddled with it, as are the worlds of fashion and academia. Professional musicians, especially if they become choir directors, are susceptible to the demonic, Jezebelian influence, as are ministers who want too much control of the church. Jezebel's spirit can operate in men, but it "prefers the disposition of a woman's nature" (101).

Frangipane also sees married life as a battleground where Jezebel must be fought. If a husband fears his strong-willed wife and does not serve as the head of the family, he possesses the Ahab spirit and is tolerating Jezebel:

When Ahab was king, Jezebel ruled. The man who cannot govern his household in godly, protective authority will not exercise his spiritual authority elsewhere. Such a man needs to repent of his fears and firmly, with gentleness, set his home in order. (118)

The husband must provide a woman with the security she feels when she knows her mate loves her. A man thus wins the war against Jezebel when he emulates Christ. A woman wins when she renounces her feminine charms and becomes meek and submissive.

Many of Frangipane's ideas are echoed by Fuchsia Pickett in her 1994 sermon-like book entitled *The Next Move of God*. Dr. Pickett, who taught at several Bible colleges, agrees that the Jezebel spirit knows no gender but is particularly attracted to women:

> It especially energizes women who are insecure, vain, jealous and dominating, having a consuming desire to control. Control is this principality's ultimate goal, and to that end it will use even sexual passion as a tool. It is not too difficult to trace the working of this Jezebel spirit in today's culture. It energizes the feminists, and is the motivator of abortion. It is especially rampant in the entertainment industry. (35)

Pickett asserts that the spirit of Jezebel was defeated at Calvary, but it is always poised to strike another blow. The Rev. Jonas Clark's 1998 work, *Jezebel, Seducing Goddess of War*, continues in Pickett's tradition and discusses the destructive Jezebel spirit that has gone unchallenged today.

There is no way to know how many times Jezebel has been mentioned by clergy down through the generations. In Sunday church services and Saturday synagogue sermons, the name Jezebel has doubtless been invoked weekly as a warning against sin. When these sermons make their way into print, they survive today and can be examined. One thing is certain: Jezebel is not going to have defenders from the pulpit.

Novels

In addition to sermons, the novel is another prose genre that conveys the Jezebel story to modern readers. Approximately thirty novels published in English in the nineteenth and twentieth centuries either self-consciously retell the biblical account or use the name Jezebel in a new story. Some of the best and worst novelists ever to put pen to paper have been attracted to the Jezebel plot. A few of the most talented, award-winning contemporary authors have been drawn to the Israelite queen's story, yet a noticeable number of pulp-fiction authors have also used her reputation to help weave tales of lust and retribution. Jezebel's well-known name is a quick and handy tool to conjure readers' prejudices. Though often lacking in literary merit, some of the novels based on Jezebel's life have had considerable appeal to the public. The sincere churchgoer, the unsophisticated consumer who is content with easy-to-digest fiction and not overly concerned with artistry, or the serious reader who occasionally desires less demanding entertainment fiction may enjoy this collection of tales.

Whether the Jezebel novels are of pulp or Pulitzer quality, they all offer fascinating insights into how her reputation and character have survived through the generations to the postmodern age. Her name elicits immediate reactions and predictable responses, and authors sometimes rely on the stereotypes and biases they assume their readers possess, substituting stereotypes for detailed character development. Using the appellation Jezebel may thus provide a shortcut for writers with less skill. On the other hand, in the hands of an artist, Jezebel allusions provide powerful metaphors for societal commentaries. Ahab and Jezebel are sometimes depicted as a loving couple in these novels, but more typically she remains cold and unresponsive to his ardor. Occasionally Jezebel has admirers among the Israelites, but usually the people hate her. By examining variations on the Bible's narrative, we can discover interesting things about how fiction is constructed. More important, however, the way novelists treat the long-dead queen reveals something intriguing about ourselves and our society's ongoing need for a fall girl.

Biblical Novels Condemning Jezebel

Few novels that retell the biblical story of Jezebel are sympathetic to the queen. In the 1930s, two historical narratives closely following the Bible's intent to vilify Jezebel emerge from London publishers and are typical of the way she is viewed. These two novels possess many similarities, fleshing out the Bible's scant details and making Jezebel appear even more evil than she is in Kings. The first of these works is Pamela Frankau's 1937 novel entitled *Jezebel,* followed in 1939 by Max Catto's *Hairy Man.*

Both novels open with similar fictional stories about how the future monarchs meet. Ahab visits King Ethbaal's court in Tyre. It is clear that Jezebel and her father believe Ahab is a weak bumpkin, but they think she can make a man out of him, teaching him how to be a worshiper of Baal and a king as well. Ethbaal believes that his proud, strong-willed daughter does not possess a traditionally feminine mind, whatever that may be. He concedes that Jezebel swears profusely with a serpent's tongue, and her many moods are compared to a snake routinely shedding its skin. She will, Ethbaal realizes, give Ahab some trouble, and the father hopes that his daughter will soon poison Ahab and claim the throne for herself alone. Frankau's young princess is also willful. In *Jezebel* Ahab visits Tyre to arrange the marriage and is amused by the beautiful girl's brash antics. Ahab considers her worthy of sharing his throne. She thinks it would be brave to marry Ahab and carry her true religion to Israel, "that barren, hateful country" (19). When Ahab ridicules Jezebel's strong religious convictions, he is forced to apologize before she will consent to wed him. She also demands in a prenuptial agreement that he serve her gods and build her a temple when she goes to Samaria. Ahab is smitten by Jezebel, admires her bold manipulations, and bends to her will. In both novels, Ahab does all of the compromising, even before the marriage takes place. Frankau and Catto fill in gaps left by the Bible story and establish early that Jezebel is the stronger character. The remainder of each novel is predicated on this notion of the regents' personalities.

Frankau and Catto deal extensively with the Mount Carmel episode. Unlike the biblical story, in which Jezebel remains in the Jezreel palace when Elijah and Baal's priests pray for the drought to end, Catto's Jezebel watches furtively from a safe distance. She is not the type of person content to stay home and wait for a report. After the rains come, Ahab is afraid of Elijah's power, but Jezebel remains defiant and spits on the ground to indicate her hatred for the prophet. She even attempts to murder Elijah with a spear as he passes Ahab's chariot on the way back to Jezreel, but her aim is bad and she kills the prophet's assistant instead. Though such details are absent from the Bible, they certainly are consistent with the Deuteronomist's view of Jezebel as Elijah's sworn enemy and would-be assassin.

Catto's Jezebel recognizes the positive attributes of her prophetic foe. She thinks about how Ahab contrasts with Elijah:

> A big man. Hairy. Uncouth and cassocked. . . . Now *there* had been somewhat of a man. Her own poor Ahab, that nervous, even conscience-stricken monarch, her spouse, had always cut so shrunken and lamentable a figure beside the awe-inspiring hugeness and passion of that hermit or prophet or priest, or whatever he was. (397)

When the rains come in Frankau's novel, Jezebel is convinced that her prayers to Baal have been answered. She does not believe that Elijah has finally ended the three-year drought, though she admires his strength. Jezebel may not fear Elijah's God, but she does tremble at the prophet's passion and influence in Israel.

The queen's steely fortitude and stoutheartedness are a foil to the king's weakness. In Frankau's *Jezebel,* Ahab is plagued by a guilty conscience after the murder of innocent Naboth, echoing biblical accounts of the king's repentance. Jezebel acted because Naboth's insult to the royal house cannot go unanswered, but Ahab is remorseful and says, "So small a vineyard; so small a thing for which to take away the life" (158). He believes the vineyard is haunted and does not speak to Jezebel for three years after seizing ownership of the property. It is Jezebel in Catto's *Hairy Man*, however, who explains what motivates her treachery: "I consider myself the arbiter of my own fate. I am guided by none, I have no fear of God, conscience does not live in me. I am *I*. I am *Jezebel!* I seek only to live insolently, to satisfy my flesh, *this personal flesh!*" (299). In both novels, Jezebel burns brightly with evil passion. She is in control of family enterprises and bullies Ahab. As Jehu approaches to kill the queen, Frankau's Jezebel—like Lady Macbeth—wishes she were a man so her advice would be heeded. In Jezebel's final moments, she prays for the courage to face death bravely, to die "with blood in my veins to hate while the knife reaches my throat" (208). Each author is convinced that the queen possesses extraordinary valor, though it is put to evil purposes.

A different perspective is found in Flavia Anderson's novel entitled *Jezebel and the Dayspring*, published in London in 1949. Jezebel is a devout Baal worshiper, but her father's religious service is perfunctory. Ethbaal is primarily a merchant and wants to marry off his daughter to increase trade with Israel. While arranging the wedding, Ethbaal is willing to bypass his own religious customs to accommodate Israelite preferences. Here the author's research adds valuable historical detail concerning the ancient practice of temple prostitution. The Canaanites demand that a girl's virginity be forfeited; the fertility goddess accepts as an act of devotion to herself the first sexual experience of a maiden. Furthermore, a sexually pure bride brings bad luck to her husband, an idea stemming from the notion that all first fruits are too sacred and dangerous for mortals to consume and must therefore be sacrificed to the gods. Failure to offer up maidenhood in the temple would be a perilous insult to the gods. Wealthy or irreligious people might pay a ransom and offer up the bride's hair instead of her virginity, but such actions demonstrate a lack of devoutness. Anderson's Ethbaal, never as strict in religious matters as he is portrayed in other novels, understands that Israelite men expect their brides to be virginal. He therefore insists that his daughter remain untouched. Jezebel is troubled by this laxness in upholding Baal's laws, preparing the reader for her subsequent conflict with Elijah.

Though Jezebel may want Baal's laws to be upheld, she is not as particular about Israel's rules. In *Jezebel and the Dayspring*, the queen handles everything in the conspiracy to kill Naboth and confiscate his land. Yet Anderson adds a unique distortion of the Bible's presentation. Jezebel has heard about Babylonian terraced gardens and wants one for herself. Naboth's vineyard is in the right location, so when he refuses to sell it, she arranges to have him stoned, but there is a mishap. Naboth climbs a rope and falls forty feet to the pavement below. Jezebel suspects that Jehu has cut the rope. Thus Anderson's novel differs from the Bible and discusses not two falls (Jezebel's and her son Ahaziah's), but three. This plot change also adds to Jehu's culpability in Naboth's murder and foreshadows his upcoming cruelty to Jezebel when he orders that she be thrown from her balcony.

Just as Anderson alters the way Naboth dies, so she changes the situation in which Elijah ascends to heaven. The new version increases Jezebel's role in Elijah's end, for the biblical narrative makes no mention of the queen. Here, however, Jezebel determines that the prophet will be executed and attempts to recreate and negate the effect of the Carmel episode. Elijah is placed on a pyre with a fire lit underneath, and frenzied priests of Baal spout their incantations. Jezebel kneels before the image of Astarte. It is dusk and people expect evening stars to emerge, but "at the highest point in the sky shone the stars that herald the Dayspring" (287). From out of the middle of the star cluster, a chariot of fire emerges and rescues Elijah, carrying him to his reward. The symbolism of the dayspring, the early dawn, is readily apparent: Elijah's exit does not signal the beginning of darkest night but the commencing of a bright, new day, for he has gone to heaven, and the people should rejoice that their prophet is with God.

In 1953 J. L. Hair published *Jezebel*. The opening line suggests the author's intemperate prose style: "It was in the days of Ahab the King, and all Israel was a seething mass of social and political rottenness that tormented the nostrils of highest heaven" (1). Jezebel is cast as the licentious, heathen queen who has driven the country to ruin, and Ahab is a spineless king hopelessly in love with the wrong woman. Hair's plot opens at the time of the drought and continues past Jezebel's brave death and Jehu's rise to power, paralleling the biblical story closely but inventing some interesting fictional characters along the way.

Though the author cannot create convincing dialogue, he does supply imaginative additions to the cast of biblical characters. Most notable of the fictitious people are David and Lois, an interfaith couple who cannot marry until David rejects idolatry. David helps develop the theme of religious conflict among ordinary people, and he is persuaded to renounce Baal worship only after witnessing the Moabites sacrifice a child to sway the course of battle. Petroth, the queen's lusty spy, ensures the defeat of Ahab's military enemies by getting them drunk before battle. Petroth is also useful because he and one of Jezebel's maids provide examples of court licentiousness and are foils to David and Lois. Episodes about the queen's headstrong daughter, Athaliah, supply motivation for Jehu to revolt against the monarchy. Athaliah and Jehu are in love but cannot marry because Jezebel considers him unworthy of a princess. Ambitious Jezebel weds her daughter off to the king of Judah, though Athaliah despises the man. Athaliah and Jehu continue their clandestine affair even after her nuptials, and Jehu feels so disgraced and angry at her family that he vows to kill them all. The Bible's motive—Jehu's desire to reestablish Yahweh worship in Israel—is thus replaced by Jehu's sexual passion as the force that compels him to act. This is Hair's most significant alteration of the biblical text, for it eliminates Jehu as God's agent in fulfilling divine will and reduces Jehu to a randy rebel.

Next, in 1955, Dorothy Clarke Wilson published *Jezebel*, which—like Anderson's *Jezebel and the Dayspring* and Hair's *Jezebel*—also examines the interesting issues of sexual heat and virginal sacrifice. One reviewer of Wilson's *Jezebel* finds that the novel holds the reader's interest from the first to the last page (*Library Journal*), while the *New York Times* dubs the novel superficial and claims that the story is painful reading to anyone but those fans dedicated to historical novels of the commonest quality.

Wilson's Jezebel faces the dilemma of forfeiting her virginity to the gods. As a young princess, in a tradition established for all Tyre's virgins, Jezebel must sell herself to a stranger, thereby consecrating herself to her deity before she marries. The money she earns as a temple prostitute is supposed to subsidize Astarte worship, but Ahab foils the goddess. He is portrayed as a cunning and brave warrior at age sixteen. Soon after he proves himself in battle, Ahab visits Tyre to meet his prospective bride, as he does in other novels. While in Tyre, he bribes a guard and disguises himself so that he can be the one who lies with Jezebel. She is angry at herself for being more of a lusty wench than a holy priestess on that night, and she vows that in the future she will always put her responsibilities to Baal ahead of her personal pleasures. Jezebel thus decides to be a crusader for her god in Israel. Wilson claims that Jezebel's name means "unhusbanded" because the queen can never have any true mate but her god. The author is concerned with the problem of how the historically documented Canaanite custom of sacrificing virginity can be reconciled with the opposite Jewish expectations, so Wilson allows Ahab himself to deflower his future queen. Jezebel's monogamous behavior is thus contrived, though the need to remain a virgin seems far more important to the sensibilities of the author than to the heroine she creates.

The historical Jezebel novels of the 1960s continue to reveal a traditionally negative approach to interpreting the queen's character. The title of Frank Gill Slaughter's 1961 novel, *The Curse of Jezebel: A Novel of the Biblical Queen of Evil*, gives a strong indication of the author's attitude toward the queen. Dr. Slaughter defines a good narrative as one in which "exciting things [happen] to interesting people under colorful circumstances" (Slaughter, Interview 493). More than sixty million copies of Slaughter's popular and commercially successful novels are in print in more than twenty countries, leading his French publisher to dub the prodigious author "the American Balzac." Critics may scoff, but the public continues to buy. *The Curse of Jezebel* combines Slaughter's interests in military, biblical, and historical themes, though it reads like the pages of a "true confessions" magazine.

In *The Curse of Jezebel*, the queen is a beautiful and beguiling seductress. Though the Bible never mentions Jezebel's loveliness, legend insists upon it and Slaughter continues the myth. Naboth explains, "She is one of those women of rare beauty who seem to possess nothing but ambition and are incapable of real love" (36). Jezebel's court is full of temptations to men. Women don transparent clothing through which their flesh gleams, hardly honoring the Hebraic custom of modesty. They adopt the Egyptian habit of wearing cosmetics, tinting their cheeks and lips red, their eyelids black, their faces white, and decorating their bodies in a manner inconsistent with Jewish tradition. They also wear heavy jewelry, for being so near Phoenicia, they can easily obtain finely crafted gold, silver, and jeweled necklaces, bracelets, and earrings. Slaughter shows that these expensive and frivolous baubles, plus other extravagances, such as Jezebel's ornate ivory furniture from Tyre, have a negative impact on Israelite values. The people develop a taste for what appears outwardly beautiful while ignoring inner qualities. They are drawn toward temporal vanities and further away from God, strong testimony to Jezebel's hold on the country.

Even the most devout and faithful men are lured into Jezebel's trap, including Michael, the fictional hero of the story and ardent follower of God. Jezebel dances nude as the incarnation of the goddess Ashtoreth, seducing Michael in the process. Due to her position as high priestess of Ashtoreth, Jezebel has secret information about potions and witchcrafts designed to bend men to her will. Jezebel's ability to dominate men comes from her knowledge of the rare plant called the "Flower of Dreams" (122). Others, including Ahab, grow it in their gardens but are unaware of how the plant can be used to control behavior. Under the spell of the drug, men can only think of love and are oblivious to everything but the queen. She uses such magical potions and her uncommon beauty to manipulate people and obtain what she wants. The chauvinistic theme, firmly established by Slaughter, is that a woman's only sources of power are beauty and sorcery.

Slaughter, in *The Curse of Jezebel*, suggests that the queen is one of the most dramatically seductive women in the Bible. Ahab is an agile warrior and able statesman who only makes one mistake: marrying Phoenician Jezebel. The union is a political and trade alliance gone awry due to Jezebel's power over men. She is able to tempt them into following her fertility gods and goddesses, earning for Ahab the denunciation of God and the prophet Elijah. Jezebel schemes to have Elijah killed because he does not succumb to her beauty or charms and is therefore a threat to her continued power.

Further condemnation of Jezebel is found in Denise Robins's *Jezebel*. Robins, writing as Francesca Wright, first published this book as *She-Devil*, which may account for the lurid cover (plate 7). The first-person narrator is the fictional half-sister of Jezebel; Ethbaal is father to both girls. They look very much alike, except that Jezebel has dark tresses while the heroine, Thamar, has wheaten hair. Thamar is ordered to court to serve the young princess. Jezebel forces the girl to wear a dark wig and impersonate the royal sister when it suits her sinister purpose. In this novel, Jezebel is as she appears in many others, cruel but beautiful. On the first page, she appears naked, except for a ruby, the symbol of her power, which she wears in her navel. Jezebel's plan, from the beginning is to marry Ahab, become the power behind the throne, and turn Israel's people away from Jehovah and toward Baal. She never lacks courage and always craves excitement. Thamar is dismayed at the pain that Jezebel inflicts upon her subjects.

Robins employs symbolic action to communicate theme. Jezebel keeps animals, for she has an affinity for wild things, especially snakes and leopards. Yet she quickly loses interest and allows her pets to die. Jezebel's pet python, aptly named Zimri, escapes from his cage during the drought. He is found loyally curled around a pair of gold sandals at the foot of Jezebel's bed. She heartlessly kills the animal and throws the carcass into the fire. Thamar sees this act as prophetic, prefiguring the end of Jezebel's snakelike power. Also, Thamar loses a scarab that Ahab had given to her in the early days of their friendship. She always wore it and sees its loss as a portent of evil things to come. One day the jewel is found in the hands of a dying leper. "But this, too, was a symbol to me of evil—of the spiritual leprosy that was creeping like a hideous film across Israel," says Thamar (295).

Thamar secretly loves Obadiah. They hide their affections for many years, until Elijah marries the couple after the Naboth episode. Thamar is with Jezebel when she is thrown to her death. Displaying the courage so typical of her life, Jezebel faces her death:

> With her face painted, her great eyes gazing steadfastly under their blued lids, her fingers sparkling with fabulous jewels, she sat there in state in her son's place; knowing that it was useless to fight, for this was no ordinary military campaign but the fulfilment [sic] of the curse. (401–2)

After the queen's death, Thamar and Obadiah live in peace with their children, glad to see Israel return to God. Robins's *Jezebel*, though hardly great literature, provides some interesting plot variations to the traditional story. The novel never rises above the most mundane style and is typical of the many lesser novels using biblical themes.

Another retelling of the biblical Jezebel story is Gloria Howe Bremkamp's *Merai: The Woman Who Challenged Queen Jezebel and the Pagan Gods*. Jezebel appears only briefly in the plot and is thoroughly villainous. Merai, the novel's heroine, never mentioned in the Bible, had been a friend of Jezebel's children.

Yet Merai worships only Yahweh and detests Jezebel. One of the themes of the novel is that Jezebel causes Israel's troubles because of her apostasy and ongoing conflict with the religious establishment. No one, not even her terrible children, can rival the queen in wickedness.

As its lengthy title suggests, religious conflict is at the heart of Bremkamp's novel. Jezebel's son King Joram plans to destroy the pillar and altar of Baal, but he insists that Jezebel not be informed until the last minute, for she is sure to be furious. She rebukes her son for pulling down *her* pillar and altar, but Joram counters that he thought they were Baal's sacred objects. Jezebel hisses, "*I* belong to Baal. And they are mine" (74). After this incident, the queen plots against her own son, feeling she cannot trust him to rule as she would have him do. Furthermore, when King Jehoshaphat of Judah dies, Jezebel seizes the opportunity to influence her new son-in-law. She sends priests to instruct the people to worship Baal in the southern kingdom. The prophet Elisha must travel to the south to counter her efforts for a Baal takeover.

The religious turmoil reaches a crescendo when Jezebel insists that a boy named Ozem, raised from the dead by Elisha, was never really deceased. Claiming the resurrection to be a hoax, the queen declares that Baal is angry about the fraud and demands that six orphan boys be sacrificed to appease the god. Elisha predicts that the country will never heal until Jezebel is killed. After Jehu orders the queen to be thrown from her balcony window, he declares, "Now that Jezebel is dead, all children will be safer in Israel" (186). Except for the resurrection of the boy, none of the events in this novel is recorded in 1 or 2 Kings. Plot variations are, nevertheless, in keeping with the general attitude of the Deuteronomist, and one feels that the biblical writer would heartily approve of all these additions to the tale of the evil Jezebel.

As the twentieth century draws to a close, the myth and mystique of Jezebel live on through the genre of the biblical novel. She has clearly come to represent a primordial type, a being of epic proportions. But myth is not static; it grows and changes as it is passed from generation to generation. The biblical novel, either loosely or strictly based on the scripture's accounts, provides especially fertile ground in which to plant new seeds of information about the queen's personality and reign. Therefore, the collection of stories that fleshes out the rather scant biblical portrait of Jezebel continues to grow as the decades pass. Though the details vary from writer to writer, there are recurring themes in most of these fictitious works. Jezebel is usually a beautiful woman who has an uncanny ability to influence many men. Her power over people is a predominant message in the biblical novels. In addition, her conflict with the religious establishment remains intact. Now and then, modern writers take Jezebel's side and display her noble qualities, but the spirit of biblical condemnation is not usually impaired by new stories about the queen.

Nonbiblical Novels Condemning Jezebel

Someone once asked Joseph Campbell what happens when myth is no longer made. He sighed deeply and responded glumly, "Read the newspaper." Humanity needs its imaginary stories of glory and glamour, baseness and blood. We need our fictitious heroes and villains, for from their actions we learn how to handle our own problems and cope with our world. The Jezebel canon is not yet closed, despite the two millennia that have passed since her death. Even today, writers feel compelled to expand the body of literature that explains her life. While many novels explore the story found in the Bible, other prose works simply use the name Jezebel as a point of departure. A character may be named Jezebel or, more typically, called a Jezebel because she has traits that are traditionally thought to be reminiscent of the long-dead queen. Yet the stories are set in more modern times and often have little or nothing to say about ancient Israel. Relying on an assumed audience knowledge about who Jezebel was, authors tell who their new heroines are. Starting with Samuel Richardson and Henry Fielding and progressing through some of our best contemporary authors, interesting novels printed in English rely on the name Jezebel to conjure up strong images for readers. In this way, her myth continues and we gain insights into the psychology of new generations that rely on old myths.

Generally considered the first modern English novel, Samuel Richardson's *Pamela; or, Virtue Rewarded* (1740) makes nine references to Jezebel. The purpose of the epistolary novel is to advance conventional religious principles, though the values expressed are often prudish and bourgeois. It is hardly surprising that the name Jezebel, the antithesis of Richardson's innocent heroine, should find its way into the story. Pamela, a maid in the home of a wealthy family, resists the repeated advances of Mr. B., the owner's son. So impressed is Mr. B. by Pamela's piousness that he marries her and tries to reform his lecherous ways. Early in the novel, Pamela writes to her parents that she has been beaten by Mrs. Jewkes. Pamela exclaims to her tormentor, "Why Jezebel, said I, (I could not help it,) would you ruin me by force?" Mrs. Jewkes responds, "I'll Jezebel you, I will so!" (129–30), transforming the Israelite queen's name from a noun into a verb. Several years after the appearance of *Pamela,* Henry Fielding (who often loved to parody Richardson) echoes the age-old connection between Jezebel and troublesome women. In *Amelia* (1751), the heroine also opposes unwanted sexual overtures, and Fielding lumps Jezebel with other famous harridans, including Medea, Messalina, and Agrippina. The last eighteenth-century novel possessing a Jezebel reference is the little-known *Memories of Miss Sidney Bidulph* (1761) by Frances Chamberlaine Sheridan. Here the queen's name is not capitalized when the author refers to a faithless woman as "that jezebel of a wife" (220). In all these cases, early English novelists see Jezebel's reputation as a convenient device for conjuring images of a wicked woman, but nearly ninety years will pass before another well-known English novelist will create a memorable Jezebelian character.

In 1847 Charlotte Brontë published her absorbing, fantastical tale *Jane Eyre,* which depicts Bertha Mason Rochester, a minor but pivotal character who resembles Queen Jezebel. Jane is a shy, mistreated orphan whose journeys take her to dismal Thornfield Hall. Intelligent and strong but not beautiful or superficially charming, Jane becomes governess to the ward of Edward Rochester, master of Thornfield. Readers soon discover the cause of Rochester's brooding melancholy: his insane wife, Bertha, is locked up in the attic of his country estate. Jane does not discover this secret until she is at the altar, about to wed Rochester. Her insistence that Rochester's marriage vows be honored, no matter how mired in madness Bertha may be, points to Jane's noble character and deepens the contrast between herself and the novel's Jezebel. Jane flees, Bertha burns down the house, and Rochester is blinded in an attempt to rescue his demented wife. Years later he and Jane are happily reunited.

Like many heroes of great literature, Jane is on a quest. She is poor, plain, and doomed to wander the earth, suffering terrible misfortunes before gradually discovering her own self-worth. The tribulations she endures at Thornfield are essential to her growth as she struggles to balance her needs for independence and security. Here, the Jezebelian Bertha has a role to play in Jane's development. The deranged Bertha epitomizes the promiscuity so often associated with the Israelite Queen Jezebel. Rochester describes his wife: "Bertha Mason, the true daughter of an infamous mother, dragged me through all the hideous and degrading agonies which must attend a man bound to a wife at once intemperate and unchaste" (275). Like the biblical queen, Bertha is the undoing of her unsuspecting husband. Furthermore, Jezebel and Bertha share a similar demise. After the mad witch, as she is called, sets fire to Thornfield, Bertha leaps from the battlements to her death and is "dead as the stones on which her brains and blood were scattered" (385). Though Jezebel does not commit suicide, both she and Bertha fall from the top floors of their homes and leave blood stains on their castle walls. *Jane Eyre* presents a Gothic fairy tale in which the heroine overcomes psychological spheres of bleakness and depravity caused partly by a Jezebel-like character.

In the late 1800s, the somber setting of Brontë's novel is traded for the lively and robust open spaces of the great American West. Starting in the 1870s and continuing for more than twenty-five years, as Americans moved west and fought

Indians after the Civil War, Beadle and Adams published paperback thrillers in what they called the Half Dime Library. The Half Dime novels usually sold for five cents, were generally printed once a week, and were aimed at young boys who could not afford the company's more expensive Dime novels. The novelettes were about poor boys who found fame and fortune in the West, detectives who solved adventure mysteries, good guys in white hats, Indian scouts with uncanny know-how, outlaws in the Jesse James tradition, and sailors who challenged the powers of the sea. Company founders provided for their stable of writers a list of instructions to follow, including mandates that nothing nasty or sexy be printed, that stories better left untold would be, that the wild and woolly tales be strong and have original plots, and that the authors be familiar with the events and surroundings they describe (Johannsen 1: 4). Some of the best minor writers of the day, including Louisa May Alcott, wrote for Beadle and Adams, but the novelettes were always called "yellow covered literature" and accused of being cheap in content, as well as in price. Authors earned about one hundred dollars per manuscript, some writing ten novels per year. Two of the nickel novels printed in 1881 used the name Jezebel in their titles to titillate readers and stimulate pamphlet circulation.

Edward L. Wheeler penned *The Black Hills Jezebel; or, Deadwood Dick's Ward;* and Thomas Chalmers Harbaugh produced *Plucky Phil of the Mountain Trail; or, Rosa, the Red Jezebel* in 1881. Full of elaborate but ingenuous plots, stock characters, and ethnic clichés, the Half Dime novels were very popular in their day. They included comic book–style black-and-white illustrations on the covers and writing that was not much more sophisticated (plate 8). The biblical Jezebel herself is entirely absent from these rough-and-tumble sagas of the Wild West, but her name remains as a stereotype and quick clue to the dispositions of newly created evil women. When the author brands a woman a Jezebel, the audience should immediately understand that she is capable of heinous acts, and the author is spared the toil and bother of developing plausible characterization.

The first of these works, Wheeler's *Black Hills Jezebel*, is the eighteenth of Wheeler's more than thirty novelettes about hero Deadwood Dick. The topographical features Wheeler describes for the area surrounding the town of Deadwood never existed, but readers found them convincing as long as they had not seen the region firsthand (Johannsen 2: 296). Stories about Deadwood Dick were so popular that Beadle and Adams hired a ghost writer to continue them after Wheeler's death in 1885. In this story, as in others of his Half Dime novels, Wheeler does not merely rely on purple prose. He worships at its altar.

In *The Black Hills Jezebel*, the piece's beautiful heroine is Kentucky Kit. She and her father travel west to Placerville to track down Kit's mother, a Jezebel figure who now calls herself Madame Cheviot. Years ago in Kentucky, she defrauded her husband of all his money and headed for the Black Hills. Kit and her father are assisted in locating the swindler by Deadwood Dick, an investigator who works on the case and who saves the father and daughter from would-be assassins hired by Madame Cheviot. Dick must repeatedly rescue the innocent Kit from her mother's cunning schemes, thus advancing the damsel-in-distress theme that Wheeler and his readers apparently enjoyed so much. Still the avaricious bandit, Madame Cheviot now intends to commit bigamy by marrying another unsuspecting wealthy man, hoping to fleece him too. In the end, she is killed, being too evil to live:

> The Jezebel was buried the next day. . . . Her funeral was largely attended, more out of curiosity than anything else, and there were few who gazed upon the cold white face of the superlatively wicked woman who did not wonder what place there would be for such as she in eternity. (15)

Five times Madame Cheviot is called a Jezebel, though no explanation of the biblical allusion is ever offered. Apparently, none is needed.

That same year, *Plucky Phil of the Mountain Trail; or, Rosa, the Red Jezebel* was published by Harbaugh and put out as a Half Dime novel. Readers still hungry for tall tales of heathen redskins and brave white settlers had ample opportunity to satiate themselves. Earlier, in 1878, the editors of Harbaugh's hometown newspaper commented that they "regret exceedingly that [Harbaugh] should add in any wise to the already overloaded market of cheap, trashy literature. It is ruining our boys and girls" (Johannsen 2: 128). Today these works are an embarrassing retrospective on culturally biased ethnic stereotypes in late-nineteenth-century America, but in 1881 sales of the pamphlets were brisk. Once again feeding on readers' predispositions against Israelite Queen Jezebel, her new incarnation is a young Sioux woman named Rosa.

The story takes place after Custer's last stand. The hero is Phil Steele, a strong and handsome seventeen-year-old captain in love with Nora Dalton. Indians, referred to as "red niggers," attack a wagon train and kill five hundred white settlers. Phil searches for the one survivor—Nora, called the "White Flower," who has been saved from the massacre by an unscrupulous trapper and ruffian named Coyote. After Coyote holds Nora hostage for a while, the Sioux kidnap her. Chief Sitting Bull is convinced that, because Nora is so beautiful, she must also be someone important, and he wrongly convinces himself that Nora is a general's daughter. Hoping to ransom her for a high price, Sitting Bull places Nora in the care of a hunchback Indian, whom Harbaugh compares to Shakespeare's Caliban and calls The Ape. Nora's keeper hides his prisoner at the bottom of a twenty-five-foot-deep canyon and delivers food and water to her by climbing a rope. Meanwhile,

Rosa has been living with Coyote and is so jealous of his interest in Nora that the Indian woman tries on several occasions to locate and kill our heroine. Only Plucky Phil can save her in this second damsel-in-distress story, which pits the color white against the color red, good versus evil.

Rosa, the Red Jezebel, like other fictional Jezebels before her, is quite a little spit-fire and is often compared to a snake. Her deep, dark eyes are reminiscent of the Israelite queen's infamous painted face, and Rosa is even called a red queen. Her fits of jealousy supposedly recall the biblical character's less admirable traits and motives. Most noticeably, murder is always Rosa's solution to solving her problems, calling to the apt reader's mind the way in which the Bible's Jezebel disposes of Naboth. In the end, after author Harbaugh introduces many characters and twists of plot, Coyote dies and Rosa returns to her tribe. Phil saves Nora's life and the two are married. Sweet Nora tries to be generous to the murderous Sioux Jezebel by commenting to Phil on how deeply Rosa must have loved Coyote. "'In her mad Indian way,' the boy smiled. 'It is the love which continually carries a knife in its hand'" (13). Happy endings (for white people) are as predictable as ethnic slurs in this story of the American West. The Half Dime novels offer a glimpse of the racist attitudes of their day. Though they cannot be cited as examples of fine literature, they can help Americans understand their own cultural history, and what they reveal is not flattering.

Across the ocean in England near the end of the nineteenth century, Wilkie Collins was also a master of fiction depending upon sensation and intrigue. Though a far more skillful writer than the authors of the Half Dime novels, Collins shared their overdependency on plot and their interest in Jezebel. Toward the end of his career (1880), he wrote a lengthy thriller called *Jezebel's Daughter.* While the ingenuity of his narratives and his gift for creating mood and atmosphere were certain, Collins's plots were often so complicated as to be downright confusing and tedious. Preoccupied with mystery during his early career, he produced dozens of popular novels and later turned his attention to fiction with a strong moral purpose. These works added little to his fame or popularity, as Algernon Charles Swinburne playfully points out: "What brought good Wilkie's genius nigh perdition? / Some demon whispered, 'Wilkie! have a mission!'" (Peters 313). Anthony Trollope agrees that Collins excelled in plot construction, though he also lamented, "But I can never lose the taste of the construction" (Peters 392). In other words, Collins's technique was so obvious that a reader had difficulty relaxing and forgetting about it.

Collins's interest in intricate storylines may be traced to his association with Charles Dickens, under whom Collins worked as a magazine staffer. The two authors helped to establish a school of thought for Victorian novelists, with thrilling and often terrifying plot as a controlling force behind all their creations. Yet while Dickens fashioned characters and then molded them to the tale, Collins reversed the procedure and created the plot first then forced characters to fit in (Baugh 1353). This procedure seems to hold true for Collins's novel *Jezebel's Daughter*, containing a wicked woman referred to as a Jezebel.

The unusual length of Collins's dedication—about ten pages— gives some hint as to how loquacious he will be in developing the novel. These opening pages explain the author's view of his purpose and main characters. Madame Fontaine, impoverished widow of a German scientist, is the Jezebelian character of this murder mystery. The widow, despite her numerous faults and terrible deeds, dearly loves her daughter, Minna. Through many twists and turns of the plot, the widow repeatedly proves that she will lie, steal, and murder (using knowledge of her dead husband's poisonous chemicals)—anything to ensure a good marriage for her daughter.

Throughout this sensational novel, Madame Fontaine is referred to as a Jezebel, though the story neither parallels the biblical queen's life nor attempts to explain the allusion. For those familiar with the Naboth episode, however, the connection is made clear indirectly: *Jezebel's Daughter* contains an unscrupulous female character who will scheme and kill innocent people to get her way. Just as Queen Jezebel is portrayed as a power-hungry woman, Madame Fontaine admits her love of control. Realizing that her husband's poisonous potions and their antidotes allow her to eliminate any enemy or save any friend, her glee is revealed:

> "Power!" she thought, with a superb smile of triumph. "The power that I have dreamed of all my life is mine at last! Alone among mortal creatures, I have Life and Death for my servants. . . . What a position! I stand here, a dweller in a populous city—and every creature in it, from the highest to lowest, is a creature in my power!" (241)

In the end, Madame Fontaine is herself poisoned. Her diary reveals the full extent of her horrific plots. Collins has created a Victorian Jezebel, updating the biblical character for his own era, yet still relying on age-old stereotypes about the Israelite queen.

The hatred that Collins has for Jezebel is shared by Haldane MacFall in her 1925 novel, *The Wooings of Jezebel Pettyfer*. In a personal note, the author refers to "the reckless heroine of these pages" going forth "arrayed to fresh adventure in this naughty world." This novel takes place in Barbados and Jamaica, its black characters speaking MacFall's idea of dialect. There is much voodoo, sorcery, and local color the author thought typical of Caribbean climes. Characters are presented in a way that is patronizing and racist, like the epithets of the Half Dime novels. For example, Jezebel Pettyfer is a dressmaker by day but is described as "a brilliant belle amongst the coloured people by night. She was certainly a most comely brown creature, with features toned down to European daintiness" (43).

This Jezebel is delighted to have an unconventional biblical namesake. She has a turbulent relationship with her live-in lover, named Jehu Dyle, but refuses to marry him. When criticized for wantonness, she defends herself by citing what she views as the interesting women of the Bible:

> I has always been loose in me affections, honey, always, dat a fact—just de same like dat dar Jezebel in Holy Writ. . . . Appears to me de only women *wid* style dat was of much account in de Scriptures, dey was almost always loose in dey affections. Dar was Jezebel, she was a real slap-up fashionable fine woman—and she was loose in she's affections. (50)

When Jezebel finally marries the owner of a rum store, she is unfaithful to him. This connection to the biblical strumpet queen, based on Jehu's 2 Kings 9.22 accusation that Jezebel is a whore, is a source of pride for Pettyfer. Near the end of the novel, she goes to a wedding, where she dresses scantily and dances hotly, recalling the dance of Salome, another biblical woman who is loosely associated with the Jezebel myth.

The Bible's balcony scene is alluded to at the end of *The Wooings of Jezebel Pettyfer*. The merchant-skipper of a trading vessel "leaned against the balustrades, bending towards [Jezebel Pettyfer] in what was meant to be an attitude of amorous tenderness, toying clumsily with the siren" (347). A drinking glass, substitute for Jezebel herself and symbol of woman's frailty, falls off the balcony and smashes on the pavement below. The skipper insightfully comments on the nature of political and sexual relations between the races, saying that "de white man puts de black man into de gutter—ho-ho!—but de white man goes into de house of de black women—hee-hee!—ho-yes!" (348). At the end of the novel, Jezebel Pettyfer is promiscuous, just as the biblical queen is accused of being. This novel, long on plot, short on artistry, tries to portray the picturesque atmosphere of the tropics and the various attitudes of characters living in this exotic environment. It is an unusual setting for a Jezebel novel, a clear departure from the quaint English villages and American towns where most renditions transpire. Filled with outdated stereotypes of black people, it attempts to identify and describe rituals and customs of the islanders.

Patricia Hill Collins sees the linkage of Jezebel to the black woman as indicative of white society's desire to oppress minorities (77). During the days of legalized slavery, it was expedient to view black women as Jezebels, whores with excessive sexual appetites. White male slave owners thus concocted a twisted rationale for raping black women. The white man's logic indicated that, if black women were by nature oversexed, they would also be especially fertile. Impregnating their slave women was a free way of acquiring the next generation of slaves and saved slave owners an expensive trip to the auction block. By associating an increased birth rate with black women, such as Jezebel Pettyfer, slave owners justified the economic advantage of their sexual assaults on black women. Viewed from Patricia Collins's perspective, novels such as *The Wooing of Jezebel Pettyfer* are more than harmless light reading. They are dangerous purveyors of society's violence against women of color.

In 1917 Fred M. White wrote *A Society Jezebel*, another of the numerous pulp novels capitalizing on the Israelite queen's name. Unlike the lowly Jezebel Pettyfer, the sinful woman in this novel is a society beauty who calls herself Lady Mary Gay. She is a phony, however, who has kidnapped the real Lady Mary and shut her up in an asylum. Three times the fake Lady Mary is referred to as a Jezebel, but the allusion is never explained. White simply assumes that his readers will understand the reference. The plot includes a prison break, murder, and diamond heist as the impostor seeks to maintain her false identity. Soon after her ploy is discovered, she perishes from gas fumes in her drawing room. There is speculation that the death is suicide, but an inquiry proves nothing, and her real identity is never revealed. Elements of the traditional murder mystery appear in *A Society Jezebel*, but the style is mundane and unsatisfying.

Another work that occasionally has unfortunate racial and ethnic slurs typical of the early decades of the twentieth century is a short story by E. Phillips Oppenheim, "Jezebel of Valley Farm," published in 1926. Oppenheim was an English pioneer of espionage and diplomatic intrigue novels enthralling to millions of readers around the world. According to Oppenheim's biographer, he was not a great or even a serious writer, yet he entertained and distracted readers with his clever plots and deserves to be called the "Prince of Storytellers" (Standish). Oppenheim developed a Sherlock Holmes–type detective named Nicholas Goade, who solved crimes as fast as they could be committed.

In this story, master sleuth Goade is traveling in the Devon countryside when he comes upon a prosperous little farmhouse. Its mistress, Mona, is immediately recognizable as a painted woman and Jezebel character. Like Rosa, the Red Jezebel of the Half Dime novel, passionate reds are Mona's signature color: "She wore a rose-coloured gown—a strange piece of colouring in the landscape of greens and golds. Her lips, parted now in a lazy smile, were almost unnaturally scarlet" (183). While Rosa's villainy is connected to her Native American ancestry, Oppenheim concludes that Mona must have Gypsy blood and comments, "She walked with delightful freedom and a faint swaying of the hips suggestive of foreign origin" (185). Clearly, no proper English lady would look or act like Mona. After Mona's lover, Mr. Delbrig, kills her husband so that Mona will be free to marry again, suspicion wrongly falls upon a caravan driver who had been seen quarreling with Mona's husband. Detective Goade must solve the case.

Jezebel's eyes, symbol of the painted hussy in the Bible, are used by Oppenheim to develop his love-triangle and adultery themes. Oppenheim writes, "More than ever one realized the beauty of her body, the restless glory of her eyes" (202). Yet when Mona meets the caravan driver at a hotel, it is *his* eyes that draw and hold her, an interesting variation on the biblical story of the seductive woman. The two instantly decide to run away together, jilting Delbrig—who has eliminated the obstacle of Mona's unwanted husband. Delbrig is furious, confesses the crime, and shouts his disdain of two-timing Mona: "Hell blast her! The Jezebel!" (204). Full of cultural stereotypes, this story uses the image of Jezebel to suggest a flirtatious strumpet.

The name Jezebel is also used as a term of abuse for immoral women in some of the twentieth century's best novels. For example, *Light in August* (1932) by William Faulkner is one of several novels set in and around the imaginary Yoknapatawpha County town of Jefferson, Mississippi. Faulkner's stories about the decline of the Old South have a somber tone and unsettling subject matter, and his elegant prose was awarded a Nobel Prize seventeen years after *Light in August* first appeared. The book revisits the author's concerns about a narrow-minded society that insists on racial and ethnic divisions among people. Ignorance, violence, and religious extremism are rampant in Jefferson. The women have an especially hard time with sexuality, and minor female characters are characterized as Jezebels.

The preacher's wife provides the novel's first link to the biblical Jezebel. The minister's spouse is an unhappy woman. She does not attend church services and disappears for days at a time. There is innuendo about her lustful appetite, which Gail Hightower, her husband, cannot or will not satisfy. One day the newspapers report that she is killed in "a house or something in Memphis" (54). Actually, "she had jumped or fallen from a hotel window in Memphis Saturday night, and was dead. There had been a man in the room with her. He was arrested. He was drunk. They were registered as man and wife, under a fictitious name" (61–62). Just like the Israelite queen who had been flung from her balcony window, Mrs. Hightower comes to a bad end. At the burial, Hightower starts to read the Bible, but another minister comes forward and removes the sacred book from his hand. Not only has the wife ruined her own reputation, but she has made it impossible for her husband, beset with his own popularity problems, to continue preaching in Jefferson. Ahab's good name and ability to perform his duties had also been hampered by his wife, a situation that Gail Hightower might well understand.

In three of the novel's flashbacks, Faulkner connects his central character, Joe Christmas, to Jezebel. Joe is delivered into this world on 25 December, born to an unwed white woman and an unnamed black man, mixing the races in ways unacceptable in the South. The lecherous doctor who delivers Joe has a mistress, repeatedly referred to as a Jezebel. It is she who sarcastically suggests the baby's last name: "And it was her, the Jezebel of the doctor, that was the Lord's instrument, that said, 'We'll name him Christmas'" (363). The second Jezebel reference occurs when Joe is five years old and accidentally witnesses a tryst between two adults. Afraid that Joe will tell on them and get them fired from their jobs, the couple fights. In a moment of anger, the man refers to his lover as a Jezebel. Lastly, the abusive tyrant who raised Joe catches him with a woman and furiously refers to her as a Jezebel and a harlot. Not surprisingly, Joe grows up with little respect for women. At one point, he realizes that he prefers the company of horses: "It's because they are not women. Even a mare horse is a kind of man" (101). Eventually Joe murders a middle-aged spinster with whom he has been living and sets her house on fire. Joe is himself killed by an angry mob, yet the reader cannot help but feel that Joe has been a victim all his life. He certainly is unlucky with women.

Chronologically, the next novel that makes a reference to the biblical queen is entitled *Jezebel's Daughter,* written in 1935 by Alan Robert Craig. Similar to Oppenheim's Mona, Craig's Cornelia Curtois is considered a Jezebel because of her bohemian lifestyle and her effect on men. Long after her death she continues to cast her spell. Some critics compliment the book's exciting plot, though others (*New York Times;* McCarthy) find that the extent of Cornelia's influence over her husband lacks verisimilitude. The biblical Jezebel's dominance of Ahab is sometimes hard to believe too.

Craig reworks the balcony scene from the Bible in *Jezebel's Daughter.* Cornelia's hotel has a balcony from which she likes to observe the nightlife of Guayaquil, Ecuador, where she lives. Her daughter, Sarah, overhears some ladies criticizing Cornelia:

> "It reminds me of—you know that woman in the Old Testament who they threw down into the street. Only I say this, Cornelia Curtois wouldn't trouble to paint her face!" A gentler voice, with laughter running through it, remarked, "Jezebel, I suppose you mean; but did Jezebel have a daughter? The Bible never tells one any of the things one really wants to know." (83)

The ladies concur that a woman like Cornelia is unfit to raise children. This is the only direct mention of Jezebel in the book, and one would prefer to assume that it is the Guayaquil society ladies, not the author, who lack knowledge of the Bible's discussion of Jezebel's ruthless daughter, Athaliah. Furthermore, Cornelia's death scene also takes place on her balcony. During a street battle as the Communists struggle to gain power in Ecuador, Cornelia is hit by a stray machine-gun bullet, a modern variation of Jehu's revolution and the weapons used to wage war. Conservative and puritanical Sarah loves her mother, but she must work hard to overlook Cornelia's lovers and unconventional behavior. Sarah later marries her dead mother's husband, but the daughter always comes in second for his affection. Just as the biblical Jezebel seems to have a special hold on men, so does Cornelia—the queen's South American imitator.

The mother-daughter conflict of Craig's work is replaced by mother-son conflict in the next Jezebel novel. Irene Nemirovsky published *A Modern Jezebel* two years later, in 1937. This pulp murder mystery is tawdry and drab to some critics, though Dorothea Kingsland of the *New York Times* praises it for having sophistication and magnetic appeal. The main character, with the amusing name Gladys Eysenach, is pure evil, her only motivation being vanity. Gladys, a wealthy woman of surpassing beauty, must be the cynosure of her world; she cannot endure the thought of growing old and losing her looks. The story begins with Gladys in a Paris courtroom where she is being tried for murdering her twenty-year-old lover, Bernard Martin. She admits killing him but denies he was her paramour. Martin turns out to be Gladys's son, and a friend of Martin's gives evidence that on the night of the murder Martin was drunk and talked about his mother being a Jezebel. The friend testifies that Martin said, "My mother Jezebel revealed herself before me" (49). The judge sentences Gladys to five years in prison. The rest of the novel is flashback that narrates the tale of Gladys's pathetic life, from age seventeen to sixty, in straight chronological order.

Once again, a writer with limited ability uses the Jezebel myth as a substitute for detailed characterization. In the Jezebel tradition, Gladys's beautiful eyes are relied upon to reveal her personality. Her future daughter-in-law notices the resemblance between Gladys and her son: "You have the same kind of eyes—What shall I call them?—Fatal?" (245). Because Gladys is a Jezebelian character obsessed with remaining young and gorgeous, questions arise in the minds of thoughtful readers about the fleeting nature of beauty. Handsome objects often carry with them demands that we try to do something about their beauty—covet it, possess it, retain it forever. The beautiful people themselves may be profoundly attached to the ideal of their own fortunate physical appearance, hoping to hang on to the exterior appearance at the expense of interior integrity. Handsome women of literature will sometimes go to any extreme to maintain this prized possession, their physical loveliness. Furthermore, surface charm may easily delude us about the true character of such individuals. This does not obtain in Gladys's case, for we have an omniscient narrator who, though unwilling to reveal secrets about plot resolution, is always ready to discuss a character's personality traits. The ugliest of thoughts and actions hide behind Gladys's graceful figure and pleasant face, perhaps teaching perceptive readers to view physical charm skeptically. The natural antagonists of youth and beauty are old age and death, for no matter how powerful the fictional character, the passage of time is always stronger. Realizing that fact is potentially tragic, as in Gladys's story. She is undone by her flaw of caring too deeply for her flawless good looks, and she commits murder as a result of her thirst for eternal youth. When Martin threatens to reveal the truth about his birth and his mother's age, they struggle over a gun, and the young man is killed. The novel may be plebeian, but the issues raised are not.

In 1939 a high watermark in twentieth-century literature was achieved when James Joyce published his last, most experimental, and highly erudite novel, *Finnegans Wake*. Because it is practically impenetrable to the unschooled reader, many tomes interpreting the meaning of this complex work exist today. The main difficulty lies in understanding Joyce's own special language, invented by the author himself, and filled with allusions to philosophical treatises, popular Irish songs, legendary folk heroes, sports, art, historical and literary characters, portmanteau words, bizarre puns, foreign phrases, and every other conceivable source. Through unconventional language and wordplay, Joyce tells the story of H. C. Earwicker and family, revealing their dreams as they lie sleeping in their beds.

The events of the family's day, their anxieties and guilt, and their darkest secrets are revealed in rambling fashion through their nightmares. In his sleep, Earwicker relives the time he accosted someone in a park, but it is never clear whether the victim is male or female. Earwicker's guilty conscience links him with various evil figures, including Lucifer. The first reference to Jezebel comes as "them bearded jezabelles you hired to rob you" (192). Sexual matters dominate the dreams, and as he sleeps Earwicker even substitutes his daughter, Issy (Isobel, a name similar to Jezebel), for his wife as a sexual partner. To avoid the problem of incest, in Earwicker's dream Issy magically transfigures into Iseult the Fair, while he himself changes into Tristram. One of the clearest facts about Issy's appearance is that she uses cosmetics, and Jezebel becomes a generic term for a troubled woman who wears makeup (Glasheen 145). It is hardly surprising that the name Jezebel would appear during the sexual machinations of the family's dreams: "a jigsaw puzzle of needles and pins and blankets and shins between them for Isabel, Jezebel and

Llewelyn marriage" (210). The line refers to a song, "Needles & pins, blankets & shins, when a man is married his sorrow begins" (McHugh 210), recalling Ahab's troubles with his wife. Finally, in *Finnegans Wake* Joyce refers to any immoral girl as "a nice jezebel" (562).

All the women in the novel gradually become associated with Earwicker's wife, Anna Livia Plurabelle, and with the River Liffey. The circular river-to-sea progression of life is one of Joyce's dominant themes. Earwicker's sin is committed in Phoenix Park; the mythological Phoenix bird is supposed to rise out of its own ashes in a five-hundred-year cycle of birth and death. Christianity teaches that the Fall of man is followed by death and resurrection, and the novel's title is based partly on the name of Irish folk hero Finn MacCool, who is supposed to return someday and save his people. Thus the cyclical repetition of good and evil is played out in *Finnegans Wake,* and the biblical Queen Jezebel plays her small part in the piece. Jezebel also seems to be connected to Bela Cohen, the aggressive madam from Joyce's *Ulysses.*

As the decade of the 1930s yielded to the 1940s, reader interest in complicated characters created by such authors as Joyce was replaced by public preoccupation with the weapons of war. One of the strangest of all the World War II–era novels is called *Jezebel the Jeep* by Fairfax Downey. It is truly difficult to believe that this novel is not written tongue in cheek, but the author seems serious, setting a new low for foolishness. The plot summary on the front cover of this paperback states:

> She was more, far more, than a quarter-ton truck, U.S. Army model, to her driver, T/5 Jonathan W. Johansen, of the Field Artillery. To him she was a jeep of jeeps. She had an impetuous individuality, manifested even on the assembly line, and a sometimes pernicious personality which kept cropping up. She was named after one of the most determined and high-handed ladies in history and she lived up to her name.

The jeep is called a "painted Jezebel," and the driver inscribes the name on the front of the vehicle, replacing the name of the girlfriend back home who jilts him. The biblical story of Jezebel reminds Johnny of how many problems a person can have by marrying the wrong woman. Johnny's father is a preacher, so the soldier remembers one of his father's sermons about the queen who caused so much trouble. Johnny's captain approves of the alliteration in the term "Jezebel the Jeep." The vehicle is called "a true namesake of Queen Jezebel who likewise brushed aside anything and everything that stood in her path" (60–61). The captain is liberal-minded enough to admire Queen Jezebel as a determined and high-spirited lady, the kind of person who would be a valuable ally during wartime. The wrecked vehicle and Johnny travel home together on the same ship, and the

Red Cross volunteer who meets Johnny on the New York dock is named Jessie Belle. Readers can only hope that the woman lives up to the jeep's reputation.

Also during the war era there is a murder mystery, part of the Red Badge Detective Series, that uses the name Jezebel to help describe an unwholesome woman. Under the name Christianna Brand, Mary Lewis wrote *Death of Jezebel* (1948), which takes place in London immediately after World War II. Isabel Drew (called a Jezebel in the character list), Perpetua Kirk, and Earl Anderson are implicated in a murder. Isabel, Perpetua, and Earl receive threatening notes promising that they too will soon be murdered. Isabel's nightly theatrical job involves ascending the steps to a balcony, and as the floodlights shift, one evening she is thrown over the low railing and lands with a thud on the floor below.

When friends moan about the passing of poor Isabel, one character cries:

> Poor Isabel? Poor Jezebel, more like! That's what Earl Anderson used to call her; and he was right. What good did she ever do, that you should pity her now, when she's met with her just deserts? . . . She was rotten: vulgar and greedy, and heartless, and immoral. (81)

The inspector working on the case recalls that the biblical Jezebel was also thrown from a second-story window to her death. Later Earl is decapitated, and the search for the killer intensifies.

The Mystery Writers of America twice awarded author Brand/Lewis with commendations for her short stories, and she was named Grand Master in Sweden. *Death of Jezebel* has a successful detective-story ending because the whodunit is solved, the reader being denied vital information that would have made it possible to predict the outcome. Plot, once again, is the focus of the work. Characterization and all other elements of quality literature are sacrificed so that suspense and surprise can be maintained, but this is conventional within the mystery genre. Craftsmanship is important to Brand/Lewis, who says in an interview published in *Contemporary Authors*, "What is my aim? To write good, readable (saleable) entertainment books and above all to write them well. I detest illiterate writing, I detest bad style, bad grammar, bad punctuation." The Jezebel reference in this book reflects Brand/Lewis's literate style and helps identify Isabel as a wicked creature who is herself capable of murder. The biblical queen's balcony death is never mentioned by the author, who apparently assumes either that readers have a sufficient understanding of the Kings narrative to comprehend the allusion or that failure to catch the reference will not impede their enjoyment of this work.

If pedestrian novels are typified by Brand/Lewis's *Death of Jezebel*, trashy paperbacks are well represented by Kate Nickerson's *Ringside Jezebel*, published in 1953. In the style of the 1950s, the book presents a suggestion of sex but no real examples of it. The cover teases the reader: "She was a girl with the smell of battling men in her nostrils, the taste of their kisses on her lips." The biblical queen is never mentioned in the text, but the heroine, Terry Hayes, is presumably the "ringside Jezebel." The reader is thus left to wonder whether it is the publisher, not the author, who made the connection between the two women and who chose the title. Actually, Terry does not behave in a manner traditionally expected of a Jezebel. She spurns a rich and powerful New York syndicate boss, opting instead for the love of a poor prizefighter. The biblical queen would surely have preferred the king of the underworld and would have relished his scheme to force the boxer to throw a fight.

A far cry from the tawdry *Ringside Jezebel* is a children's book by F. N. Monjo entitled *The Jezebel Wolf*. It is based on a true story that Israel Putnam often told about a wolf hunt in the winter of 1742–1743 near Pomfret, Connecticut. Twenty years after the hunt, General Putnam was one of George Washington's most able officers in the Continental army. At the Battle of Bunker Hill, it was Putnam (Old Put) who told the men not to fire until they could "see the whites of their eyes." In the preface, Monjo says that he wants to tell modern readers about the wolf hunt because "it is a gripping story in its own right and one which embodies an act of frontier courage that backward-looking addicts of nostalgia [such as himself] would like to believe to be distinctively American." To assist him in recreating an American pioneer story, Monjo refers to the ancient queen of Israel. Once again, the background for the Jezebel reference is not explained in the text, even though his intended audience of youngsters is probably not familiar with the biblical queen's exploits. Israel follows "the she-devil" into her lair and, after a great battle, finally kills the animal. She is an intelligent, formidable opponent who leads her pursuers on a long and exhausting chase. Israel is forced to enter her cave three times before he is able to kill and drag her out. After the wolf dies, all the neighbors have a big celebration "on account of killin' that sheep-murderin' Jezebel at last" (40–41). They hang the wolf high on a beam for all to see before Israel skins her. Adults may notice a slight resemblance between the wolf's death and the queen's, but juvenile readers will not. Nevertheless, the story preserves an interesting American legend, for the wolf's den is reputedly still in existence today.

In 1993 Canadian literary luminary Margaret Atwood published *The Robber Bride*, a bestseller and winner of the Trillium Award. Atwood is no stranger to critical praise, and this work received the acclaim due the most talented writers. The novel contains a Jezebelian character, Zenia, whose "name is enough to evoke the old sense of outrage, of humiliation and confused pain. Or at least an echo of it" (11). Yet citing an adage that a nonbiting rattlesnake teaches one nothing, Atwood suggests that contact with Zenia/Jezebel, devastating though it surely is, provides valuable learning experiences for her victims, and *The Robber Bride* has plenty of victims. Everyone who comes into contact with Zenia is deeply harmed by her deceptions and tricks. Zenia's three former college classmates (Tony, now a history professor; Charis, an ex-flower child; and Roz, an entrepreneur) believe that Zenia was killed by a Lebanese terrorist's bomb. United by their hatred of the dead woman, as the novel opens they see Zenia—alive and well—in a Toronto restaurant. Zenia is back in town, like the black-hatted villain in a Western movie. Through a series of flashbacks, the novel explains how her mendacity has disrupted, if not destroyed, the lives of the three friends. Conjecturing about Zenia's motive for seducing and stealing away the men they love and for generally causing havoc in everyone's life, Tony thinks, "Maybe she lied and tortured just for the fun of it" (208). Shocked that Zenia is still alive, the women wonder what to do next.

Atwood's sarcastic, spicy tone is evident when she describes Zenia's physical appearance. In her current reincarnation, Zenia is plumper than the three friends remember her, especially her breasts, which have been surgically enhanced with silicone implants. Tony, Charis, and Roz speculate that when a person dies and is cremated the implants will not burn: "that's the rumour going around, about artificial boobs. They just melt" (89). Voluptuousness, breasts, symbols of feminine allure and nurturing, must be purchased by evil Zenia, who has no natural attributes linking her to womanly softness. Roz imagines the stitch marks where Frankenstein physicians have worked their magic. She daydreams about the fault lines along which Zenia might split open. Adventurers, Atwood tells us, live by their wits, but adventuresses live by their tits. As in Jezebel's case, Zenia's cosmetics and eyes receive attention from the author. Zenia's curiously immobile, masklike face always looks made up, even when it is not. Her mascara does not run because it is not mascara; it is Zenia's own sinister black eyelashes.

Jezebel connections become more direct as the novel progresses. For example, when Charis was a little girl, her grandmother read one Bible verse each week. She would open the scriptures, close her eyes, stick a pin down randomly on a page, and read only the one sentence where the pin landed. One day the grandmother reads, "Now the dogs shall eat Jezebel by the wall of Jezreel," but she does not understand what the verse means. On another Sunday, she asks Charis to stick the pin down. Revelation 2.20 comes up, the story of the Bible's second Jezebel. After Zenia reappears at the restaurant, a grown-up Charis again takes down the Bible and does the pin trick. It falls on 2 Kings 9.35, the passage about nothing being left of Jezebel's body when Jehu's men return to bury the dead queen: "It's Jezebel thrown down from the tower, Jezebel eaten by dogs. *Again,* thinks Charis. Behind her eyes there is a dark shape falling" (322). Charis fantasizes about throwing Zenia out a window. The body is light, as though disease has hollowed and rotted out Zenia's insides. Charis dreams of throwing Zenia's body over the balcony rail and watching it float down, hit the edge of a fountain, and burst open like an overly ripe squash. Later Zenia's dead body actually does end up in a fountain under her hotel window. Really deceased this time, Zenia is cremated. Her three friends take an urn containing the ashes to disperse them over water, but the vase cracks in two. "It pleases [Charis] that Zenia would attend her own scattering, making herself known. It's a token of her continuation. Zenia will now be free, to be reborn for another chance at life" (526).

Atwood uses Jezebel as a symbol of eternal evil, reborn in every generation. The details of how a wicked life plays out will change with each reincarnation, but the general nature of depravity is always the same, causing the Jezebel/Zenia character to seem unidimensional. The symbol of amorality is not supposed to be a well-rounded human being. One interpretation is that ruthless, self-centered Zenia is too bad to be true; another is that she embodies all the evil impulses that the three heroines have conquered in their quest to be credits to womanhood. Forming Zenia as a flat character marks a change in Atwood's feminist perspective, for rarely does the author acknowledge that a woman may embody all that troubles the world. As usual, each main character in the novel—Tony, Charis, Roz—is an intelligent, pained, confused woman absorbed in her search for identity and struggle with relationships and career. The difference in *The Robber Bride* is that the source of angst is another female, a wolf in designer clothing, a Jezebel. Appearing in the guise of a beautiful and vulnerable friend, this femme fatale comes to seduce the three heroines' men, men who are so weak that they can hardly be trusted to take the dog for a walk around the block, much less ward off the advances of a cunning woman. Yet perhaps Atwood achieves a more balanced sort of feminism here, one that considers women, not just men, as possible destroyers of the dream of a happy life.

Atwood does not need to explore the complexities of Jezebel's character or suggest alternatives to the stereotype of her depraved nature. Instead, the Israelite queen is the unquestioned representation of the dark side of human nature, and Atwood uses Jezebel/Zenia to relate complicated stories about the betrayal of trust. On the surface, the three protagonists also seem to be mere stereotypes: Tony, the clever academic; Charis, the New Age earth mother; and Roz, the successful businesswoman. Atwood quickly moves beyond these clichés to build the theme that power plays underlie relationships. Zenia is called a robber bride, a variation on the robber bridegroom story for children wherein beautiful maidens searching for husbands are lured to the woods and chopped into pieces by handsome strangers. Zenia's friends conclude that "Robber Broad" is a more apt title for her because she is nothing more than "an up-market slut" (332). Jezebel's image as a vamp who controls men through sexual appeal is perpetuated by the Zenia character. While a few authors doubt that Jezebel could actually have been as terrible as her reputation, Atwood uses that reputation to help build the theme of evil's constant presence in the world. Malevolence takes female form in Atwood's *Robber Bride*, linking this novel to its many earlier counterparts that hold women responsible for mankind's troubles, but it develops the message with wit and graceful prose.

The final example in the category of nonbiblical novels that condemn Jezebel is *Serpent's Tooth* (1997), a *New York Times* bestseller by detective novelist Faye Kellerman. This thriller compares Jezebel to the beautiful female mastermind behind a mass murder in Los Angeles. The Jewish detective in charge of the case jokes that perhaps he should consult the holy books for advice about what to do when being harassed by an evil woman. The Elijah–Jezebel conflict works for Kellerman as it has for other writers in other generations. The trend of using the Israelite queen's name to assist in modern storytelling is unlikely to stop in the near future, but there are also a half dozen lively and interesting novels more charitable to the ancient queen's memory.

Jezebel Redeemed

Redeeming Jezebel's character and reputation is no simple task, yet some novelists portray the queen in a favorable light. One of the first novels to do so was published in America and retells the Kings story: *Jezebel: A Romance in the Days When Ahab Was King of Israel*, written by Lafayette McLaws and printed in 1902. It has four illustrations by Corwin K. Linson, placed at strategic points in the story (plate 9). Though not a great work of art, the novel contains unique additions to the biblical plot and is one of the few biblical novels that is generous to Jezebel. The unchauvinistic tone is developed by the narrator, an Egyptian dwarf who is Jezebel's loyal servant and who tells in first person what he sees at the palace. The dwarf loves his queen, finds her to be beautiful and kind, a faithful wife and devoted mother, and usually a wise ruler of her people. McLaws's positive portrait is uncommon in fictitious accounts of Jezebel's reign. Rarely does an author's development of Jezebel's character show the queen's ability to inspire affection and trust in others.

Jezebel's relationship to God is explained in a sympathetic manner in McLaws's novel, diametrically opposed to the biblical account. The queen is portrayed as a dutiful wife who knows her place and honors her husband's deity: "I lead [the Israelites] not away, for I, Jezebel, bend the knee to Jehovah because he is the God of King Ahab, and it is seemly for a woman to worship the gods of her lord" (86).

She sincerely believes, however, that Yahweh shows his clenched fists more frequently than his protective arms and that the Jews need a more merciful deity. She thinks God is sometimes cruel and rules by threats. Her native god Baal is a kinder, gentler alternative. It also has not escaped Jezebel's notice that Mosaic law is hard on women, and she treats Israelite women as sisters and encourages Ahab to grant them greater freedom.

The long drought is as depressing to Jezebel as it is to ordinary citizens of Israel. Though no mention of the queen's generosity is mentioned in the Bible, in McLaws's novel Jezebel opens palace storehouses and feeds the hungry from her own table. (More kind words are heaped upon the queen later in the story when Samaria is besieged by Ahab's enemies. Jezebel labors tirelessly and turns the palace into a hospital, where she personally assists the physicians in caring for the sick.) During the drought, a sinister change bubbles and churns to the surface of Jezebel's personality as a result of her long feud with the prophet Elijah. In her anger and frustration over Elijah's intolerance, Jezebel learns to be cruel. Ahab also senses a change in his queen. In a good example of McLaws's brand of symbolism, Jezebel is described as a finely crafted sword; and Ahab, though proud of his valuable possession, also fears the blade's sharpness.

The novel contains long subplots about fictional characters not mentioned in the Bible, notably palace spies and the virtuous Ruth, daughter of Naboth, whom Ahab's father, Omri, had once considered as a potential bride for Ahab. The most astonishing and intriguing departure from the Bible and from every other Jezebel novel involves Ruth. She and servant Amon are placed in a situation recreating the biblical story of Shadrach, Meshach, and Abednego in the third chapter of Daniel. Because they disobey Jezebel, now hardened with care and woe, Ruth and Amon are placed in a fiery furnace. Ruth goes into the blaze like a bride meeting her beloved groom. Just as Nebuchadnezzar, the sadistic despot in the Book of Daniel, is foiled by the three Jewish men who remain steadfastly loyal to God, both of McLaws's characters also emerge from the flaming death trap unharmed. In a miraculous change of heart, contrary to the spirit of the biblical account, Jezebel experiences a complete reversal of faith after Ruth and Amon's episode in the fiery furnace. In no other adaptation of the Jezebel story does this sort of Aristotelian recognition and reversal take place. Here McLaws's story ends; Jezebel becomes a faithful believer in Yahweh. She is treated sympathetically by the author, and now the reader can see why. The queen redeems herself by converting. She renounces her pantheon of gods and embraces the one true divinity.

It is not until 1961 that another biblical narrative favorable to Jezebel appears. *The Painted Queen* by Olga Hesky is a thoughtful novel possessing passages of theological insight. Yet its pedestrian style embarrasses reviewers, who tire of the shrill defense of Jezebel (e.g., *Spectator; Times Literary Supplement*), for the author insists that the queen is always an obedient wife and Israelite patriot. Hesky is definitely skeptical about the truth of biblical accounts, especially those concerning the prophet Elijah.

The author distrusts Elijah and poses the reasonable hypothesis that Ahab practices religious tolerance in the land. Other deities had always been worshiped in Israel, not at the instigation of Jezebel but simply because the people were attracted to other gods. While Ahab himself follows Yahweh and gives all his children names that reflect his faith, he has no intention of denying religious freedom to any of the citizens, including Jezebel with her devotion to Baal and Astarte. It is precisely this liberal attitude that causes the conflict with Elijah, and Jezebel is the prophet's natural target because she is a public figure who does not accept Yahweh as the exclusive divinity of the Jewish people. Despite his penchant for respecting other religions, Hesky's Ahab is reluctant to build a temple to Baal in Samaria, for he already has begun to have trouble with Elijah and the priests of Yahweh.

In *The Painted Queen*, Elijah dictates his version of events to a scribe and is not concerned with facts. Rather, he wants "history" to be written in a manner that suits his religious purpose of elevating Yahweh's position. Elijah feels this manipulation of detail is righteous because the public is not capable of discerning right from wrong and because future generations will only know what is found in scripture. Elijah realizes that the words will be read in the future by people who were not eyewitnesses and who have no way of knowing what actually transpired. Hesky states, "Only the words will remain. And so it is that history is made, not by events, but by the writing; not by kings and not by peoples, but by the prophets who dictate the records and the scribes who write them" (34). Therefore, Elijah wants to control what is written, for as something is called, so it becomes. Hesky alleges that this is what happens in the Carmel, Naboth, and fiery chariot episodes.

One event that Elijah misrepresents in scripture is the Mount Carmel contest. Hesky maintains that no drought is ever unexpected in this arid land. Every person who lives to middle age can recall a similar extended period when little or no rain fell. In *The Painted Queen*, the people do not care whether it is Yahweh or Baal who stops the drought, just so long as the parching of people, cattle, crops, and land comes to an end. Hesky's Elijah uses a trick to light the sacrificial fire on Mount Carmel during the duel of the gods: a handful of "precious and mysterious stones," "queer-looking pebbles" (140), which the prophet procures from desert nomads. He throws them onto the pyre. Shafts of smoke rise from the wood; then it suddenly catches fire.

According to Hesky, Elijah also contrives an outrageous lie about Jezebel framing the innocent Naboth. Shahar, the scribe whom Hesky invents to assist Elijah, warns the prophet that the Naboth story is a limping, implausible tale that will never be believed, but the scribe dutifully records it as his mentor demands. Hesky states that God gives Elijah vital information that could have saved Naboth's life but too late, for God desires the vineyard owner's death. Jezebel and Ahab are thus God's tools, so the couple's actions should be appreciated instead of condemned. Finally, Hesky maintains that the flaming chariot carrying Elijah to heaven is merely an example of another tall tale created for future generations to read as "history." In her novel, nobody knows when or where the phantomlike Elijah dies; his passing is as mysterious as his coming. Whenever the great prophet is mentioned, Hesky offers a counterbiblical explanation for events, and her ideas have a clear, plausible ring. *The Painted Queen* emerges as a Jezebel novel that critically questions the politics of biblical sources.

The next Jezebel novel also treats the heroine favorably but for radically different reasons. Richard Pryce's *Jezebel* (1913) begins in an English village where the Lord of the local manor has, in a fit of jealousy and unfounded suspicion against his Lady, just made the shocking decision to christen their daughter Jezebel. Pryce is keenly aware of the biblical story and draws upon the passage in 2 Kings 9.22 in which Jezebel is accused by Jehu of practicing witchcraft. In her childhood years, Pryce's Jezebel performs her special magic and sorceries, believing she has the power to make lightening strike and people die. The child is called Jessy so that the townspeople are spared the shock of dealing with the name of a notorious fallen woman, but the girl herself prefers Jezebel. It is a magnificent challenge, she thinks, to possess a unique name:

> There were no Jezebels in books, only Jessys that are Jessicas. *She* was a Jezebel, the only Jezebel, the one Jezebel in the world. It was glorious. The thing became a pride and an unbreathed boast. She hugged it to herself together with the triumph of the blasted oak. She was not like other people. (94)

She reads the Bible and adores the part about Jezebel painting her face, fixing her hair, and looking out of the balcony window. Imitating the ancient queen, the girl surprises a servant one day by looking down at him from the nursery casement, her cheeks painted vermilion and her hair piled high on her head. She yells, "Had Zimri peace?" Always a high-spirited creature, this fictional Jezebel revels in the notoriety obtained from having a spunky biblical namesake. The novel was positively received by reviewers in 1913, some critics noting that Pryce was well versed in the study of women. The *New York Sun*'s comment, however, is that the author's "harping on the poor joke of his heroine's name is tiresome" (4).

Pryce's Jezebel becomes involved with a well-born gentleman, Philip Malmsey, but years of circumstances—including the interference of family, travels, education, and their own pride—keep them apart. Philip thinks his beautiful and fiery Jezebel is made of "snow, blood, and ebony" (135). Over the years, Jezebel matures and gives up her malicious ways. In an astonishing shift from the biblical queen's diabolical image, Pryce allows his character to be called "Jezebel-Mary." Yet when she goes to a ball and looks down from a balcony, Philip's mother still wishes the high-spirited girl would be thrown down, as was her Israelite predecessor. The reformed Jezebel and Philip do not wed until the last page of the novel, where-upon Jezebel becomes a respected family name among the Malmseys. This rever-sal of fortune, where the evil woman is transformed into the good heroine, is not unheard of in the Jezebel novels, but actually associating her with the Virgin Mary is unprecedented. Furthermore, the evil connotations of the name Jezebel are overcome by the headstrong heroine. Pryce suggests that virtue can be found in the darkest of hearts and that change is always possible.

Events during and immediately after World War II are discussed in *Jezebel's Dust* by award-winning Scottish author Fred Urquhart. Published in 1951, this novel is the story of Bessie Campbell, a young woman living in Edinburgh and London during the 1940s. Like most young people, Bessie likes escapist films and talks endlessly about movie stars, reflecting the interests of author Urquhart, who was also a script reader for Metro-Goldwyn-Mayer and a scout for Walt Disney Productions. Bessie is influenced by her friend Lily, who drinks, smokes, goes to dance halls, and sleeps with any man who pleases her. In what may (or may not) be intended as a Jezebel reference, a colonel raises his glass to toast Lily's eyes: "To your eyes, Miss Lily, to your beautiful immoral eyes!"

Encouraged by Lily, Bessie begins to have affairs, one with an abusive and vio-lent Polish soldier and another with a man who leaves her pregnant when he goes to the front. Bessie marries him, but to her relief, baby and husband both die. Bessie sometimes likes to read and has a copy of *The Poems and Sermons of John Donne,* although she says that his funny spellings and obtuse sentences are beyond her comprehension. Bessie and Lily read Donne's sermon about Jezebel's dust, but neither understands it. At the end of the novel, Bessie marries an American sol-dier and goes to live in his hometown. They have two children, and Bessie tells them war stories. The optimistic message of this lackluster novel apparently is that a Jezebel can reform. The difference between "good girls" and "bad girls" is sim-plistic, but at least it indicates that a person is capable of change. In the end, Bessie becomes a conventional and harmless wife and mother as the dust of Jezebel settles.

The last book in this section of novels sympathetic to Jezebel is composed by a gifted contemporary writer, Tom Robbins, who uses references to Jezebel to help develop theme. Here, in the hands of a clever creator of literature, the depths of

Jezebel's character are fully explored in fiction. Robbins's wild and controversial *Skinny Legs and All,* published in 1990, has a fablelike quality. At the same time, it is also raucous and irreverent, an entertaining and frightening look at modern politics, race relations, religion, art, sex, and marriage. Robbins mixes the sublime and the ridiculous.

The heroine of *Skinny Legs and All* is Ellen Cherry Charles. She and her new husband make their way to New York, where they both have contributions to make as artists. Working as a waitress in a restaurant co-owned by an Arab and a Jew and located across the street from the United Nations, Ellen Cherry has astonishing adventures. Through it all, Robbins's tone is playful as he relates his deadly serious commentary on life. The presence of Jezebel, ancient queen of Israel, is felt throughout as Robbins reexamines her biography and poses probing questions about her character.

Robbins's sympathy for Jezebel is apparent from the start. Heroine Ellen Cherry reads the Bible and tries to understand why Jezebel has such an evil reputation, but the Bible does not answer Ellen's questions. She finds only a few sentences on Jezebel and no proof that the queen is ever anything but a faithful wife to Ahab. The king involves himself in a suspect real estate acquisition, and Jezebel is supposed to have started a rumor that led to the landowner's death. It seems to Ellen that a right-winger named Jehu accuses the couple of idolatry because he has designs on their throne. The idolatry charges probably stem from the fact that Jezebel is a foreigner and does not wholeheartedly worship Yahweh. Aside from involvement in a shady land deal, however, "she apparently had been as properly behaved as, say, Queen Elizabeth" (33).

Ellen is especially bothered by Jezebel's being thrown out the window, her body left as food for the dogs. Why is the queen so criticized for applying makeup and fixing her hair? So what if the old queen is trying to flirt with Jehu when he comes to her balcony? For that little bit of lash batting, she has received eternal condemnation, although coquetry is hardly a capital offense. What are we supposed to conclude from the episode? "That Satan is a hairdresser? That Elizabeth Arden ought to be fed to the poodles?" (33). Ellen Cherry simply cannot comprehend why "in the Bitch Hall of Fame, Jezebel had a room of her own; nay, an entire wing" (33), and is deeply confused by the biblical condemnation of the queen as the Slut of Samaria and Queen of Tarts. Author Robbins suggests that Jezebel has been framed. Why? "Because veils of ignorance, disinformation, and illusion separate us from that which is imperative to our understanding of our evolutionary journey, shield us from the Mystery that is central to being" (51–52). In his novel, one by one the veils begin to fall away.

In *Skinny Legs and All,* a hick preacher, the Rev. Buddy Winkler, provides readers with anticlerical chuckles. He uses crude animal imagery to explain to Ellen Cherry's mother, Patsy, why Jezebel applied cosmetics. He says that a baboon's rump is bright red, yellow, and blue because the garish colors attract other baboons to mate. Jezebel paints her face for the same reason. Modern woman's fondness for makeup is, Winkler contends, a continuation of Jezebel business. He blames overly painted and coiffured Tammy Faye Bakker for her televangelist husband's downfall. When the most influential preachers in the country take painted hussies as wives, the end of the world must be approaching. When Jezebel "frescoed her eyelids with history's tragic glitter" (20), she set in motion an evil model for a hundred thousand generations of women to follow. In addition to Jezebel's wicked influence concerning the way women adorn themselves, the queen's most serious misdeed, the Rev. Buddy says, is that she stole hearts away from God.

When examining religious worship, Robbins suggests that Yahweh is a "Yahny-come-lately" (49) in Jezebel's time. The novel genre gives an author ample opportunity to lay plot aside momentarily and philosophize, as Robbins frequently does. He writes, for example, that Astarte, mother goddess of us all and light of the world, is the most ancient and revered deity in human history. She was beloved of the people for her life-giving and nurturing qualities. Using informal language a scholar could never get away with, Robbins gives his view of why the Deuteronomist tries to kill Jezebel and the goddess she represents:

> Because the uterine magic of [Astarte's] daughters had since the dawn of consciousness overshadowed the penis power of her sons, resentful priests of a tribe of nomadic Hebrews led a coup against her some four thousand years ago—and most of what we know as Western civilization is the result. Life still begins in the womb, cocky erections still collapse and lie useless when woman's superior sexuality is finished with them, but men control the divine channels now and while that control may be largely an illusion, their laws, institutions, and elaborate weaponry exist primarily to maintain it. (50)

Today, the author claims, men may be reminded of the goddess's power with every ejaculation, earthquake, or full moon, but in Jezebel's day masculine Yahwehism had only a precarious hold on a few zealots in Israel. No wonder patriarchs of the religious establishment—"angry old geezers with bad breath and impotence anxiety" (100)—fight the Phoenician queen when she comes to power in Samaria. To eliminate the appeal of voluptuous Astarte, Queen Jezebel has to be slandered, framed, and finally killed. The goddess has made a comeback, however. Her last gasp does not occur in 2 Kings after all, for Robbins and other writers revive her. Robbins's sympathetic treatment of Jezebel and the goddess is both funny and probing.

Prose Adaptations of the Jezebel Story

⊗⊙⊗

Prose writings may be as short as officially recorded debates and personal conversations, as formal as theological opinions and sermons, or as fanciful as biblical and nonbiblical novels. In all types of prose, Jezebel makes her appearance. Down through the centuries, the ancient queen of Israel has been the inspiration for religious and political propaganda. Sometimes she is mentioned once; sometimes she is pivotal to the plot. After moving beyond the early sermonizers who universally take the Bible literally and therefore despise the queen and women thought to be like her, more contemporary prose writers have varying attitudes toward Jezebel. Treatments of her story are contained in prose literature of widely divergent length and quality. Diverse authors—from detective-story writers to retellers of the biblical narrative—have used the very name of Jezebel to provide clues about their imaginary heroines' characters. In fact, sometimes they invoke the three syllables of Jezebel's name as a substitute for genuine character development. Other times writers explore in depth the soul of Jezebel and any modern reincarnation they might invent. Both pulp novelists and prizewinning authors are attracted to Jezebel because her name is well known and recognized by readers. Little exposition about her is required, though some authors prefer to take no chances and fill in a few background details. In these updates of her story, Jezebel is condemned often, derided occasionally, and praised rarely. This chapter provides a sample, not an exhaustive catalog, of Jezebel prose written or translated into English. We learn from these generations of authors that, more than two thousand years after her death, the appeal of Jezebel remains intact. The queen is as enigmatic today as she was in the ninth century BCE. The debate continues over her sexuality, idolatry, and lawlessness. The degree to which she, as a symbol of the archetypical evil female, is to blame for tempting man down the wayward path is still discussed. Definitive answers about Jezebel's character may never be available, but provocative questions will always be investigated—as long as the questions of love, religion, and law interest writers and readers.

5

Jezebel in Poetry

ဇ္ဇၑ

Brightness falls from the air;
Queens have died young and fair.

—Thomas Nashe,
"In Time of Pestilence"

IN A FOUR-LINE TRIBUTE TO JOHN DONNE, SAMUEL TAYLOR COLERIDGE calls poetry "fancy's maze and clue, / Wit's forge and fire-blast, meaning's press and screw" (433). And so it is. With felicity and economy of language, the best poetic compositions vividly and imaginatively convey life's experiences. Poetry includes our hymns of praise, songs of love, and verses of despair. Definitions of poetry are common, but good talk about poetry is rare. Readers cannot be bullied into appreciating the lyrical beauty of poetry, but we can bring ourselves pleasure by learning to understand individual poems. When we read a prose story, we focus on plot, character, conflict, resolution. Authors may make long digressions, for time and space are not at a premium in novels and unity of purpose is not required. Some poems are narratives too, but plot is secondary to image, metaphor, allusion, rhythm. Every syllable counts in a poem, so we pay close attention to individual words. As far back as Horace, the "Art of Poetry" argues that the charm of verse derives from its ability to keep words to a minimum. Poems say only what must be said and defer other discussion. Indeed, if a poem is well constructed, the omission of a single word can cause the whole work to fail.

It is not enough for the language of poetry to be succinct. It must also be affecting. If poets bring their intelligence and wisdom to the language of poetry, their words produce or amplify a particular mood, thus delighting the reader's soul, regardless of whether we feel cheerful or somber. The result is emotional transport, an elevation of the spirit. Poetry is perfect when it imitates and reflects human experience, as Aristotle says in the *Poetics*. Poetry is valued because of its power to arouse passions, instruct gently, and bring joy.

We may also discover the truth behind the paradox of poetry's ability to be contemporary to our time, as well as to its own time. The result of a fortunately composed poem is mental music, which enters the mind through the eyes and resonates in the heart. The music can cause us to glide through a new dance or put flesh on the skeletal remains of passions we thought dormant or dead. The rhyme or meter can drum a beat of admiration, sympathy, or disgust for the poem's themes and protagonists. The symbols and other poetic devices can subtly tap ideas into our heads. When explicating poems devoted to the much picked over carcass of the ancient Queen Jezebel, we find that in many cases the old bones still rattle around, knocking at the door of our memories and rapping a lively tune.

The name Jezebel never appears in the works of early poetic giants. Dante, Chaucer, and other literary luminaries—interested though they are in human beauties and foibles—do not mention the Israelite queen. Jezebel might seem a natural choice for such poets who know the Bible well and are eager to touch the face of boldness and evil, but her name never surfaces in their writings. There are three types of poems that do discuss Jezebel, and none of them has a kind word for the queen. First, there are poems of general condemnation, which record various complaints against her character. Some of them are retellings of the biblical story, while others simply use the name Jezebel in reference to the poets' newly created female characters. The second category of poems condemns Jezebel specifically because she is a seductress. These are among the most vehement attacks on the queen, blaming her for the Fall of man. Third are poems that condemn Jezebel because she offends the poets' political or theological sensibilities. In this group of poems, Jezebel's name is used to assist authors in formulating their protests of contemporary governmental or religious institutions.

Poems of General Condemnation

In the seventeenth century, there are several British poets who give attention to Jezebel. All condemn her on general principle. First is Joseph Beaumont, who was born in Suffolk and became a master at Peterhouse, Cambridge. In 1648 he penned *Psyche*, a long narrative poem, in which he mentions Jezebel twice as he retells the biblical story. The queen is vilified in canto 12 for threatening Elijah's life. Later, in canto 13, Jezebel's coconspirators in the Naboth murder regret their actions and "wish'd all hell / Melted into the heart of *Jezebel*" (lines 257–58). Beaumont thus ascribes to Jezebel's helpers remorse that is absent in 1 Kings. Around the same time, Richard Brathwait, in his 1658 poem *The Honest Ghost; or, A Voice from the*

Vault, also refers in rhymed couplets to Jezebel's sin against Naboth, though it is in a context of larger evil:

> For tell me, can that liberty be given
> On earth, which never was allow'd by heav'n?
> Shall *Naboths* blood cry for revenge and have it?
> Shall *Abels* cry for vengeance and receive it?
> Shall snarling Curs, as scattered stories tell,
> Lick up the blood of wicked *Jezebel,*
> To shew how ev'ry creature seems to smother
> Their just revenge, whose hand's deep dipt in murther?
>
> (199–206)

Beaumont and Brathwait, two minor poets, share a common perception of Jezebel's evil nature.

Two centuries later, we come upon *Jezebel: A Poem in Three Cantos,* by Canadian poet Charles Heavysege. Originally published in the *New Dominion Monthly* of January 1868, the poem retells the biblical story of Jezebel's struggle against God and the prophets. In Heavysege's biblical works, King Saul is arrogant; Jephthah is foolish; Jezebel is randy. They are treated like romantic rebels and placed into a sort of Shakespearean world where order is restored before the tale ends. Heavysege's protagonists are sinners, and the author has a strong, simple, black-and-white sense of morality, which might not appeal to some contemporary readers. If it were not for the fundamental truths expressed in Heavysege's psychological portraits, plus the occasional flashes of brilliantly crafted verse, the poet might well be left in obscurity. Yet his poem *Jezebel* deserves to be revisited because of its artistry and insights.

In the first canto, Ahab gives Jezebel the news of the Carmel contest's outcome, including the death of her priests. Jezebel claims that she will destroy Elijah and that dogs shall tear *him* to pieces:

> I will have him rent
> Piecemeal before me; and Samaria's dogs
> Shall fill their slack and famine-wrinkled hides
> With his torn carcass.

The irony is not lost on those who know the biblical story of Jezebel's being eaten by the dogs of Jezreel. This is foreshadowing in reverse.

Much of the power of Heavysege's *Jezebel* is in his metaphors. The queen is compared to a serpent, a tigress, a closed door, and anachronistically a Judas. Though similar comparisons are made by numerous writers, Heavysege's felicity of expression makes them seem fresh. For example, Jezebel is furious when caitiff Ahab hedges about what has become of her four hundred Baal priests. She says,

"I was not tempered to be jested with, / No more than to be fondled was the serpent." She accuses Ahab of disgracing himself by cowering before Elijah. When she is angry at the prophet, she is "like to a tigress at the smell of blood." During the Naboth episode, Jezebel feels contempt for her husband's political impotency and refuses physical contact with him. When Ahab tries to kiss his wife, her lips and heart are locked as tightly as prison doors. Then, using a New Testament sinner as a point of reference, Heavysege writes that after the Naboth episode, Ahab

> Then ran unto his house, and in the hall
> Met Jezebel, all unattended, sole.
> As once Iscariot distracted rushed
> Into the presence of the Sanhedrim,
> And there threw down the dread, accursed price
> For which he sold the Saviour of the world;—
> So Ahab stood in presence of his wife.

Heavysege's vivid images of Jezebel and Ahab give life to the poem. Ahab is often depicted as a solitary figure—alone, lonely, and at the mercy of his unsympathetic wife, who says, "Thou didst discrown / Thyself. Unmonarched man!" He walks by himself through his newly acquired vineyard and looks like a "scarecrow in a field." Though Ahab does penance and his soul is healed, to the bitter end Jezebel retains her icy aloofness. Knowing that she will be killed, she adorns herself to show "the stately, cold composure of a Queen." She never fears her enemies or stops hurling insults at them. Sandra Djwa, in an introduction to a volume of Heavysege's works, has a high opinion of Heavysege's language, terming the poet "an irrepressible creative spirit whose works reflect the literary flavour of an age" (Heavysege, ix).

Another narrative poem, purporting to be an ancient manuscript written by Jezebel to Ahab, is a 1911 effort called *An Epistle to Ahab King of Israel*, "transcribed" by E. Van Der Meulen and C. S. Hulst. The poem contains indefinite meter and rhyme scheme and purports to be a private letter from Jezebel to her husband. The plot is based directly upon events recorded in 1 Kings 22–23 and 2 Kings 9, the aftermath of the Naboth episode and the queen's death.

The introduction indicates Jezebel's devotion to Ahab. She says that she "bows low in obeisance" to the king and hopes he will live forever. The next stanza informs Ahab of Naboth's death and advises that Ahab "shrink not though the soil with [Naboth's] life-blood is red." The bulk of the epistle is her justification, her rationale, for the vineyard owner's murder and for confiscating his property. Ahab should not, Jezebel counsels, feel ashamed for killing Naboth. She begins her argument by stating that the vineyard keeper acted arrogantly before His Majesty, and such insolence could not be tolerated:

Should the king of a mighty nation
. . . .
Be brought to shame and confusion
By a semi-civilized yeoman?
Play not the part of a woman
Oh King of transcendent worth.

She further argues that Ahab is in the best position to make good use of the land, and all Israel will benefit from his action. Jezebel believes that "the thing that we did was but technical wrong" and that, in any case, her code of ethics is superior to the old laws of Israel. She also argues that it is actually Ahab's duty to take the land and improve it. She says that even Naboth's kindred will be grateful to Ahab for his wise ameliorations to the property. After this, the queen maintains that Ahab deserves the vineyard as compensation for all his hard work as Israel's monarch. If Ben-hadad, a king, pays tribute to mighty Ahab, why should Naboth not pay? Jezebel concludes this portion of the letter by pointing out that Naboth is a traitor who has gotten his just deserts for not accepting the king's generous offer of compensation.

Ironically, Jezebel also invokes as a positive example the image of Jacob swindling Esau out of his birthright in exchange for a little stew. While Genesis may obliquely suggest that Jacob is the better man to take Isaac's place as patriarch, Jacob's underhanded methods of obtaining Esau's birthright are never lauded in the Bible. Jezebel, however, is impressed with Jacob's trick to get what he wants, and she encourages Ahab to follow his ancestor's example.

The queen adds a postscript to the letter, indicating that it is to be kept "strictly private." Here she whispers in Ahab's ear not to let Elijah know what has happened with Naboth. Readers familiar with the Bible story understand the dramatic irony, for nothing can be kept hidden from a prophet of God. Having indirectly raised the subject of religion by mentioning Elijah, Jezebel plunges into a full frontal attack on Yahwehism. She implores Ahab to give up his silly worship of God and follow Baal instead. Her reason is that "the worship of Baal, the god of Power, / Is the worship best suited a King's condition." Baal will not object if a citizen, such as Naboth, has to be killed now and then; the god will see the murder as a sacrificial offering. She ends her private note by begging Ahab to learn from this Naboth experience, to gain enough wisdom to put aside worship of Yahweh.

An Epistle to Ahab King of Israel is a long narrative. It is primarily an exploration of Jezebel's motives for killing Naboth, interesting because the Bible seldom looks into a person's mind to investigate thoughts and feelings. Authors Van Der Meulen and Hulst add an appropriate quote from Shakespeare's *Macbeth* at the conclusion of the poem. The line reminds readers that Macbeth achieves all his goals because of the wicked deeds he performs: "Thou hast it now, King, Cawdor, Glamis, all / As the Weird Women promis'd; and I fear / Thou play'dst most foully for it." The theme of this narrative poem about Jezebel is that there is a heavy price to pay for sinfulness. Even the highest born eventually have to answer for their misdeeds.

Ella Wheeler Wilcox expresses similar disdain of Jezebel in her poem "Devils." Not only do women achieve nothing of lasting significance, they are also demons. The queen is grouped with other familiar biblical women who represent earth's evils:

Then into forms human
Each came as a woman
Delilah, and Jezebel, Lilith and all
Females who stand but that others may fall:
And females who gossip and stir up strife,
And are thorns in the flesh of the neighbourhood life.

(17)

Regardless of whether the neighborhood is ancient Jezreel or a modern city, this poem concludes that the Jezebels of the world will be there to cause trouble for all of humanity.

No trace of goodwill toward Jezebel is found in modern biblical poetry, including "Song for the Clatter-Bones" by F. R. Higgins. This poem carries the unique distinction of accusing Jezebel of being a Jew, or at least like a Jew. It is either ignorance of her Phoenician origin or just plain anti-Semitism that motivates Higgins to mistake the queen's homeland and religion. Nowhere else in literature is Jezebel called a Jew. The text reveals that the "Jewy" queen's evil song can still be heard today:

God rest that Jewy woman,
Queen Jezebel, the bitch
. . . .
And so she was thrown from the window;
Like Lucifer she fell
Beneath the feet of the horses and they beat
The light out of Jezebel.
. . . .
And as once her dancing body
Made star-lit princes sweat,
So I'll just clack: though her ghost lacks a back
There's music in the old bones yet.

(249)

The Eternal Jezebel
ᗌᗏ

In Higgins's poem, Jezebel is compared to the devil. She falls from her window, paralleling Lucifer's drop from the sky as he is evicted from heaven. One of the many intriguing legends about Lucifer is that he was at one time God's greatest admirer. He adored God and desired to serve only the deity, so much so that he was unable to comply when God commanded Lucifer and the other angels to serve humanity. The Lord then ejected Lucifer from heaven for the crime of disobedience. He fell to hell, where he still rules and now tries to undermine humankind's relationship to Yahweh. The image of Jezebel's fall from grace being linked to Lucifer's fall is thus quite poignant. The second allusion in "Song for the Clatter-Bones" is to Salome, the young girl who danced for Herod and pleased him so much that she was given the head of John the Baptist for a reward. Jezebel is called a "dancing girl" here, even though the Bible never mentions her dancing. Those who espouse their shared wickedness and temptation of men frequently link Jezebel and Salome.

The poetry of Edward Henry Bickersteth, the bishop of Exeter, includes hymns and biblical poems of a didactic nature, including *Yesterday, To-Day and For Ever: A Poem in Twelve Books,* wherein a single reference to Jezebel can be found. In the 1866 preface, the author states, "If it may please God to awaken any minds to deeper thought on things unseen and eternal, by this humble effort to combine some of the pictorial teaching supplied by His most holy Word, it will be the answer to many prayers" (v). The first-person narrator, named Oriel, dies at the poem's opening. With a guide, Oriel enters eternal life and encounters spirits who lived and died in sin, but he continues on the road to heaven, where he sees God and famous persons from the Bible and from history. In book 11, "The Last Judgment," Jezebel is found among

> . . . crowds of miserable idolaters,
> Of whom I mark'd lascivious Jezebel:
> Sinners of every age and every type;
> The proud, despiteful, fierce, implacable,
> Unthankful, and unholy, and unclean;
> And they who lived in pleasure, dead the while;
> Haters of God; and whosoever loved,
> And whosoever wrought the devil's lie.
> (lines 779–86)

Following this description of Jezebel and other enemies of God, Bickersteth concludes by giving an account of the bliss existing after God's final judgment and the many kingdoms under divine rule, all surpassing Eden in delight.

Whether poets are writing biblical or nonbiblical poetry, there is not a single positive allusion to the Israelite queen. The message is a simple one: her reputation is so tarnished that her name is enough to warn readers of her destructive influence. The mere mention of the word *Jezebel* is usually sufficient to achieve the poets' purpose of summoning readers' sensations of evil. Her name serves as a sort of shorthand, a quick and efficient allusion to sinfulness. Many of the poets, never bothering to explain who Jezebel is, assume that their audiences will associate Jezebel with misconduct.

Through the centuries, numerous poets move away from directly retelling the Bible story toward simply alluding to Jezebel as a well-known, undisputed example of waywardness, especially pride. For example, Benjamin Keach, a Baptist, in his poem entitled "Distressed Sion Relieved, or, The Garment of Praise for the Spirit of Heaviness," mentions (once, at line 4374) a contemporary woman, a new Jezebel who surpasses the ancient queen in sinfulness: "Her proper title is (Great Babylon) / Who in great pomp and Royal State doth ride, / Excelling haughty Jezebel in pride." In 1677 Samuel Speed, later to be a prisoner in London's Ludgate Prison, wrote a poem entitled "On Beauty." Like Keach, Speed also has a single, unflattering reference to Jezebel: "Thus we adore those whom we think excel / In Beauty, though a painted Jezebel" (lines 9–10). Beauty is an outer deception that masks inner reprehensibility.

Of the numerous poets who cite Jezebel in nonbiblical works, some have lively style and interesting content. George Crabbe—a strict moralist, ordained minister, and friend to Edmund Burke and Samuel Johnson—created convincing characters and narratives. Crabbe's poetry is still read today because of its poignancy in describing middle-class life. Crabbe had humanitarian impulses, though he tended to blame poor people for their own misfortunes and to accuse them of being intemperate. He is often regarded as a transitional writer between the neoclassic and romantic periods. In "The Convert," one of Crabbe's *Tales,* published in 1812, the protagonist is fatherless John Dighton, who works hard and thrives, though he also indulges in vices, such as card playing, lying, and reveling of all sorts. Dighton becomes ill and resolves to change his evil ways; but virtue wanes, and churchmen must continue to try to convert his heart to good. Finally he repents and dies but not before Crabbe sermonizes by comparing John Dighton's wife to Jezebel: "John, thou hast made thy wife a Jezebel: / See! on her bosom rests the sign of sin, / The glaring proof of naughty thoughts within" (3: 392). In *Tales,* Crabbe's last work is the verse story "Sir Owen Dale." Here Crabbe demonstrates his skill in writing heroic couplets as he alludes to the biblical queen of sin:

> I loved a lady, somewhat late in life,
> . . . .
> but when she knew my pain,
> Saw my first wish her favour to obtain,

And ask her hand—no sooner was it ask'd,
Than she, the lovely Jezebel unmask'd;
And by her haughty airs, and scornful pride,
My peace was wounded—nay, my reason tried;
I felt despised and fallen when we met,
And she, O folly! looks too lovely yet;
Yet love no longer in my bosom glows,
But my heart warms at the revenge it owes.

(5: 16–17)

After Crabbe's somber "Sir Owen Dale," a Jezebelian bagatelle was composed by London poet and punster Thomas Hood, author of "The Song of the Shirt." His humorous piece entitled "A Tale of a Trumpet" (published posthumously in 1880) is typical of Hood's lighthearted verse and good-natured satire on human foibles. In it a deaf woman, Dame Eleanor Spearing, receives a recently invented hearing aid, or ear trumpet, from a peddler who promises that, if Dame Eleanor purchases the device, she will hear "even what people are going to say." At first she refuses to buy, though the peddler keeps lowering the price. Finally she relents and finds that she can now hear all the ugly tidings offhandedly exchanged among the townspeople. In spreading all the unpleasant news she now hears, Dame Eleanor upsets the entire village. Instigating a witch-hunt to locate Dame Eleanor, the citizens call her a Jezebel, crush the trumpet, and kill her cat: "Oh! then arises the fearful shout— / Bawled and screamed, and bandied about— / 'Seize her!—drag the old Jezebel out!'" (29). The moral against gossip is obvious at the end of "A Tale of a Trumpet." In 1 Kings, the biblical Jezebel is guilty of spreading malicious rumors about Naboth, resulting in the man's murder and confiscation of his land. Therefore, the allusion to Jezebel in "A Tale of a Trumpet" seems a logical interpretation for a modern reader. Though Jezebel is never even accused in the Bible of some of the crimes that she commits in postbiblical sources, the Naboth story writer insists that she is a spreader of lies, as is Hood's old Dame Eleanor. The epitaph on Hood's tombstone reads, "Here lies one who spat more blood and made more puns than any man living." If the poet spits more blood upon Jezebel, it is in keeping with traditional interpretations of her evil loquaciousness.

In 1924 Vachel Lindsay goes much further in his poem "A Curse for the Saxophone," which holds Jezebel responsible for deliberately playing life's murderous music. Killers throughout time—Cain, Jezebel, Judas, Nero, Henry VIII, and John Wilkes Booth—are connected to jazz belted out on the sax. Each of these evildoers orders saxophones to be played; Booth even takes hold of the horn and blows it himself. Lindsay allows jazzy music to symbolize life's harsh, discordant strains, for "none but an assassin would enjoy this horn." He urges us to "forget our jazzes and our razzes and our hates" and to listen instead to the world's softer, more romantic melodies. Flutes and Irish harps create beautiful tunes that soothe human beings at day's end. Jezebel tolerated no such pleasing arrangement of sounds and instead decreed that the saxophones should play

> When Jezebel put on her tiaras and looked grand,
> Her three-piece pajamas and her diamond bosom-band,
> And stopped the honest prophets as they marched upon their way,
> And slaughtered them, and hung them in her hearty wholesale way,
> She licked her wicked chops, she pulled out all her stops,
> And she ordered the saxophones to play.

Lindsay hopes that society will banish discord and the steamy music of the red-hot sax. This entertaining, well-written poem pleads for an end to the Jezebel music that has permeated society.

Also in 1924, "Jezebel" by Scudder Middleton won first prize in a poetry contest sponsored by the *Nation*. A woman of the town, referred to only as Jezebel, lives isolated and alone on a hill. Occasionally people wonder about her street-walking past, but mostly people forget about her as they go about their daily work. Seldom does anyone visit Jezebel, yet all are subliminally aware of her constant presence among them, and sometimes townspeople venture up the briar pathway to her house. This Jezebel personifies evil, and people of all ages have been touched by her at some time. After experiencing the wickedness that Jezebel symbolizes, the townspeople (who narrate the poem in the first-person-plural *we*) return to their normal lives, forget unpleasant things, and are happy. Middleton successfully conjures up the image of an ostracized and outcast woman, but one whom all the people recognize as being a real part of their lives. In this lovely poem, the biblical queen and details of her story are absent, but Jezebel's name is sufficient to spin webs of sinister intrigue and mystery, as this excerpt demonstrates:

> We know she lives upon that thorny hill,
> We see her lights and watch her chimneys spark—
> . . . .
> Remembering when she came, her ways were dark,
> And that her only name is Jezebel.
> . . . .
> We never wonder more of Jezebel.
> We have our work to do and God is hard.
> Serving the wheels or guiding straight the plow
> Leaves little thought of frankincense and nard.
> Yet, she is like deep water of the Spring
> Running along our minds; down at the roots.

The Eternal Jezebel
&&

. . . .
We have gone up through briars and the night,
And seen the secret face of Jezebel.
There, in that still confessional where she waits,
We all have had the blessing of her breast,
As over us she learned to blow the light.
                                    (lines 1–5, 15–20, 31–35)

Middleton's "Jezebel" evokes the tone and mood of Nathaniel Hawthorne's short story "Young Goodman Brown." Evil lurks on the edge of the village. Citizens covertly experience the shady side of life, then return to the brightness of daily routine. Middleton's Jezebel character is, as with William Faulkner's Miss Emily from his 1931 story "A Rose for Emily," a care and a burden to the townspeople. They are curious about her but also try to avoid contact. They are at once attracted and repelled by her omnipresence and her darkness. If the people display little affection toward Jezebel, she certainly returns the favor in her sentiments regarding them.

Not all poems are confined to the printed page; some verse is also set to music and performed. Young singers from the recording industry have seized the opportunity to capitalize on the Jezebel story. In the 1980s and 1990s, several rock groups latched onto Jezebel's tainted reputation, sometimes using it to promote their counterculture images. In 1998 Acid Bath had a hit song entitled "Jezebel," which describes how she screams in agony as her fingers are cut off. "Jezzebel" by Boyz II Men, a much tamer group, tells of a man who meets an alluring woman while riding on the B train. The singer cannot discern her nationality but is instantly drawn to her. "Juke Joint Jezebel" by the band KMFDM and The Reverend Horton Heat's song "Jezebel" also appeared on pop charts. A group called 10,000 Maniacs, with vocalist Natalie Merchant, wrote a song called "Jezebel" for their collection *Our Time in Eden*. The singer laments that she is a married woman and a Jezebel because she wants to leave her husband. Other groups employ the name Jezebel in their band titles. Gene Loves Jezebel is a five-piece British glam-rock band that was the darling of MTV watchers in the 1980s, and there is a four-member band from Quebec known as Jezebel's Children. Though these pop stars reveal no deep knowledge of their biblical source, Jezebel's unwholesome reputation is still well known enough to enter present-day musical verse.

Poems of Sexual Condemnation

The next group of Jezebel poems concerns sexuality. Very little early poetry dealing with Jezebel is extant today. One Latin poem entitled "Altercatio inter virum et mulierem" is found in a single manuscript, dates from the fourteenth century, and may have been composed by Warner of Rouen, France. It discusses many biblical persons whose stories are famous for their sexual content: Eve, Lot, Tamar, Potiphar, Bathsheba, Solomon's wives, Herodias, and of course, Jezebel. Preconquest Normandy is not well known for its rich literary atmosphere (Ziolkowski 38), but in the brief glances into the culture that are available to modern readers, the character Jezebel emerges as a prototype for wickedness connected to sexuality.

Jezebel is the principal character in a Norman poem, an anonymous nonbiblical effort in Latin that probably dates from eleventh-century Rouen. Called "Jezebel," it is a fascinating 141-line poem, the unique extant copy located today at the Bibliothèque Nationale in Paris. The poem, translated and edited by Jan Ziolkowski, is a stichomythic dialogue between two people who are exact opposites. The man's identity is never revealed, and the woman is called Jezebel. The poem directly mentions her name five times, but the female speaker's soul in the poem is far blacker than her biblical counterpart. This new Jezebel's language is filled with bawdy humor, lewd imagery, and unrelenting irreverence. She seems to lick her chops in unrestrained merriment as she contemplates the young men she can debauch and the erotic passion she can arouse. Her one aim and pleasure in life is her frank sexuality. She is acquainted with biblical locales traditionally associated with sin, such as Babel; she is intimately connected to pagan gods, such as Venus; and she is dedicated to hedonistic lifestyles, such as Epicureanism. Her partner in the interlocution is as pious as she is promiscuous. Each line of "Jezebel" consists of his innocent questions and her vulgar answers or his protestations and her flippant replies. For example:

Whence do you come, Jezebel? — From the foul prison of Babel-Babylon. /
Whence do you return, woman? — From the vaulted brother of Topheth. /
. . . .
What power keeps you laughing? — Practice as a prostitute. / For what do you search above all? — Priapus, in a hundred whorehouses. / What do you seek constantly? — To be mounted, pressed down. / What do you desire least? — People chaste in body. / What do you abhor most? — Divine laws, I suppose. / Which god is in your heart? — The one who reigns in the garden. / Which people is most ignoble, in your opinion? — The generation of the just. / Why are you pale in the face? — I am consumed by love of young men. / But why are you red on the brow? — I harvest on the brow injuries of the haunches. /
. . . .
You are the snare of youths. — I pray to be their tomb. / What do you accomplish in anger? — That the sad eunuch should flee from the garden. / What do you wish to happen, when you pray? — That I may deserve to become the goddess of promiscuity. / Tell now what would happen. — Every manly thigh would be available. / But for whom? — For Jezebel, tried in the flesh.

(lines 8–9, 14–22, 81–85)

The virtue-and-vice dialogue continues, as the man and Jezebel speak like characters in a one-act play. In every line, the couple's contradictory views on life and love are juxtaposed.

"Jezebel" has two noteworthy features. First is the absence of detail concerning the people's identities, the time, and the place. The reader is never certain who the speakers are, though it seems that the Jezebel character is a fictitious creation who is a contemporary of the poet and modeled loosely on her biblical namesake. By comparison, the Jezebel of 1 and 2 Kings seems tame indeed. No clue is provided as to the male speaker's identity. Furthermore, setting is unspecified. Readers are not informed where or when the conversation takes place. The poet thus intends this poem, containing a cat-and-mouse dialogue of intriguing questions and sarcastic answers, to have a high degree of universality. Since no particular person, date, or locale is noted, the possibilities are endless. Any two individuals of opposite temperament could be arguing, anytime, anywhere. (An alternative interpretation, of course, is that the actual biblical Jezebel is debating Elijah.) A second salient aspect of the poem is that the woman constantly misinterprets the man's questions and replies in a brash, sacrilegious manner that is sure to insult him. The vocabulary is characterized by blasphemous puns and sexual double entendres; the meter depends upon stretched syntax and unusual words. In every instance, Jezebel rudely answers challenging questions; she never poses one. For the most part, critics have been harsh with "Jezebel" because of its murky, idiosyncratic style. Nevertheless, it is one of the few early extant poems, and we are fortunate that it has been translated into English from its original Latin.

"Jezebel" contains considerable artistry and impressive contrasts, despite the poem's quirkiness, and it provides valuable insight into how the name of the ancient Israelite queen was used in medieval Europe. The poet recreates an acid-tongued vixen who gives her worst of thoughts the worst of words and is a foil for the righteous man. In this poem, the duality of humankind is revealed, with woman embodying the evil half. Jezebel—the eternal Jezebel—leads men to sin.

Next is George Barlow's 1882 poem entitled "Jezebel." It suggests, in strong trochaic tetrameter, the queen's enduring seductive power, recalled in England many hundreds of years after her death. An excerpt:

Who felt the touch of her swift hands,—
What lord of sunstruck Eastern lands?
Who felt the soft white bosom swell
Of Jezebel, of Jezebel?
. . . .

Jezebel in Poetry
&

Slender wast thou,—or matron-wise
Shaped, with black subtle serpent-eyes
Where are the strong men who could tell
To us the glory of Jezebel?

They all are gone along with thee,
And we who pace by grey-blue sea
What know we of the souls in hell
For thy sake, deep-haired Jezebel.

Could one but tell us of thy form
One mouth that kissed thy red lips warm
We too might madden 'neath thy spell
O poison-lipped sweet Jezebel!
(lines 1–4, 13–24)

The eternalness of Jezebel's seductive beauty remains alive in "Jezebel," a theme often seen in literature that recalls the queen's name. Those in Eastern lands who had firsthand experience with the enchantress's lips have all perished, and Englishmen never knew her touch. Yet thanks to the poets, Jezebel remains in the collective memory of humanity, the embodiment of dark woman magic. Should this particular femme fatale appear in our midst again, poets claim, men would be as vulnerable as ever to her lure, driven to madness or to hell by her irresistible charms.

Also in this general time frame is a curious volume of English poetry, entitled *Jezebel; and Other Tragic Poems,* written in 1899 by Aleister Crowley under the name Count Vladimir Svareff. An English author and magician, Crowley became interested in spells and witches during the late nineteenth century's revival of magic. Along with W. B. Yeats, Crowley was a member of the Order of the Golden Dawn, but he was expelled from the society because of his extremism. Later driven out of Italy for continued bizarre practices, Crowley was rumored to have orchestrated ceremonies involving infant sacrifice, wild orgies, and drugs. Many of his associates died under suspicious circumstances, including his wife and child. Crowley loved his reputation as a beastly, wicked man. His fascination with Jezebel is therefore germane to this study, and his morbid interest in her stranglehold on men and her gory, unnatural death are evident throughout the poem. In his autobiography, he wrote that Jezebel "held her place as my favourite character in Scripture" (*Confessions* 409).

"Jezebel" has two parts, the first taking place before and the second after Ahab's death at Ramoth-gilead. The whole composition is in six-line stanzas of iambic tetrameter, though enjambment keeps the strong *a,b,a,b,c,c* rhyme scheme from being obtrusive. The dominant image throughout this poem is the flames of passion; practically every stanza contains a metaphor or image of fire that sears the hearts of the characters. This burning consumes the soul of the narrator and Jezebel.

Identifying the first-person narrator is like solving a jigsaw puzzle, for he calls himself a prophet who has been to Carmel and must now go to court to rail against Ahab. A cryptic footnote in the text, presumably supplied by Crowley, indicates that the poem's narrator is "not Elijah, as the sequel shows. Foolish contemporary reviews, however, made this silly blunder" ("Jezebel" 1.1). Yet the mistake is not so ludicrous, for the unnamed prophet bears many similarities to the queen's perennial foe. He is long suffering, feels the burden of God's word, and believes he is called by God to preach doom to the sinful monarchy. Nevertheless, this narrator is very different from the 1–2 Kings description of Elijah, for he is truly an unholy prophet whose strongest desire is to become a lover of Jezebel's. In part 1, he pants for her night and day and is ablaze with the heat of his ardor, though he is clearly dismayed at her demonic power.

The physical beauty often associated with Jezebel is absent in this poem, but she is regally attired and possesses a devilish magnetism that pulls the prophet into her orb. A metaphysical conceit compares her tongue and teeth—not to cherries and pearls as readers might expect in love poetry—to a flash of fire and prison bars:

> . . . her tongue
> (A flame from the dark heart of hell,
>   The ivory-barred mouth, that stung
> With unimaginable pangs)
> Shot out at me, and Hell fixed fangs.
>
> (1.30)

Her lips are "crimson snakes," and her glossy black hair "glistens with unholy lights." Upon seeing the prophet, bare-breasted Jezebel spits on him, the spittle scorching his cheeks and causing him to crave her body for a "sacrament of shame." Despite his internal misgivings, the narrator says, "I lust for her, and hell, and death. / I see that ghastly look, and yearn / Toward the brands of her that burn." The queen is compared to an adder sucking at the prophet's chest, yet he cannot control his love of (and hate for) the evil temptress. The tormented prophet longs to possess her.

In part 2 of Crowley's "Jezebel," the narrator fights at Ramoth-gilead. There he observes Jehu and realizes that the would-be crown usurper will kill the queen, the prophet's beloved to whom he claims his soul is now lost. As Jehu is taunted by Jezebel from her balcony, the narrator watches and feels that he himself dies when she is flung from the window. (In the Bible, Elijah's end comes before the queen's, of course.) The "tigress woman" does not die immediately, as the Bible leads us to believe, but speaks with the prophet:

> "Ah! prophet, come to mock at me
> And gloat on mine exceeding pain?"
> "Nay, but to give my soul to thee,
> And have thee spit at me again!"
> She smiled—I know she smiled—she sighed,
> Bit my lips through, and drank, and died!
>
> (1.132)

Scavenger animals gather as the spirit leaves Jezebel's body. Near the conclusion of the poem, an unhallowed Last Supper is suggested, recalling the body of a crucified Christ:

> The host is lifted up. Behold
> The vintage spilt, the broken bread!
> I feast upon the cruel cold
> Pale body that was ripe and red.
> Only, her head, her palms, her feet,
> I kissed all night, and did not eat.

After the death of his beloved, the narrator/prophet longs for death so that he can mate in hell with his harlot. Together they two will conquer God.

The tone of Crowley's narrative poem reflects the occult that interested him so greatly. Jezebel is a demon lover who, in siren fashion, makes a righteous man long to possess her and die. The relentless fire images show the prophet to be scorching with illicit sexual appetite, the sin compounded because of his position as one chosen by God to be a model of morality for the people. "Jezebel" has considerable aesthetic appeal, though its content may be disconcerting. The biblical queen's reputation is not just sullied by her treatment in this poem; it is annihilated. Crowley uses his artistic skill to create new plot and imagery damning to the queen. He sounds notes up and down the scale of sexual suggestion. Sometimes language is merely laden with lewd nuance, while other times it bombards readers with the queen's unrestrained depravity. Here is one of the most brazen examples of Jezebel as the prototype for shameless wickedness.

One of the period's best-known poets to use Jezebel references is Robert Browning, though his most famous poems are not among those that cite the queen. "Red Cotton Night-Cap Country or Turf and Towers," a nonbiblical poem of four thousand lines written in 1873, has a single citation (7: 398) of Jezebel's name in describing woman:

The Eternal Jezebel
ஐ

—finally conclude
To leave the reprobate untroubled now
In her unholy triumph, till the Law
Shall right the injured ones; for gentlemen
Allow the female sex, this sort at least,
Its privilege. So, simply "Cockatrice!"—
"Jezebel!"

(lines 3974–80)

The poem tells a true story, a tragedy concerning mental aberration. Browning changed the peoples' names to avoid a libel suit stemming from this long narrative poem. It is one of his least satisfying works, not containing the dramatic style of his successes. The hero of the story kills himself in remorse for behaving badly toward his mother. The event, Browning himself says, "was likely to have been occasioned by passionate woman-love" (Browning 7: xv). The poet suspected, however, that the hero's suicide was not intentional. A second Browning poem, "Pietro of Abano" from *Dramatic Idyls* of 1880, also refers to the queen as "powder-paint-and-patch, Hag Jezebel" (9: 316). The queen provides Browning with a quick, easy reference to evil.

Modern Jezebels must make restitution for their sexual misconduct. In 1914 critic and poet Arthur Symons writes an intriguing verse about the death of a prostitute. The opening leads readers to believe the main character is perhaps from Ahab's court, but later references to such things as chimney sweeps and hospitals date the setting to more modern times (Shakespeare mentions chimney sweeps). "Jezebel Mort" is both the heroine's name and the poem's title. No direct mention is made of the Israelite queen, but a knowledgeable reader recalls the ancient connection between her name and whoredom.

In this first-person narrative poem a streetwalker speaks directly to the reader and discusses the plight of women who make their living on their backs. Each line of the poem contains a double rhyme, one in the middle and one at the end. Take, for example, the opening: "My name is Jezebel Mort: you know the thing that that means; / If ever one comes into Court, they call us pleasure-machines."

A major theme of "Jezebel Mort" is innate depravity. Some girls are born to sin, which is compared to a mire:

Nay, none were born a saint, for we were born on the earth
To be tainted by sin's taint; some girls of us even from birth
Had it just in their blood: sin, the veritable sin,
That drenches one in the mud, up from the knee to chin.

The circumstances of this new Jezebel's birth leave her without much chance for a decent life, for she is born in a bawdy house and is sinful by nature. Yet women are not the only ones whose souls are corrupted by original sin. Men are also compared to demons that crave women's bodies and cause women to fall into sexually degrading traps:

> Vice, I tell you, is in all; is a virtue to some, perhaps.
> We, girls after our fall, are caught in sinister traps,
> Just as they snare the birds; for brute men are snares, I say.

All women are metaphorically sold in meat markets and used by men. Until Judgment Day, the situation will not change. The poem's final image is of a leafless tree, suggesting the emptiness of Jezebel Mort's existence and the loneliness of her death: "Well, there's an end for me; just perhaps, where, there nod / Branches of a barren tree: and, this night I go to my God." Her body is covered with a shroud as her sad case comes to a close.

Before the close of the nineteenth century, American poet Henry Wadsworth Longfellow refers briefly to Jezebel. In a dramatic poem entitled *Cristus: A Mystery*, he lumps Jezebel with other alluring biblical women, though his reference to her is not as damning as others that treat her as a seductress. Throughout the centuries, the sexuality of Jezebel reappears in the poetry of the great and near great. Their unanimous judgment is that the Israelite queen's reputation as a painted hussy shall endure.

Poems of Political and Religious Condemnation

The third category of Jezebel poems condemns her because of the author's personal beliefs. The nineteenth century was a time when religious and political poems made reference to Queen Jezebel. A good example is "Czar Peter" by Martin Farquhar Tupper. In this poem, the Russian ruler is deemed a worthy leader, despite the unsavory influence of a woman in the czar's life, a woman so like Jezebel that the two could be related:

> . . . to thee, great prince,
> Despite a Jezebel-sister's cursed plan
> Of luring thee to pleasure's guilty ways,
> Justly belongs the honourable praise
> Of waking a barbarian world of slaves
> To fame and power, that have not faded since.
>
> (lines 5–10)

The gilded opulence of the Russian court is described here, and governmental leaders are mildly criticized for decadent dalliances. Yet the despot somehow remains able to rule the common people and bring glory to the nation.

Closer to the English hearthside, other poems use a Jezebel reference to describe the religious-political conflict in Britain. William Edmondstoune Aytoun, a Scottish professor of belles lettres at the University of Edinburgh, wrote *Bothwell: A Poem in Six Parts* in 1856. Narrated by the husband of Mary, Queen of Scots, the poem discusses the exploits of evangelist John Knox, who often compared Catholic Queen Mary to Baalist Queen Jezebel:

> Then to a drove of gaping clowns
> Would Knox with unction tell
> The vengeance that in days of old
> Had fallen on Jezebel!
> (lines 297–300)

In a similar political-religious vein, Percy Bysshe Shelley wrote but never finished "Charles the First," which contains one reference to Jezebel. As in Aytoun's poem, the Catholic monarch is compared to the heathen from Phoenicia:

> Good Lord! rain it down upon him!
> Amid her ladies walks the papist queen,
> As if her nice feet scorned our English earth.
> The Canaanitish Jezebel! I would be
> A dog if I might tear her with my teeth!
> (490)

Shelley's narrator is so hostile toward the Catholic queen that he longs to be like a dog that bites her viciously. The image vividly recalls the aftermath of Queen Jezebel's assassination, when her unburied body is attacked by animals. Anti-Catholic sentiment does not stop here, however. John Moultrie mentions Jezebel in a blistering diatribe, "The Black Fence." He pleads for the Protestant Church to retain its purity and resist the immoral influence of Rome:

> God give her wavering clergy back that honest heart and true,
> Which once was theirs, ere Popish fraud its spells around them threw;
> Nor let them barter wife and child, bright hearth and happy home,
> For the drunken bliss of the strumpet-kiss of the Jezebel of Rome.
> (lines 165–68)

The Catholic Church is compared to an evil woman, and her name is Jezebel.

Chronologically, the next Jezebel political poem written in English is composed by Thomas Hardy. Hardy published a flood of work—eight poetry volumes and seventeen novels—all characterized by his pessimistic philosophy of an unkind fate blindly dealing blows to good people. The heroine of *Tess of the D'Urbervilles*, for example, is a simple country girl finally driven by ill fortune to commit murder. Though Hardy was highly acclaimed in his day, he was nonetheless attacked for sympathizing with Tess, whom he called "a pure woman." After *Tess* was virulently criticized, Hardy turned his attention to poetry, which he considered superior to prose. Perhaps because critics were alarmed by Hardy's compassion for Tess, he professed no such love for Jezebel in "Jezreel: On Its Seizure by the English under Allenby, September 1918." Always interested in military stories, especially Napoleon's threatened invasion of England, Hardy penned numerous war poems. "Jezreel" thus reflects themes common to the Hardy canon and describes the advance of the English army into land formerly known to the Tishbite prophet Elijah, Jezebel, and Jehu:

> Did they catch as it were in a Vision at shut of the day—
> When their cavalry smote through the ancient Esdraelon Plain,
> And they crossed where the Tishbite stood forth in his enemy's way
> His gaunt mournful Shade as he bade the King haste off amain?
>
> On war-men at this end of time—even on Englishmen's eyes—
> Who slay with their arms of new might in that long-ago place,
> Flashed he who drove furiously? . . . Ah, did the phantom arise
> Of that queen, of the proud Tyrian woman who painted her face?
>
> (lines 1–8)

In London the *Times* reported the advance of the British army, led by Gen. Edmund Allenby on 23 September 1918. Hardy's poem was dated the next day and also published in the *Times*. Allenby crossed Palestine's Plain of Esdraelon, and Hardy immediately recognized the geography as the same area populated in ancient times by Ahab and Jezebel. A letter from Hardy to Mrs. Florence Henniker describes the poet's thought processes during the poem's composition:

> It was written very rapidly . . . , it being just a poem for the moment. I thought people did not seem to realize that Esdraelon and Jezreel were the same. Well, as to my having any affection for Jezebel, I don't think I can admit that: I have the same sort of admiration for her that I have for Lady Macbeth, Clytemnestra, and such. Her courage was splendid. (2: 511)

Though Hardy's poem stops short of praising Jezebel, "Jezreel" is the kindest of the political poems that refer to the queen.

One of the more recent Jezebel poems to satirize governmental leaders is by Gillian E. Hanscombe. Born in Australia, she moved to London and found employment as a teacher, clerk, journalist, and salesperson. In 1979 she graduated from Oxford, where she wrote a thesis on feminist novelist Dorothy Richardson. The following is an excerpt from Hanscombe's political poem, "Jezebel: Her Progress":

The Eternal Jezebel
୫୦

Mrs. Snatcher Thatcher
runs the land.
. . . .

She believes in sin.
The sin of the poor is their idleness;
the sin of the sick is their dependence;
the sin of the children is their ignorance;
the sin of the women is their helplessness;
the sin of the workers is their discontent.

Sweat and tears do not placate her.
She snatches back
what she says has not been earned
and juggles it abracadabra
into a missile
which she says will defend the
poor
sick
children and
women and
workers

(lines 1–2, 7–23)

In this political protest poem, Hanscombe uses ordinary, modern language to voice dissent about the domestic and foreign policies of Prime Minister Margaret Thatcher. A staunch defender of government spending to build nuclear arsenals, Thatcher had the axiomatic view that the weapons of war help keep the peace and ensure prosperity. This philosophy is at odds with the poet's immediate concern for the unemployed, hungry, sick, and degraded. Thatcher's anxiety for the needy is denied. The title of the poem, "Jezebel: Her Progress" historically links Jezebel, Sinner of Samaria, to Margaret, Trumpeter of Toryism. There is an implied comparison between the ancient queen and the former British leader; both are supposedly examples of rulers who do not adequately care for the welfare of the citizenry. "Mrs. Snatcher Thatcher" believes in the sinfulness of lazy people and blames the victims for society's crimes against them. Jezebel's "progress" is that her unfeeling imperialism is reinvented in late-twentieth-century Britain. The theme is that when in every age unsympathetic government rears its ugly head, its face belongs to Jezebel.

Perhaps the most powerful contemporary poem to use the image of Queen Jezebel is by British poet laureate Ted Hughes. *Birthday Letters*, his 1998 collection of verse about his dead wife, American poet Sylvia Plath, includes a memorable poem entitled "The Dogs Are Eating Your Mother." Hughes compares Plath, who committed suicide in 1963 when she was just thirty-one years old, to Jezebel. Just as Jezebel's dead body was consumed by dogs after she was thrown from her balcony window to the street below, so have what remains of Sylvia Plath—her poems—been devoured by a public that lacks understanding. "The Dogs Are Eating Your Mother" is addressed to the couple's two children:

> That is not your mother but her body.
> She leapt from our window
> And fell there. Those are not dogs
> That seem to be dogs
> Pulling at her.
> . . . . .
> Let them
> Jerk their tail-stumps, bristle and vomit
> Over their symposia.
> (lines 1–5, 36–38)

Clearly angry with readers and critics who tear apart Plath's life and work, "pulling her remains," Ted Hughes lashes out in a bitter condemnation of her audience. He warns his children that trying to protect their dead mother is a useless endeavor. Instead, they should go on with their lives. When writing *Birthday Letters,* Hughes, nearing the end of his unsuccessful battle with cancer, attempts to have the last word on his much publicly picked over relationship with his ex-wife. Hughes's allusion to the morbid dismemberment of Jezebel's corpse explains his concept of how Plath's poetry has been treated. It has been chewed to pieces by dogs. It has been persistently gnawed and diminished by an overly curious public, an audience that has sensationalized the death of a brilliant young writer.

In conclusion, Israelite Queen Jezebel can be counted among the highly influential biblical sources for the poetic imagination. The term *poetry* describes a wide variety of written styles and patterns, and each successful poem is unique. Poetry can stretch our intellects, arouse our emotions, inspire our deeds, and increase our insight into the human condition. Under the best of circumstances, poetry can cause us to examine or define our ideas and attitudes. Topics can cover the range of experience, including love, death, war, politics, and religion. Biblical characters and themes are enduring subjects for poetry, and Queen Jezebel has certainly received her share of negative attention. A poet who staunchly defends the ancient queen has yet to come forward. Treatments of Jezebel are negative in poetry, and she is especially condemned as an evil seductress.

The Eternal Jezebel

Numerous poets use Jezebel either as the subject of their biblical poems or as a point of reference in their secular examinations of good and evil. Her name carries extremely strong poetic connotations, all of them negative. In many poems, from the early Latin efforts, which are little more than sermons in verse, to the songs of poets still living, the mere mention of Jezebel's name is sufficient to conjure up strong feelings within a reader. Poetry is the music of the ages, and Jezebel music is everywhere in our society.

6

The Smell of the Greasepaint
Jezebel in Drama

ରେ

Thro' all the drama—whether damned or not—
Love gilds the scene, and women guide the plot.

—Richard Brinsley Sheridan, *The Rivals*

A LOOK AT SERMONS, NOVELS, AND POEMS ABOUT JEZEBEL REVEALS MANY
highly dramatic moments. As a literary genre, drama is in some ways similar to prose and poetry. Novels contain conversations that are like scenes in a play;
Margaret Atwood, for instance, wrote dialogue in *The Robber Bride* that could be
lifted out of the book and inserted into a screenplay. More pedestrian fiction,
including Beadle's Half Dime novels, slips into melodrama. Essays and sermons
testify to the drama of human history while they seek to influence the outcome
of events, as when John Knox blasted Mary, Queen of Scots, by calling her a
Jezebel. Sometimes the distinction between play and poem is minimal. Plays may
be written in poetic form (including blank verse and rhymed couplets). Poems,
such as Arthur Symons's dramatic monologue "Jezebel Mort," possess language
that is a unique sort of drama, similar to a one-woman show staged in the theater.
When a work is called *dramatic,* it has emotional intensity and resembles a theatrical performance in passionate content or plot progression. All forms of literature distill human experience, and drama therefore lends its name to other genres when they are especially vivid. Nevertheless, drama is a distinct way of telling
a story.

Aristotle, in the *Poetics,* called drama "imitated human action," emphasizing
the importance of plot, character, thought, diction, spectacle, and song—in that

order. In a play, which is composed of dialogue plus stage directions, the narrative is "told" by actors who impersonate fictional characters before an audience. Unfortunately, people seldom have an opportunity to view live performances. We could wait years before a playwright's work is produced, and we may never have the opportunity to see particular plays. In the absence of live presentations, people must tolerate the alternative: reading a play while trying to pay attention to its theatricality. Digesting any genre poses special challenges, but a reader's solitary, silent scanning of a play's lines may impoverish the genre. Drama springs to life when it is performed. A director's singular interpretation; an actor's variations in tone of voice and gestures; the visual effect of sets, lights, and costumes; the sounds of background music; and the impact of the shared experience of an audience are all lost when one reads a play. The reader of plays must therefore appreciate the literary aspects of drama while remaining especially sensitive to the theatrical idiom. In addition to presentations in a theater or on film, plays may also be acted out on the stage that exists in the reader's mind. In fact, reading drama can enhance a person's understanding, especially if the play's language is challenging or the action is complex and difficult to follow. A play's survival as literature depends upon generations of readers returning to the text to examine structure and theme.

An individual interested in dramatic interpretations of Jezebel may have to settle for reading obscure or quirky plays about the queen; live performances are unlikely. A few Jezebel dramas acknowledge the queen's complex personality and bravery, but most condemn her.

Biblical Drama

Not all dramas about Jezebel are accessible to the English-speaking public, for they have not been translated into English. Yet two early Latin plays, composed in the sixteenth century, are available in editor Nigel Griffin's book entitled *Two Jesuit Ahab Dramas*. Both plays were written by Spanish Jesuit rhetoric teachers and were performed publicly in the writers' colleges. The first is *Tragoedia Cui Nomen Inditum Achabus* by Miguel Venegas (b. 1531), composed in the elevated Latin prescribed by Jesuit preferences for the theater. It was originally seen in 1561 at Coimbra in the Portuguese province where it was probably staged and directed by the author. The play closely follows the Vulgate story, only detailing a few episodes in the life of Queen Jezebel, but it also presupposes a knowledgeable audience familiar with the Bible. Little exposition is given concerning the reign of Ahab. The second drama in this volume is *Tragaedia Jezabelis,* probably from Castile and postdating the first play by ten to fifteen years. Though this second drama is anonymous, it is attributed to Juan Bonifacio (1538–1606). It is a less elaborate dramatization of the Jezebel story, composed in the vernacular and uneven in quality, with some parts written in prose and others in poetry. It possesses the vocabulary and tone of a work intended for a far less formal occasion than the first play and was probably intended to be more entertaining than instructive for students of rhetoric. Together these plays provide modern readers with a glimpse of the degree to which Jesuit drama uses Israelite history for inspiration (Griffin x).

The Vulgate's *Regum* (today divided into 1 and 2 Samuel and 1 and 2 Kings) is the primary source of information on which these two plays are based. Perhaps the Jezebel saga in Kings appealed to the Jesuits because it fit their sense of biblical morality and because it conformed to Aristotle's description of tragedy in the *Poetics*, wherein individuals with great power are brought low due to flaws in their character. The accounts of Ahab and Jezebel in the Hebrew Scriptures give three episodes popular with Jesuit writers: the exile of Elijah after his challenge to pagan gods under the patronage of Queen Jezebel; the death of Naboth and annexation of his land by Ahab; and the revolt of Jehu, plus the abolition of the House of Ahab. These stories provide an opportunity to expound upon the ephemeral nature of power and beauty. Also evident is Counter-Reformation theology concerning the rigors of maintaining the right to rule and the accuracy of prophecy in Holy Scriptures (Griffin vii).

Living in turbulent times, full of threats to established religious order, the Jesuits deemed restoration to be their duty. They believed it imperative to restore their church's power and prestige over the rising tide of Protestantism, just as Elijah and Elisha reinstated the authority of Yahweh over Baal and his acolytes in Jezebel's time. Jesuit dramas involve Lutherans, Huguenots, and (with more than a small touch of anti-Semitism) Jews as heretics who prostrate themselves before false gods, such as Baal and Melkaart. Audiences were exhorted to imitate Elijah's example and to oppose vigorously the new breed of Protestant idolaters. *Tragoedia Cui Nomen Inditum Achabus* and *Tragaedia Jezabelis* also indulge the Jesuit misogynistic penchant. Women were banned from stage and playhouse during the college literary festivals, when the plays were performed. The all-male audiences probably reveled in these chauvinistic attacks on the female sex. The Kings books are repositories for material railing against women who cause man's downfall, and these two plays follow their biblical source carefully. The intention behind the virulent attack on Queen Jezebel is to restore masculine and religious order.

Religious matters were also often on the mind of French dramatist Jean-Baptiste Racine (1639–1699), whose plays are still noted for their beautiful poetry and realistic characters. Racine is considered one of the greatest world dramatists, a master of tragic pathos. Many of his stories, drawn from history and Greek tragedy, possess perfect form and structure. Placed within the flawless architecture of his dramatic compositions, Racine's historical protagonists act in ways believable for our own times. His psychological insight into the characters and his felicity of expression have frequently been compared to Shakespeare's. Racine is praised today for his exquisite verse and passion. Educated by strict Catholic churchmen of the Jansenist sect, Racine broke away from them to devote his life to literature and a more libertine lifestyle. Winning the favor of Louis XIV, Racine was elevated to the status of nobleman as he continued to produce great plays, such as *Phèdre*. When his works received hostile attacks, Racine gave up drama for a time. Near the end of his career, he returned to writing and published two tragedies based on biblical stories, *Esther* (1689) and *Athalie* (1691).

Athalie (Athaliah, Jezebel's daughter) is Racine's last play and is sometimes regarded as his most sublime (see Solomon, in Racine 2: 372). Voltaire, always tepid about the value of non-French authors and culture, proclaimed in 1764 in the *Dictionnaire philosophique* that *Athalie* was the "chef d'oeuvre de l'esprit humain" and again in a letter to a friend that it was "le chef d'oeuvre de la belle poésie" (qtd. in Racine 2: 372). Athaliah's character is drawn in a manner consistent with the Bible's treatment of her famous mother. Athaliah—herself a queen in Judah—is ambitious and greedy, courageous and defiant, and she acts as though compelled to pry into God's business. The play was first performed by schoolgirls of Saint-Cyr on 5 January 1691, without benefit of costumes and with scant critical praise. The Comédie-Française revived the play in 1716 to much more positive notices.

In Racine's own preface to the play, he calls Athaliah "no less wicked than her mother" and a queen "who dragged the King, her husband, into idolatry" (2: 372). The preface indicates that, when Athaliah hears that Ahab and Jezebel have died, she determines to eliminate the House of David. Though the play's plot does not focus on Jezebel, she is mentioned seven times in *Athalie,* and the strong connection between mother and daughter is clear. In act 2, Athaliah is referred to as "this other Jezebel," and the daughter is determined to avenge the deaths of her parents and undo God's holy work. Racine's attitude is in keeping with the traditional view of Jezebel as a monster. Athaliah relates a dream that demonstrates Racine's knowledge of the biblical story and his tone of unyielding disgust for the Israelite queen:

> My mother Jezebel appeared before me
> Arrayed in pomp, as on the day she died.
> Her pride was quite untamed by her misfortunes;
> Immaculate as ever were the unguents
> With which she never failed to deck her face
> To hide the hideous ravages of time.
> "Tremble," she said to me, "my worthy daughter.

You too, the cruel Jewish God must slaughter.
I pity you, when in His fearful hands
You fall, my child." With these words, but with dread,
Her spirit seemed to lean towards my bed;
And I, I stretched my hands out to embrace her.
Yet all I found was but horrid mush
Of bones and mangled flesh, dragged in the slush,
Of bloody strips, and limbs all shameless scarred,
That bit by bit the wrangling dogs devoured.

(2.5)

The manner of Jezebel's death holds no romantic appeal for Racine, who seems to revel in the gory biblical details. He writes (in 1.1) of the queen being trampled by horses and "thirsty dogs licking her barbarous blood, / Tearing her hideous body limb from limb." Perhaps the severity of his Jansenist upbringing, set aside during his middle years, was not lost upon the dramatist as he aged.

Nearly two hundred years later, in 1872, American Peter Bayne (1830–1896) published a five-act play, *The Days of Jezebel: An Historical Drama*. The author's preface points out traditional reasons for Jezebel's bad reputation: "The records we possess of her reign were composed by Hebrews for whom it was both patriotism and religion to hate her with a perfect hatred" (ix–x).

Bayne allows Jezebel to speak for herself, often achieving eloquent poetry in the process. Nevertheless, the language may make *The Days of Jezebel* unappealing to today's action-loving theatergoer. There are choral hymns sung by loquacious minor characters. For example, Micaiah, son of Imlah (one of God's priests), takes up prophecy and leads the group in chanting poetic passages. For those who appreciate Bayne's artistic skill, the poetry is often lovely, though it can run tediously long.

One of the most interesting elements of Bayne's drama is its discussion of God, referred to as Jah, a diminutive of Yahweh or Jehovah. Early in the play, Jezebel claims that she will respect the Israelite God, though Phoenician deities claim her special loyalty. She calls Jah "an old and strenuous god," clearly preferring Baal and Ashtoreth, who are "bright, kind, loving, glorious" (35). Tolerance wanes as Jezebel becomes angry when Jah's prophets howl slanders against her and stir up the people against their queen. Furthermore, Jezebel dislikes the exclusivity of Jehovah worship and demands that her gods too be paid homage. She is outraged that in Israel only Jah reigns, an unfair situation from the queen's point of view. As revenge for this injustice, Jezebel desires to kill all God's prophets, so Obadiah is obliged to hide them. Elijah predicts the dismal end of Ahab and Jezebel. His words against the queen are especially forceful as he condemns her polytheism:

Thou, Queen of Israel, madest it thine aim
To quench the nation's vital spark, to kill
That which is Israel's soul, inbreathed from heaven;
To change the Hebrew worshipper of One,
A Spirit, infinite, invisible,
Into a heathen bowing reckless down
To many things called gods.

(225)

The climax comes when Jezebel defends herself by saying that Solomon also acknowledged many gods. Elijah reminds her that Solomon lost God's favor. Furious, Jezebel draws a dagger and stabs at Elijah, at the same time mocking Ahab for not being man enough to kill the prophet. Here the play ends, an interesting variation on the biblical story. In the Bible, Jezebel has many faults but never directly attempts to murder the prophet. In this play, he is almost eliminated by a malicious, mortal queen.

Jezebel's cruelty is her most dominant quality in Bayne's retelling of the tale. Her presence casts a dark shadow in each of her scenes. Her father, Eithobal (Bayne's spelling), kills his elder brother and usurps the throne. Jezebel admires this sort of fortitude, and her taste for strong, violent men is directly connected to her upbringing. When Ahab emulates Eithobal's ruthlessness, Jezebel is proud of her husband. Ahab's success at war causes her to note that only on the battlefield is Ahab her "hero unimpeached" (108). When Ahab balks at stealing Naboth's garden, Jezebel is disgusted by her husband's lack of conviction and feels that she must intervene to "refix [his] wavering diadem" (111). Jezebel refuses even to kiss Ahab when she feels he is being weak, and she wishes her husband were more like her father. Bayne's Jezebel is born into palace life where treachery reigns, and her bloodthirsty expectations cause conflict with her husband.

The queen's preference for merciless men is also reflected in the demands she places on her coconspirators in the Naboth incident. They know they must do her bidding and are too afraid to disobey. Yet they are not happy about their assignment and, along with Ahab, do not really meet Jezebel's standards for manliness. Ehud, for example, compares his scruples to something that must be strangled, for he does not wish to harm anyone: "I take my conscience by the throat, / When it rebels, and choke it" (120). Jezebel requires obedience from her men.

Some playwrights concentrate on the cruelty of Jezebel's daughter as much as on the notorious meanness of the queen herself. Moving forward in time just over two hundred years from Racine's *Athalie*, Athaliah appears in the twentieth century's first play concerning Jezebel. For a long time, biblical themes could not appear on the English stage unless set to music (Jackson 16). Then comes *Jezebel: A Drama,* published in London in 1904 and written by P. Mordaunt Barnard, rector of Headley, Surrey. It is a play in three acts, much of it in either lovely blank verse or iambic tetrameter. Barnard sometimes uses a strong rhyme scheme (*abab, cdcd, ee*) and rather frequently incorporates biblical quotations.

From the outset of Barnard's prologue, Ahab is a true believer in Baal, delving far more deeply into idolatry than indicated by any biblical accusation made against the king. In their effort to teach the people by example how to worship and behave, Ahab and Jezebel offer sacrifices to the gods. The priests dance and chant, offering up beautiful poems along with their harvest and animal sacrifices, but Baal desires blood to satisfy his appetite, and the priests faint and fall to the ground from self-inflicted wounds during the ceremonial frenzy. Elijah witnesses these abominations and declares that, as a result of priestly and kingly apostasy, no rain shall fall. In act 1, Jezebel's father, Ethbaal, sacrifices to Melkart (Barnard's spelling), and the rains begin again. Jezebel rejoices, believing the god has answered their petitions: "The rain descending at my father's prayer, / Makes me feel, what I am, a queen" (17). Meanwhile, Ahab has undergone a transformation at Carmel and now believes God to be the supreme, the only divine being. Jezebel thinks her spouse a weakling and a hypocrite. Gathering strength he never finds in the Bible or in most postbiblical portraits of the king, Ahab lashes out at his queen in act 1:

I married thee a foreign pest
To Israel's tribes, and thou hast brought a dower
Of Hellish plagues, of rank idolatry,
Upsetting the pure worship of the land
With antic-working priests and idols foul,
That joy in things impure, in witchcraft vile
And whoredoms unrestrained.

(22)

This husband-wife conflict remains throughout the drama and even escalates as time passes. In act 2, Ahab is depressed because he has been chided for letting Ben-hadad go free. He believes that possessing Naboth's vineyard will cheer him up, for the king genuinely seems to love the beauty of nature. Jezebel asks for his signet ring and says she will obtain the vineyard, but Ahab does not trust her to keep trouble away from the royal household. After obtaining the property, Ahab voices his resentment of Jezebel's interference in royal matters:

Affairs of state demand her instant care!
She treats me like a child, gives me a toy,
And bids me play with it, while she attends
To state affairs, frames policies and leagues.

(37)

Ahab wishes Naboth were still alive and fears Jezebel has made him culpable for the death, saying: "I feel another Cain" (40). He complains to Elijah that Jezebel is responsible for Naboth's demise, but Elijah refuses to allow the king to think of himself as innocent in the matter, indicating that Ahab is "slave to the worst of women" (43). As usual, Jezebel is the cause of man's undoing.

In act 3 of *Jezebel: A Drama,* the husband-wife conflict is replaced by mother-daughter misunderstandings. Athaliah is in Jezreel visiting. Jezebel confesses her affinity for the young woman, calling her "from childhood's years the partner of my thoughts" (50), and feels elated that they are two widowed queens who can unite David's mighty realm under Ethbaal's name. Athaliah believes Jezebel is too old to understand the revolt that is brewing in Jehu's camp. Jezebel, a practitioner of witchcraft, says she will put a hex on Jehu, but Athaliah flees to avoid being killed by Jehu in the coming rebellion. Heartlessly, she refuses to take Jezebel with her into safety, hissing: "Follow me not, or I will strike thee dead" (56). Barnard's Athaliah is so selfish, proud, ungrateful, and opportunistic that even Jezebel is alarmed. Before being thrown to her death from the balcony window, the dowager queen curses her own daughter. The characters that Barnard draws are in keeping with the spirit of the Bible, though the details of interpersonal relationships mark a far more serious rift within the royal family than the Bible ever suggests.

Family tension is focused directly on the royal couple in the next Jezebel play. England's lord chamberlain licensed the public performance of Gwen Lally's *Jezebel: A Play* in 1912. It was the first biblical drama approved by the country's official censor and contains four acts written in blank verse. It is set in Israel's grove of Astarte and palace of Jezebel, described as "a magnificent specimen of barbaric architecture." The stage directions describe Prince Ahab as weak, vacillating, and artistic in temperament. Before his marriage to Princess Jezebel, he goes to the grove of Astarte to pray; there he acknowledges that Jezebel is cruel but strong. Despite warnings that his kingdom will drip blood because of Jezebel and that he will come to hate her, her beauty has ensnared him, and he cannot resist the princess.

In an interesting variation on the biblical story, Ahab is violently jealous of his new wife, accusing her of adultery with Bidkar, captain of the army, and Amon, governor of Jezreel. She uses these men to help her achieve her evil ends but seems to have genuine affection for Amon, who assists her in securing false witnesses against Naboth. Ahab's love of Jezebel fades, and in the style of a Shakespearean hero, a deeply troubled Ahab sees the ghost of Naboth. Jezebel, of course, cannot see the apparition but realizes that Naboth's blood is on her head. At the end of the play, the queen's beauty has departed but not her strong will. Though the population has turned against Jezebel and wants Jehu to rule, the queen is defiant to the end. She tells a handmaiden just before being tossed to her death:

Come, tie my head,
And make fresh roses bloom upon my cheek.
I, Jezebel, have never known defeat.
I'll play this part—a kingdom is at stake;
And though I perish, yet I shall not feel
That I have weakly bowed my head to fate.
(64)

This Jezebel is fearless to the end. She is killed but not conquered, and Lally's treatment of the queen is more evenhanded than others'. Jezebel is brave, but she acts in defense of an evil cause.

A one-act play entitled *Jezebel*, written in 1915 by Robert Gilbert Welsh, depicts as degenerate a picture of Jezebel as is found anywhere. Stage directions indicate the author's concept of Jezebel's toxic effect on her environment. For example, when the servant girl Mara presents a bouquet of blue irises to the queen, "Jezebel leers. She lifts them to her lips. When her breath touches them they fade into an ashy grey" (653).

The first time Jezebel's name is mentioned, she and her priests are said to be "in a drunken slumber, after their night of abominations" (648). Throughout the play, the queen's sexual escapades are condemned. The virginal servant, Mara, is forced by Jezebel to become a priestess of Astarte and give herself, in keeping with Phoenician custom, to the first man who comes to her. But Mara is in love with a young soldier, Loammi, who is devoted to God. Ironically, Loammi (לֹא־עַמִּי, meaning "not my people") is the name of the third illegitimate son of Hosea's adulterous wife in the Hebrew Scriptures, but in this play Loammi is loyal to God. Jezebel nags her High Priest Beloth to use his magic to make her young and beautiful again so she can seduce Loammi. Beloth cautions Jezebel to think about more pressing political matters and warns that a storm in Tyre has torn off two branches of a tree planted by her father, Ethbaal, at her birth. The symbolic tree has fallen, and Beloth thus predicts that Jezebel and her two sons will be vanquished, partly because of Jezebel's sexual intemperance. Jezebel, as priestess of Astarte, feels that she is as one with the goddess and proclaims, "I am Eve, and I am Lilith! I am the first of women and the best! I am she whom all men seek for their delight! I am she whom all the sons of men desire" (658).

Heavily didactic, Welsh will not let the queen possess dignity after such an outburst. While trying to seduce Loammi, Jezebel (in shades of Herod and Salome) says that she will grant him any request if he will sleep with her. His desire is that she become God's instrument in Israel. When Jaho (Welsh's spelling of Jehu) comes to claim the throne, having killed Jezebel's two sons, he compares her to the predatory she-wolf. He calls her a "profaner of Jahweh's name, dishonorer of the faith of Israel, the despoiler of other men's lands, the spiller of innocent blood!" (660) and commands that she be thrown to her death. The queen possesses no redeeming quality.

Several years later, a one-act play by Dorothy Stockbridge, *Jezebel: A Play*, was first performed at Vassar College. It too tells the biblical story but presents its own startling departures from traditional ideas about the ancient queen. The opening of the play corresponds to the period of biblical time close to the queen's death. Jezebel kneels before a golden bull and prays for her son Joram's safety in his battle against Jehu. The queen owns a slave, the fictional Melkah, who has been given to Joram as a concubine. Believing the slave to be a loyal confidant, the queen confesses that she has no real religious convictions. Jezebel then declares to the golden bull:

> If I gave thee my heart to eat thou wouldst still grin as the smith made thee. Thinkest thou I have forgotten how thou wert made of my jewels—the jewels King Ahab gave me when I was a bride? . . . Dost think that I do not know that they are jewels and not eyes? These I wore in my ears. Dost thou think I can believe that the goldsmith hath made a god of my vanities? (553)

Nowhere does the Bible suggest that Jezebel is actually an atheist or hypocrite concerning her idol worship; the Deuteronomic historian would probably not have been able to conceive of someone with no religious beliefs at all. When the slave Melkah suggests that the queen pray to God if she cannot offer sincere petition to the golden bull, Jezebel cannot bring herself to do that either. The play suggests the despondency that occurs in the heart of one who has absolutely no faith, a powerful and universal theme, but not a concept typically applied to Jezebel.

Seduction is another theme in Stockbridge's play. Though the Bible is silent about Jezebel's reasons for dressing up before her death, Stockbridge clearly believes that Jezebel is trying to seduce Jehu. Melkah helps the queen with her makeup, and Jezebel, like Cleopatra awaiting Caesar, hopes that she is not too old to be alluring. She reasons that Jehu has made love to her in the past, thereby confessing to adultery that is never specified in the Bible and that would, in the Deuteronomist's mind, make Jehu wholly unsuitable as the next king of Israel. Yet in this play, Jezebel wonders whether Jehu would love her again. Melkah finally reveals her long-concealed antipathy for her mistress: the slave is actually the daughter of Naboth. Years earlier she had begged Jezebel for mercy and had been slapped by the heartless queen. In the end, Jezebel commits suicide, flinging herself from the balcony window rather than being hurled by Jehu's allies.

In its revelations about relationships and in the manner of Jezebel's death, Stockbridge's *Jezebel* is a complete departure from the Bible and even from tradition. It is highly doubtful that Jehu would have received the sanction of the Deuteronomic historian had the rebel ever been intimately involved with sinful

Jezebel. Such an alliance would have tainted Jehu irreversibly. Furthermore, it is important in the Bible that the queen be killed, for at issue is the fulfillment of Elijah's prophecy and the matter of who is in control, Jezebel as the force of darkness or Jehu as the representative of light. If she takes her own life, then Jehu is denied the honor of ending the line of Ahab and reestablishing masculine dominance. Stockbridge's Jezebel dies, but she retains the dignity and privilege of determining her own exit, and this indicates the author's grudging admiration for the queen. Once again, Jezebel is shown to be wrong-minded but strong willed.

Respect for Jezebel is also found in *A King's Daughter: A Tragedy in Verse* by English poet laureate John Masefield (1878–1967). A well-known lover of the sea who was driven ashore by failing health, Masefield became a poet, novelist, and dramatist. His interest in biblical material is confirmed by two of his later works, plays entitled *The Trial of Jesus* (1925) and *The Coming of Christ* (1928). On 25 May 1923, the first performance of his Jezebelian drama, set in the palace of Samaria, premiered at the Oxford Playhouse. The biblical queen is proud, able, and willing to act in Israel's best interest, yet she is also tormented by her lack of understanding for her adopted country. Ahab vacillates between the determination of David and the desperation of Saul. His ignorance assures his innocence in the Naboth incident. Jehu is Jezebel's foxy antagonist, strident in his political opportunism and supremely confident of his skill (Clarke 230).

While these characterizations sound rather routine, Masefield adds his own original touches to the Naboth story. For example, as a consequence of the episode, son Joram demands that Jezebel be dethroned and exiled. Ahab concurs, and the queen accepts the royal decision with grace, if not relief, though she calls her own son evil. In act 1, Jezebel herself rues the unhappy moment when she ascended to the Israelite throne: "in an evil day I became Queen / Over these strangers in Samaria" (211). She is later dismayed that the people blame her for the vineyard fiasco just because she is a foreigner. She claims that she and Ahab do not desire the property for themselves. They want to acquire it for the city, to enclose it properly inside the city walls because Jehu, minister of Jezreel's defenses, has urged them to do so for security reasons. Ahab mopes and Jezebel is forced to fill the void and rule. She proclaims: "I govern, I am King" (223).

In addition, Masefield's Naboth, often a speechless victim in other retellings of his story, plays an unusual role in the episode. Unlike his biblical counterpart, this Naboth is willing to negotiate a deal for the vineyard. He will give it to the foreign queen if she will make a sacrifice to the God of Israel, but that price is too high for Jezebel to pay. When she refuses his offer, Naboth is enraged and finds his bold tongue:

You smeared with spice, painted, and dripping perfume,
A shameless woman, chaffering with a man,
And he, the King, a dallier with God's foes,
Conspiring thus to cheat me of my vineyard.
. . . .
I spit upon you both and bid God curse you,
Curse you to ruin and to rottenness.
As here I curse you; him for making peace,
Where no peace is, and you, you insolent woman,
For being, like the King, a curse on Israel,
A bringer down into the pit of hell.

(242)

Ahab is also angry with Jezebel for having Naboth stoned. The king believes that she has ruined his chances of governing well, as Masefield creates some interesting moments in the play.

Masefield's handling of Jezebel's death scene begins with predictable but powerful condemnations of the queen. Pashur, a mere messenger, freely blasts Jezebel as he tells her that Jehu has killed Joram and is about to kill her too. Using powerful parallel phrases, he declares her to be a

scarlet whore,
Abominable in the face of God,
You manless, soulless, crownless foreigner,
Shall taste the wrath of God and of God's people.
Now for your spicery there shall be stink,
And where the delicate hair has known the comb
There shall be baldness, and where silk has lain
There shall be nakedness.
And where the red lips mocked God delicately
There shall be broken teeth biting on dust:
It shall be done to you ere this day passes.

(305)

Yet the author presents a fascinating twist to the ending of *A King's Daughter*. Knowing that her time has arrived, Jezebel refuses to flee but thoughtfully saves her romantically named handmaidens, Rose-Flower and Moon-Blossom. Then as she prepares alone for death, Jezebel dons a robe that had belonged to the beauteous Helen of Troy. Jezebel's father had won it at Rhodes long ago, and possessing it confers on Jezebel an aura of respect for the timelessness of feminine power and influence. She adorns herself for the meeting with Jehu so that no one will think her cowardly, and she paints herself, "lest men should think me pale / And say that I, the Queen, am pale from fear" (308). The play's final judgment on Jezebel comes from surprisingly sympathetic Micaiah, the seer: "She was too good a woman to be Queen / In such a land as this, at such a time" (312).

A King's Daughter possesses unity, passion, moving atmosphere, and tragic pathos. Jezebel is, like the heroes of classical tragedy, a highborn person at the mercy of time and circumstance but also a victim of her own inner conflicts and personal failings. She struggles to break free of the net that catches and surrounds her and her family, but it closes too tightly and she is tangled in its mesh. At the last, she succumbs to a situation too terrible to overcome, but she maintains a regal and elegant instinct for handling the inevitable with style.

In 1924, one year following Masefield's play, the Shakespeare Head Press published H. M. McDowall's *Jezebel: A Tragedy*. It is a play in three scenes, each one possessing a Jezebel who reclines on cushions and is fanned by servants. The play is written in nicely phrased blank verse.

McDowall's language produces a torrent of images and possesses metaphors appropriate to a foreign queen native to coastal Phoenicia but caught in landlocked Israel. He uses the geographical differences in the two countries to underscore Jezebel's feelings of alienation. For example, in scene 1, Jezebel dreams that she is back home near the beautiful ocean and muses: "I love to wait and watch and wonder till / Myself seems not myself, and I am lost / In the o'erwhelming glory" (8). But she always wakens to find herself in Israel's scorching desert, "Far from the sea, in this abhorred place." Still tied to the undulating shores of her homeland in scene 2, Jezebel uses sea imagery to describe the ebb and flow of her feelings:

I scorn these Israelites! I scorn the king!
He knows not his own mind. They follow him
In all his vacillations. When the sea
Is rising, all the lovely, delicate
Sea plants incline one way, and when it turns
They change, and softly outwards yearn again.
So with these people.

(16)

The water images cascade over the audience, which must recognize how spiritually parched Jezebel feels in her adopted land.

The queen is bound to Phoenicia in another way also. She remains loyal to Baal, believing him to be the benevolent sun that kisses the earth, the source of corn that grows in abundance, and the giver of life for man and beast. Jezebel's god encompasses all of nature, and when Ahab is distraught by the long drought, he admits that in his heart he too prefers Baal worship. Though this reverence for Baal causes inevitable conflict with Elijah, Jezebel feels great affinity for the stern Jewish prophet. She may hate all other Israelites, but she admires Elijah's lack of fear and recognizes it as being akin to her own courage. When Elijah runs ahead of Ahab's chariot to herald the coming rain, Jezebel says, "Mine eyes beheld a victor passing by; / That was no man, but storm in human shape" (19). She also believes that she must make it impossible for Ahab ever to worship God again. Therefore, without his knowledge, she breaks laws to obtain Naboth's vineyard. She performs the evil deed in Ahab's name so that the people will suspect he no longer honors God. Then, she hopes, he will have to turn to Baal exclusively, a flawed plan that fails.

McDowall's play is at times reminiscent of Shakespeare's tragedy *Macbeth*. For instance, Jezebel is appalled at Ahab's inability to stop the execution of her four hundred priests. In Lady Macbeth style, Jezebel responds, "Oh! God! If only I had been a man!" (21). Further, in a "dagger of the mind" scene, Ahab has two guilty visions of dead, mangled bodies with swooping birds above them—a premonition of his two dead sons. Unlike Shakespeare's queen, however, Jezebel does not lose her mind or die pitifully offstage. Instead she vows to face her end by cloaking herself in majesty as though heads of state await her.

In a three-act tragedy entitled *Jezebel* (printed c. 1924), H. R. Barbor incorporates biblical quotes into the characters' dialogue, and stage directions provide both exposition and character analysis. The author invents several unique plot twists in the Jezebel story, though act 1 presents a fairly routine picture of Ahab, Jezebel, and Elijah at the time of the Carmel contest. Jezebel despises not only her spouse but most of her retinue, considering them to be mere pawns. As in McDowall's version, the queen does respect the great prophet Elijah's power, and the "strong tower" of Israel is the epithet used for him. Everyone admits that Israel has prospered since Jezebel ascended to the throne; and she brags, "I bade [Sidonian and Tyrian merchants] trade oil and wine, for kingdoms wax where marting is brisk and where the merchants repair." Thinking of troubled times that lie ahead for Israel, Obadiah answers coldly, "That's true. Kingdoms wax" (20). Ahab's ivory palace is supposed to serve as a "sign to the people that they shall look upward from their lands and outward from their boundaries and make for themselves a great land in which they shall prosper and grow fat" (63). Yet Obadiah insists that the people cry for spiritual not material things, though they have been blinded by Baal and Ashtoreth, who have obscured "the bright wonder of Yhwh" (20). Meanwhile, Ahab is a weakling dominated completely by his sinful wife. She calls him a "pulling manikin," a dummy. Jezebel considers him to be "no King, rather a blade of grass tossed in the air" (22) when he relates the news that Baal has lost at Carmel.

In this play, as in others, Jezebel is not only an idolater but a fornicator as well, and Barbor introduces a unique idea about the queen's partner in adultery. Here it is Naboth who has secret assignations with Jezebel and who then pays dearly for his romantic trysts. Stage directions indicate that at the play's opening Jezebel is a "splendidly built, full-figured woman of thirty" (10), and she is a beautiful seductress throughout the play. Jehu reveals that he was selected to sing at court and provide background entertainment during Naboth's clandestine dalliance with Jezebel. Jehu was also the watchman who led a veiled Jezebel, dressed in Bedouin women's clothes, back to Ahab's palace after her adultery with Naboth. As proof, Jehu produces a gold bracelet that he claims the queen presented him as payment for his assistance during the affair, circumstantial evidence that actually proves nothing. In other renditions of the Jezebel story, Naboth is portrayed as an innocent victim; but in Barbor's version, the vineyard keeper's behavior is tawdry as he betrays his king and becomes his queen's lover.

The seduction theme is continued in act 3 of Barbor's *Jezebel* when the queen seeks to seduce Jehu. She has "tender words to whisper to this seeker after glory" (137). Just prior to her death, serving girls deck Jezebel's hair with pearl ropes and paint her face. She believes that her body is still worthy of a man's desire. To the approaching usurper of her family's throne she says, "For I am not spent in years, and my trusted loveliness endures. Wear me for Israel's delight and yours" (142). At the play's end, after Jezebel is thrown to her death and Jehu sits down to his feast, servants find only a pearl and a disembodied, cold hand belonging to Jezebel. Barbor's original plotting and fine tragic detailing are chilling to readers, and this Jezebel has no redeeming qualities to make us admire her courage or mourn her passing. Perhaps we cannot help but feel regret that her remains have been so grievously neglected, but we also must be relieved that her terrible reign is at an end.

In 1929 a very different view of the queen appears in Edith Lombard Squires's (1884–1939) one-act play, in verse, *Queen Jezebel*. Everything surrounding Jezebel glitters and glistens in majestic splendor. The opulence of the Jezreel palace is so great that Jezebel's brilliant, golden room reflects the sun. Her attire is equally glorious, as a stage direction indicates: "She is clad in white with a deep purple hem to her gown. Her thick, red hair, held by a golden cord, catches the last rays of the setting sun. Her wide blue eyes scan eagerly the golden curtain before the divan" (617).

Set against this luster is the darkness that approaches. Ahab encourages his wife to wangle Naboth's land away from him, claiming that she would do it if she truly loved her king. After Jezebel does the deed, the court's splendor grows dim as Jezebel tells Ahab: "Naboth is dead. His vineyard land is thine. / Turn on thy couch and tell me thou art glad. / I love thee, Ahab, and the darkness comes" (619). Immediately thereafter, Elijah makes his gloomy prediction. Jezebel fears not for herself but for her husband, whom she adores.

Squires's short dramatic narrative is often at variance with the Bible story. Jehu desires for Jezebel to reign beside him and be his queen. She commits suicide, preferring to throw herself over the parapet rather than succumb to Jehu's lustful urges. The new king orders a proper burial for Jezebel, but dogs find and devour her body before the grave diggers arrive. Jehu clutches Jezebel's plush golden scarf, symbol of the court's former brightness, and buries his face in it as the curtain drops. The Deuteronomist certainly never intended such a bond to form between Jezebel and Jehu. After all, she is intended to represent biblical disgust with foreign idol worship; his role is to symbolize Israel's return to godliness. Squires sees Jezebel as alluring enough to tempt Jehu, God's chosen monarch.

A more familiar looking Jehu reemerges in Australian author M. W. MacCallum's (1854–1942) *Queen Jezebel: Fragments of an Imaginary Biography in Dramatised Dialogue,* published in 1930. The play has five "incidents" and spans the thirty years from 915 to 885 BCE: Jezebel's marriage, the end of the famine, the death of Naboth, the death of Ahab, and the revolt of Jehu. The opening incident includes all characters who will be important in the drama. Bidkar is impressed with Jezebel's beauty, but devout Jehu is immediately skeptical, lest she "Should graft on Israel these fond vanities / That the Sidonians prize" (21). Bidkar is convinced that Jezebel will be like Ruth, making Israel's God and people her own. Obadiah is practical, seeing how fit it is that Omri's son should take the king of Tyre's daughter for a wife and tolerate images worshiped by others, since foreign gods do no real harm.

MacCallum's play examines the power of its female characters. The author insists that Athaliah is Ahab's sister and not his child with Queen Jezebel. Yet the two women have much in common, and in scene 2 Jezebel feels familial affection for Athaliah. The sister-in-law acknowledges her debt to Jezebel, for she "Hast shown the mark at which a queen should aim / And the craft to aim aright" (41). The women discuss how it feels to be in a harem, but Jezebel does not begrudge Ahab his other women, as long as she is allowed to help him rule. Even after the Mount Carmel episode, Jezebel is not alarmed because she, not Elijah, still rules in Israel. Athaliah pledges that, if the prophet flees south to Judah, he shall not find sanctuary in her land. Jezebel believes that Elijah is a sorcerer who has charmed Ahab and taken away the king's manhood.

MacCallum eloquently summarizes Jezebel's attitude toward God:

And what a thing is this,
The fear of Israel's God! A grievous yoke,
A bridle and a bit, it weights them down,
Rules, checks, and thwarts and galls them, changes them
To beasts of burden. In our happier Tyre

Great Melkarth is appeased with precious gifts,
And, even when most incensed, with human blood.
But no burnt offerings buys Jehovah's grace:
His worshippers, in spite of their own desires,
Must do His will in all and make it theirs,
Obey His statutes, and with heart and mind
Follow what He accounts a righteousness.
What king can walk in leading-strings like these,
What kingdom stand o'erladen with such laws?

(83)

As with several other writers, MacCallum allows Jezebel to utter grievances against God that make her preference for Phoenician deities seem less unreasonable. In the final scene, she sees her death as a sacrifice to Baal, cursing Israel as she is about to die.

The last half hour of Jezebel's life is the subject of a one-act play by Nora Ratcliff, published in 1939 and simply titled *Jezebel*. All the characters are female—the queen and six of her attendants—ranging in age from seventeen to over forty. Most are frightened but steadfast followers of Yahweh, and loyalty to God is a primary theme of this drama. The other main character is Naomi, fictional widow of Naboth, who has been in prison, where she is so ill-treated that her body—but not her faith—has been broken. Jezebel had "obviously been beautiful in her youth, but now her extravagant make-up only serves to accentuate the ravages of time and an evil life" (87). The pivotal influence in that evil life is Baal, "the god who calls for human flesh" (83).

An anthropomorphized God is central to Ratcliff's play. For example, when Jezebel commands her women to pray to Baal for Jehu's overthrow, some are afraid to defy the queen, but a servant named Miriam says, "The Queen's arm is long indeed. We, who have suffered, know that. But the arms of Jehovah encircle the world, and in the hollow of his hand he holds both us and all we love" (82). Jezebel intends to offer a human sacrifice. She calls for wine and spills it over her hands, symbolizing the connection between Baal worship and bloodshed. She is so arrogant as to believe that her son Joram is victorious over Jehu and God, and she is convinced that her power, not theirs, will continue. She brags, "Was it not I who slew the prophets of Israel's puny god, and set up altars to Baal?" (88).

The theme of Jezebel's misplaced pride dominates the play. Ratcliff's queen convinces herself that Joram's continuation on the throne is secure, so the motivation for dressing and applying makeup is different here than in most renditions of the tale. Jezebel wears her finest clothes and jewels to greet Joram as he enters Jezreel, victoriously, his mother thinks. Her ladies try to persuade Jezebel that she is mistaken, and the queen briefly seems to understand the situation better. Nevertheless, she is convinced that she can seduce Jehu: "I am beautiful, beautiful! Men look upon me and their hearts grow hot with desire. What is Jehu that he should not be as other men when his eyes meet mine?" (92). She compares her beauty to a spear, believing that it can sink deep into a man's flesh. Even to the very end, Jezebel maintains her foolish pride. The crowd boos her as she is about to be thrown from her window, and an attendant comments, "Poor crazed thing! See, she acknowledges that howl of hatred as if they were cheering her—" (93). This Jezebel has no moment of recognition or reversal when she truly realizes her situation and copes courageously. She is in denial at the end, out of touch with the meaning of events swirling around her.

Though Ratcliff's Jezebel is proud, she is replaced by an even meaner spirited woman in *The Vineyard: Being the Story of Elijah, Ahab and Jezebel,* by the sixth earl of Longford (Edward Arthur Henry Pakenham [1905–1961]). First produced at the Dublin Gate Theatre in March 1943, the drama is sometimes characterized by a mundane, unimpressive prose style, except when the author is alluding to biblical sources. For instance, act 1 takes place in the Sidonian city of Zarephath, where Elijah revives a dead child whose parents have fled Israel due to conflicts with Ahab and Jezebel. Echoing the powerful rhetoric of Amos 1–2, the play begins with the lament: "Woe unto Zarephath! Woe unto all the land of Sidon! For three transgressions of Sidon, yea for four, I will not turn away the punishment thereof!" (1). In act 2, an angel who feeds Elijah in the desert refers to the spiritual quality of food, comparing it to the bread and water of life and paraphrasing the words of Jesus (John 4.1–42 and 6.22–66). The author also achieves good transition between acts by introducing the subject matter for act 2 at the conclusion of act 1 and repeating this procedure for act 3 as well.

The earl of Longford's Jezebel is a thoroughly contemptuous character. The Jezebel–Elijah conflict, so clearly stressed in the Bible, is the subject of much of the play's first and second acts. When Obadiah introduces himself to Elijah as the governor of Ahab's household, Elijah responds, "I always thought the governor of Ahab's household was Queen Jezebel" (16). The queen has the reputation of constantly bossing her husband around. Examples of Jezebel's meddlesome and controlling nature develop as the play moves into act 2. Hearing of the Carmel contest, Jezebel is unwilling to wait patiently for news of the outcome. Instead, she erects a pavilion near the mountain summit so that she can observe the event unseen. She possesses a terrible temper and routinely "upset her dressing table, beat her maid and kicked the King's dog" (22). In the palace, she is so jealous that courtiers are not allowed to look at any woman other than the queen. Vanity is not the worst of Jezebel's traits, however. She is also a raging anti-Semite, disgusted that the Jewish homeland is populated by the Jewish people: "Jews! Jews! Jews! Nothing but Jews. Obadiah, is there anyone here but dirty Jews? What a country!" (28). Her hostility and lack of understanding of Israelite worship customs are also evident: "What a people! No religion! Nothing but hairy prophets on top of inaccessible mountains! They deserve to be conquered by the Syrians" (29).

The sexual customs around the palace are another subject that interests Longford. Jezebel uses sex to get her way at court. For instance, Ahab says he is not interested in Naboth's vineyard and promises its owner not to try to confiscate it. Jezebel is furious and insists that no one will respect the crown if the king cannot show his power and do as he pleases. She is repulsed by Ahab's weakness and will not allow him to touch her, reminding him often that she is the daughter of a genuine king, if not the wife of one. In act 3, Naboth refuses to give up his land to Queen Jezebel, calling her a painted strumpet. Furthermore, Princess Athaliah's boredom with life is reflected in her attitude toward the type of sex required for the worship of her gods: "I'm bored stiff with sacrifices and dreary prayers and still drearier orgies. You've no idea how boring an orgy can be when it's all in a good cause, with prophets and priests buzzing round like flies to make sure everyone enjoys themselves" (28). A courtier named Aram jovially comments that Baal worship is indeed "a very exhausting religion" (52), but it has more of what the people want than does the strict Jewish faith, with its admonitions about permitted and forbidden sex.

A radical change of pace is available in a funny, mischievous piece loosely based on biblical stories and exploring the nature of God. Robert Nathan's 1953 play, *Jezebel's Husband*, contends that God uses humor to teach. The drama contains a strong woman who chooses to be called Jezebel. She is born Jehosheba but changes her name after Queen Jezebel dies, is food for the dogs, and has much distinction heaped upon her. The play is set in Israel in 731 BCE in the home of Jonah the prophet. This new Jezebel is the wife of Jonah, who had earlier achieved fame by surviving for three days in the belly of a whale and then visiting Nineveh to warn of the city's impending destruction. The prologue to the play warns that this Jezebel "is not to be confused with the infamous queen" (3), yet the two women have much in common. Jonah is a weakling, who also bears a striking resemblance to King Ahab.

The plot and characters are whimsical. Nathan's Jezebel has a private room with a balcony, through which sightseers are led on guided tours of the palace. The tourists are unimpressed with the place and with Jonah's plaques commemorating his trip to Nineveh. God has not spoken to Jonah since the whale episode, so the prophet is disappointed in his career and wishes to retire. He would like to be as famous as Elijah—only not so poor. Jezebel is "attractive, but hard as a peach pit, and as voracious as a pariah. . . . She is possessive, ambitious, ruthless, and efficient. She has made Jonah what he is; and means to have credit for it" (10). Their characters are developed with imagination and fantasy mixed with some biblical facts and insight into human nature.

The central conflict of *Jezebel's Husband* involves humanity's relationship with God. The people are facing war, want God on their side, and desire a message of hope and comfort from a prophet. Messages of doom like the ones delivered earlier by Elijah and Jonah are not appreciated. The people need a vision reassuring them of divine love. Encouraged by Jezebel, Jonah brings news the public longs to hear, even though he knows his words of consolation are false. War begins, and King Tiglath of Nineveh wants to hire Jezebel as his court visionary because, he says, the prophecy she forces Jonah to deliver is "a corker. It told us all we needed to know—that you people were trusting to dreams again, instead of chariots. Still,—it was a powerful speech" (105). Jezebel and Jonah separate, she taking a new job as prophetess of Nineveh and he retiring to a cave though he never liked caves. The play is a silly little caper, but there are moments of wit and wisdom, and the effect of the whole is a charming diversion as long as no one takes it too seriously.

In the 1950s, Hollywood tried to dramatize the biblical Jezebel story. *Sins of Jezebel*, a movie spectacle starring Paulette Goddard and directed by Reginald Le Borg, opened in 1954 to miserable reviews. The film industry was attempting to compete with television, but it was also struggling with conflicting impulses of its own: the need to moralize by issuing severe warnings to evildoers and the need to sell tickets by revealing bare midriffs. When characters hold forth on Jehovah while jumping from bedroom to bedroom, the result seems falsely contrived.

Nonbiblical Drama

Not all plays in which Jezebel is mentioned directly involve the queen or other biblical characters. As with novels and poems, much drama makes brief use of the queen's name without bothering to retell her story. For example, Shakespeare refers to Jezebel in *Twelfth Night*. In the gulling of Malvolio scene (2.5), Sir Andrew Aguecheek speaks while outside Malvolio's range of hearing and refers to the foolish Malvolio as a Jezebel. It is unprecedented for a *man* to be called a Jezebel, but Sir Andrew is disgusted with Malvolio's ridiculous political ambition, lust, and pride in thinking he can win the affection of a gentlewoman well above his station. Sir Andrew is also a fool and therefore compares Malvolio to the haughty queen of Israel.

A bit later, English dramatist William Congreve (1670–1729) wrote his urbane comedy of manners *The Old Bachelor,* produced in 1693 with John Dryden's assistance. It was a great success and helped revive public interest in the theater after a slump in popularity; Congreve's sophisticated wit was widely acclaimed, assuring him a place of respect among the pack of Restoration playwrights. In *The Old Bachelor,* as in *Twelfth Night,* there are plot intrigues concerning people in different social strata, and Jezebel is mentioned (4.4) in a quip with context similar to Sir Andrew Aguecheek's. The play's stock characters include Puritan banker Fondlewife, his spouse Laetitia, and Bellmour (who is disguised as a preacher and intent on making a cuckold of the banker). Fondlewife is suspicious and says to Laetitia and Bellmour, whose stomach is upset:

> But what—not to be cured of the Cholick? Don't you know your Patient, Mrs. *Quack?* Oh, lie upon your Stomach; lying upon your Stomach will cure you of the Cholick. Ah! I wish he has lain upon no bodies stomach but his own. Answer me that, *Jezabel?* (93)

Such social vignettes with their humorous implications and sexual undercurrents are quintessential Congreve, and his good-natured levity makes up for his thin plots and weak characterizations.

At least twenty-five other pre-1900 nonbiblical British dramas briefly mention Queen Jezebel. Not once is she portrayed with special sympathy. Authors as diverse as poet-playwright John Dryden (*The Kind Keeper* [1680]), actor-playwright David Garrick (*The Chances* [1773]), novelist-playwright Henry Fielding (*Don Quixote in England* [1734]), and critic-playwright Algernon Charles Swinburne (*Bothwell: A Tragedy* [1874]) each make one reference to Jezebel. She is far from the focus of their work, but she appears in the dialogue long enough to be called a painted hussy or a demon.

Though a far cry from Shakespeare or Dryden, a nonbiblical comedy written in America in 1916 is Charles Hiram Chapman's *Jezebel: A Comedy.* Published at his own expense, the play contains feminist ideas well ahead of their time. The author (b. 1859) appears to delight in shocking the middle classes of his generation. The entire drama, composed in rhymed couplets of mostly trochaic tetrameter, is a radical departure from previous treatments of the Jezebel story and makes no references to ancient Israel. It is funny in many places and one of the few plays to apply the biblical heroine's name to a contemporary woman. It mixes imaginary and real characters, including President Theodore Roosevelt and social reformer Anthony Comstock. Comstock (1844–1915) led crusades against vice that resulted in the coining of a new term, *Comstockery,* meaning "overzealous censorship due to alleged immorality."

The plot of *Jezebel: A Comedy* is based on a ridiculous premise: the president of the United States offers a million dollars to any mother who has produced sixteen legitimate children, all within a marriage to the same husband. The male characters in the play, especially Comstock, attempt to find such a deserving woman. Their efforts are foiled by a woman named Jezebel who advocates birth control and causes quite a bit of consternation among the men. Once again it is a Jezebel who will upset the masculine power structure.

In the opening scene, Comstock asserts the misogynistic sentiment that predominates in all the play's male characters: "How pure we'd live would God exempt us / From woman's wiles" (3). He is so prudish that he cannot bear to hear the words *arm* and *leg* uttered publicly. Comstock and the town mayor comment on the appropriateness of the new Jezebel's name, for they fear that she will adversely influence all modern wives. Implying a comparison of this contemporary Jezebel and the Genesis serpent, the men complain that there is no stopping her:

> We've fined her, jailed her, cracked her skull,
> But night or day there's scarce a lull
> In her demoniac propaganda.
> Thruout the city she has fanned a
> Flame to both church and state destructive
> With poisonous serpent breath seductive.
>
> (8)

Two of the play's major themes are man's desire to play God and woman's desire to be emancipated. At the height of the Women's Suffrage movement but years before the Women's Liberation movement, Chapman, a man, is supportive of feminist issues, and the play has an abundance of praise and blame to suggest. The new Jezebel is run in on a rail to answer charges leveled against her by the townsmen. A lawyer claims she has broken obscenity laws by championing the cause of birth control, and Jezebel counters that the men behave as though they know God's will, which is unknowable. The men—acting as prosecuting attorney, judge, jury, and executioner—take the law into their own hands and decide to burn Jezebel at the stake, Joan of Arc style. Her defense is that women need to be encouraged to take control of their own lives:

> What then
> Were women but mere toys for men
> Ere I inspired them chains to break,
> Live their own lives, possession take
> Of their own souls?
>
> (14)

In *Jezebel: A Comedy,* all different types of men are unsympathetic to women. A greedy entrepreneur, an industrialist who could be straight out of a Dickens novel, wants women to be breeders of babies to provide him with a cheap, constant supply of labor. He is not interested in well-educated, high-minded people, just in drudges who toil in his factory and ensure his profits. A minister wants women to have lots of infants so that he can save their souls. He is concerned about the immortal character of children never conceived: "They wander damned thru space forlorn / All unredeemed because unborn" (21). His warped logic tells him that anyone who never lives will never benefit from Jesus' sacrifice or heaven's joy; therefore, women must be baby-making machines and bring the opportunity for redemption to souls yet unborn.

Finally the men locate a beggar woman, appropriately named Angeline. Her drunkard husband is in jail, but her sixteen children qualify her for the one million dollars. She relates the sad tale of her life, how her aspirations for education and missionary work were dashed by her early marriage and numerous progeny. Her current poverty, weakness, lack of ambition, and ill health are due, she says, to her overly large family. The men suspect she's been influenced by Jezebel, but Angeline says her opinions come directly from her own experience. She believes she has sunk too low ever to rise again. Fearing the worst for their campaign to elevate the birth rate, the men decide to execute both Jezebel and Angeline. The minister advises Jezebel to trust in God's salvation, but she scoffs: "The old song. / I'm tired of God's procrastination. / His saving mercy waits too long" (45). In the town, people march in demonstrations of solidarity with Jezebel. They seize Comstock and demand that Jezebel and Angeline be released. The women are freed, providing the happy ending demanded by comedy. Selfless Angeline, apparently forgetting about her family's plight, donates her prize money to spread the message of birth control. Such is the influence of Jezebel.

Perhaps the most intriguing drama to mention the name of the Israelite queen is the story of the Old South, *Jezebel*, by Owen Davis, Sr. (1874–1956). The play ran briefly on Broadway in 1933–1934 and was rewritten for the movies in 1938. The heroine is Julie, the spoiled, headstrong southern belle who combines elements of emasculating temptress and captivating innocent. She pouts when she does not get her way and connives to control her world. The play was not successful on the stage (Krutch 28; Young 226) and soon closed, but Bette Davis revived the part in the more critically acclaimed and financially successful film version, giving one of the best performances of her career (plate 10).

In 1937, as Metro-Goldwyn-Meyer's David O. Selznick searched for the perfect Scarlett for the film version of *Gone With the Wind*, Fred Warner attempted to steal some of the attention by coming out with his own tale of the twisted South, an adaptation of Owen Davis's *Jezebel*. At Warner Brothers, Bette Davis (who had coveted the role of Scarlett) and director William Wyler threw themselves into a professional and personal collaboration on the screenplay of *Jezebel*. The film had some interesting moments and was nominated for Academy Awards for Best Picture, Best Score, and Best Cinematography, in addition to the two categories for which it won Oscars, Best Actress and Best Supporting Actress. In purple prose, the trailer to Warner's film proclaimed:

> From the picturesque glamour of the old south a great actress draws the scarlet portrait of a gorgeous spit-fire who lived by the wild desire of her untamed heart. . . . The story of a woman who was loved when she should have been whipped. . . . Jezebel. Pride of the south that loved her. Shame of the man she loved. (Jeter 31)

The opulence of biblical Jezreel's ivory palaces is echoed in the film's setting, which is drenched in local color. *Jezebel* takes place in New Orleans in 1852, and the set drips in Spanish moss, sloshes in mint juleps, and sweats in stately antebellum rooms. Characters remain flat and stereotypical. Julie—in a manner reminiscent of the biblical queen—is a charming, impulsive vixen who flaunts her disdain for convention. Julie is in love with Preston Dillard (played by Henry Fonda), an equally willful young banker who does not immediately capitulate to Julie's demands. Sparks fly when the couple appears at the Olympus Ball, where unmarried girls traditionally wear white. Julie is adamant about appearing in a daring red gown. When Julie becomes embarrassed that she is making a spectacle of herself, Pres insists that she remain at the party, bravely dancing and facing the indignant crowd. Pres breaks off the romance and leaves Louisiana to work at one of his family's northern banks. When he returns three years later, Julie has learned her lesson and behaves in an obsequious manner Queen Jezebel would never have sanctioned. Julie swallows her pride and humbles herself before Pres, hoping that he will forgive and marry her. He's already married, however, to a northern woman.

At this point, *Jezebel* becomes a morality play centered on Julie's realization of her shortcomings. To stir up trouble, she claims that she has been dishonored by Pres, manipulating his brother and a southern gentleman named Buck Cantrell into fighting a duel. When Buck is killed, Julie finally begins to understand her evilness. Aunt Belle chides her niece: "I'm thinking of a woman called Jezebel who did evil in the sight of God." Like her biblical counterpart in the Naboth story, Julie causes an innocent man's death.

According to Hollywood conventions of the 1930s, Julie must be made to regret her transgressions. Pres is stricken with yellow fever, and Julie successfully argues that it is she, not his bride, who should accompany him to Lazarette Island, a leper colony where the sick are exiled. If anyone can save Pres's life, Julie is the one with the scrappiness to do it. Yet at this point in the history of American drama, the

Production Code of the Motion Picture Producers and Distributors of America dictated that bad women had to be punished (Jeter 43), a concept not found in Owen Davis's Broadway play. The notion of Julie not paying the price for her independence was unacceptable to film censors of the 1930s. She could atone for her haughtiness by unselfishly nursing the mortally ill Pres and facing almost certain death herself. The denouement of the movie occurs when the couple rides on a cart bound for the quarantine island. Julie, symbolically seated beside a nun, appears resolved, serene, and perhaps even spiritual. Some audience members may assume that her expiation through suffering is complete. More cynical observers see Julie's act as her last selfish attempt to control others and regain her lost lover. There is sufficient ambiguity to support both interpretations. In fact, writer-director Edmund Goulding advised Warner executives before filming began on *Jezebel* that, even if a redemptive finale were added to Owen Davis's original script, it could "only tell the story of the triumph of bitchery" (Schatz 22). The biblical Jezebel never repents, but both Julie and her biblical counterpart face their ends with courage.

Jezebel is a transitional film for Hollywood, standing between America's romantic and decadent visions of southern life. Between the U.S. stock market crash of 1929 and the beginning of American involvement in World War II in 1941, Hollywood produced no fewer than seventy-five movies nostalgically glorifying southern pre–Civil War society—patrician, agrarian, and built upon concepts of white superiority. In later decades, films based on the writings of Lillian Hellman, Tennessee Williams, and William Faulkner would be made. These authors employed Gothic and sexual perversion motifs to depict the decline and fall of southern aristocracy, so Hollywood's adaptations of these works mark a significant shift in attitude. *Jezebel* exhibits elements of both viewpoints (Jeter 32), as represented by Julie's conflicts with good and evil. It is her maverick personality that ultimately leads her to be called a Jezebel. While the biblical Jezebel never seeks forgiveness, her film namesake undergoes a change of heart. The alteration in Julie's character may be implausible, but it did satisfy Hollywood's film censors of the 1930s.

Sometimes Jezebel's name is used in film, and sometimes it is appropriated in drama set to music. Highbrow composers have relied on stereotypes of the queen, and the polyvalent image of Jezebel has found its way into classical suites. Jezebel references appear in the 1956 award-winning opera of lust and greed, *The Ballad of Baby Doe,* music by Douglas Moore and libretto by John Latouche. Based on a true tale of America's Wild West at the turn of the twentieth century, a love triangle forms among Elizabeth ("Baby") Doe, wealthy silver miner Horace Tabor, and Tabor's wife. Tabor leaves his spouse to marry Baby, thus earning her the reputation of a Jezebel. Baby's wedding is a grand event attended by President Chester

A. Arthur, but predictably, Tabor's career is ruined because of his second marriage. Once again a Jezebel character causes a man's downfall and death. Baby remains true to Tabor's memory, but she too comes to a pitiful end, freezing to death near an abandoned silver mine. Her image as a destructive temptress is unmitigated by years of devotion to Tabor.

Today's movie and television dramatists frequently use the queen's name. In the popular film *Steel Magnolias,* the hairdresser played by Dolly Parton jokingly calls her sidekick a Jezebel for applying makeup before attending a Christmas festival. The film *Antonia's Line,* winner of the 1996 Oscar for Best Foreign Language Film, features a Jezebel reference that highlights the foibles of the clergy. A hypocritical village priest implies that Antonia's daughter Danielle, pregnant and unmarried, is a Jezebel whose lust is responsible for the downfall of man. Ironically, the priest himself is soon caught performing a sexual act in the confessional. Numerous television scriptwriters for such shows as *I Love Lucy* and *Little House on the Prairie* invoke Jezebel's memory as a slur against any female character who commits a misdeed or is dangerously seductive. Desi Arnaz sang "Jezebel" in one of his 1950s television nightclub scenes with Lucille Ball. The song claims that Jezebel is a devil without horns. In 1996 a Jim Henson television production, *Muppets Tonight!,* premiered on ABC. Actress Michelle Pfeiffer and muppet Miss Piggy supplied the conflict for the first episode. Jealous of the show's human guest star, Miss Piggy (in her inimitable porcine way) repeatedly accused Pfeiffer of being a Jezebel. The list of Jezebel references grows daily and seems endless.

In conclusion, from the Latin plays written by the Jesuits to the films produced by Hollywood, Jezebel makes her appearance in numerous dramas. Some of the best and some of the most mediocre playwrights in history have relied upon the queen's presence in their texts. Though there are a few comedies that use the Jezebel character, in the final analysis, most of the Jezebel dramas are morality plays and tragedies. Jezebel exhibits little virtue in these dramas of her life, and her vice is brought to such a bad end that the strictest moralist must feel vindicated. Plays about the life of Jezebel or characters named after her are usually tragedies of spiritual disharmony. The main characters flounder in the imbalance of body and soul. The subject matter is often the decadence of the queen and her unholy court. In some plays, the queen assumes an air of tragedy that links her to the unfortunate heroes of classical drama. Doomed by an understandable human failing and by the ravages of circumstance, a person of high position, important to the history of a race or nation, dies. In Jezebelian drama, she usually dies well. The character often has some moments of grand behavior, but she ultimately sinks into a quagmire from which there is no escape. Jezebel does speak a few lines in the Bible, but in a drama she can become as lyrical or obstreperous as the playwright's imagination allows. The style of the play may be one of sustained elegance when written by a great author, such as Racine. Through viewing or reading plays about Jezebel, we learn something important about the queen and ourselves; at times we are repelled by her foibles and at times sympathetic to her plight. At the conclusion of the drama, we experience a catharsis, or what John Milton calls a "calm of mind, all passion spent."

Works Cited

Index

Works Cited

ꙮ

Ackroyd, Peter R. "Goddesses, Women and Jezebel." *Images of Women in Antiquity*. Ed. Averil and Amelie Kuhrt Cameron. Rev. ed. London: Routledge, 1993. 245–59.

Andersen, Francis I. "The Socio-juridical Background of the Naboth Incident." *Journal of Biblical Literature* 85 (1966): 46–57.

Anderson, Flavia. *Jezebel and the Dayspring*. London: Chapman, 1949.

Aristotle. *Poetics. Criticism: The Major Texts*. Ed. W. J. Bate. New York: Harcourt, 1952. 19–39.

Atwood, Margaret. *The Robber Bride*. New York: Bantam, 1993.

Avigad, N. "The Seal of Jezebel." *Israel Exploration Journal* 14 (1964): 274–76.

Aytoun, William Edmondstoune. *Bothwell: A Poem in Six Parts*. 3rd ed. Edinburgh: Blackwood, 1858.

Barbor, H. R. *Jezebel: A Tragedy in Three Acts*. London: Arthur Brenton, [1924].

Barlow, George. "Jezebel." *Song-Spray*. London: Remington, 1882.

Barnard, P. Mordaunt. *Jezebel: A Drama*. London: Griffiths, 1904.

Baugh, Albert C., ed. *A Literary History of England*. New York: Appleton, 1948.

Bayne, Peter. *The Days of Jezebel: An Historical Drama*. Boston: Gould, 1872.

Beach, Eleanor Ferris. "The Samaria Ivories, Marzeah, and Biblical Text." *Biblical Archaeologist* 56.2 (1993): 94–104.

Beaumont, Joseph. *Psyche in XXIV Cantos. The Complete Poems of Dr. Joseph Beaumont*. Ed. Alexander B. Grosart. 2 vols. Edinburgh: Edinburgh UP, 1880.

Benet, William Rose. *The Reader's Encyclopedia*. 2nd ed. New York: Crowell, 1965.

Ben-Sasson, H. H., ed. *A History of the Jewish People*. Cambridge: Harvard UP, 1976.

Bewer, Julius. *The Literature of the Old Testament*. Revised by Emil Kraeling. 3rd ed. New York: Columbia UP, 1962.

Bialik, Hayman Nahman, and Yehoshua Hana Ravnitzky, eds. *The Book of Legends:*

Works Cited

Legends from the Talmud and Midrash. Trans. William G. B. Braude. New York: Schocken, 1992.

Bickersteth, Edward Henry. *Yesterday, To-day, and For Ever: A Poem in Twelve Books.* 1866. London: Rivingtons, 1873.

Bin Gorion, Micha Joseph. *Mimekor Yisrael: Classical Jewish Folktales.* Trans. I. M. Lask. Ed. Emanuel bin Gorion. Vol. 1. Bloomington: Indiana UP, 1976.

Brand, Christianna [Mary Lewis]. *Death of Jezebel.* New York: Dodd, 1948.

———. Interview. *Contemporary Authors.* New Revision Ser. 13: 324. Detroit: Gale Research, 1994.

Brathwait, Richard. *The Honest Ghost; or, A Voice from the Vault.* London: 1658.

Bremkamp, Gloria Howe. *Merai: The Woman Who Challenged Queen Jezebel and the Pagan Gods.* San Francisco: Harper, 1986.

Brontë, Charlotte. *Jane Eyre.* 1847. Pleasantville, NY: Reader's Digest, 1984.

Browning, Robert. *The Works of Robert Browning.* Ed. Sir F. G. Kenyon. 10 vols. 1912. New York: AMS, 1966. Vols. 7 and 9.

Campbell, Joseph. *The Power of Myth, with Bill Moyers.* Ed. Betty Sue Flowers. New York: Doubleday, 1988.

Carmichael, Calum. "Biblical Laws of Talion." *Hebrew Annual Review* 9 (1985): 107–26.

Catto, Max. *The Hairy Man.* London: Secker, 1939.

Chapman, Charles Hiram. *Jezebel: A Comedy.* N.p.: Chapman, 1916.

Christensen, Duane L. "Huldah and the Men of Anathoth: Women in Leadership in the Deuteronomic History." *Society of Biblical Literature Seminar Papers* 23 (1984): 399–404.

Clark, Jonas. *Jezebel, Seducing Goddess of War.* Hallandale, FL: Spirit of Life, 1998.

Clarke, George Herbert. "John Masefield and Jezebel." *Sewanee Review* 32 (1924): 225–42.

Coe, Edward B. "Jezebel." *Women of the Bible by Eminent Divines.* New York: Harper, 1900. 121–34.

Coleridge, Samuel Taylor. *The Poems of Samuel Taylor Coleridge.* Ed. Ernest Hartley Coleridge. Oxford: Clarendon, 1912.

Collins, Patricia Hill. *Black Feminist Thought: Knowledge, Consciousness, and the Politics of Empowerment.* Perspectives on Gender 2. New York: Routledge, 1991.

Collins, Wilkie. *Jezebel's Daughter.* 1880. *The Works of Wilkie Collins.* Vol. 27. New York: AMS, 1970.

Congreve, William. *The Old Bachelor.* 1693. *The Plays of William Congreve.* Ed. Herbert Davis. Chicago: U of Chicago P, 1967.

Crabbe, George. *The Works of the Rev. George Crabbe.* 5 vols. London: John Murray, 1823. 3: 381–401; 5: 3–47.

Works Cited

Craig, A[llen] R[obert]. *Jezebel's Daughter.* Garden City, NY: Doubleday, 1935.

Crowley, Aleister. *The Confessions of Aleister Crowley: An Autobiography.* Ed. John Symonds and Kermuth Grant. New York: Hill, 1969.

———. *The Works of Aleister Crowley.* 3 vols. New York: Gordon, 1974. 1: 129–32.

Davis, Owen, Sr. *Jezebel.* Warner Bros., 1938.

Di Lella, Alexander A. *The Wisdom of Ben Sira.* Anchor Bible 39. New York: Doubleday, 1987.

Donne, John. *Complete Poetry and Selected Prose.* Ed. John Hayward. London: Nonesuch Lib., 1955.

Downey, Fairfax. *Jezebel the Jeep.* Illus. Paul Brown. New York: Dodd, 1945.

Dryden, John. *The Kind Keeper.* London: Bentley, 1680.

Ellis, Peter F. "1–2 Kings." *The Jerome Biblical Commentary.* Ed. Raymond E. Brown, Joseph A. Fitzmyer, and Ronald E. Murphy. Englewood Cliffs, NJ: Prentice, 1968. 1: 179–209.

Faulkner, William. *Light in August.* 1932. New York: Vintage, 1972.

Fausset, Hugh I'Anson. *John Donne: A Study in Discord.* London: Cape, 1924.

Fielding, Henry. *Amelia.* 1751. New York: Dutton, 1930.

———. *Don Quixote in England.* London: Watts, 1734.

Frangipane, Francis. *The Three Battlegrounds: An In-Depth View of the Three Arenas of Spiritual Warfare: The Mind, the Church and the Heavenly Places.* Cedar Rapids, IA: Advancing Church, 1989.

Frankau, Pamela. *Jezebel.* London: Rich, 1937.

Fraser, Antonia. *The Wives of Henry VIII.* New York: Knopf, 1992.

Frost, Stanley B. "Judgment on Jezebel, or a Woman Wronged." *Theology Today* 20.4 (1964): 503–17.

Fuchs, Esther. "Who Is Hiding the Truth? Deceptive Women and Biblical Androcentrism." *Feminist Perspectives on Biblical Scholarship.* Ed. Adela Yarbro Collins. Chico, CA: Scholars, 1985. 137–44.

Garrick, David. *The Chances.* 1773. *The Dramatic Works.* London: Millar, 1798.

Glasheen, Adaline. *Third Census of Finnegans Wake: An Index of the Characters and Their Roles.* Berkeley: U of California P, 1977.

Gray, John. *I and II Kings: A Commentary.* 2nd ed. Philadelphia: Westminster, 1970.

Greenspahn, Frederick. "A Typology of Biblical Women." *Judaism* 32 (1983): 43–50.

Griffin, Nigel, ed. *Two Jesuit Ahab Dramas.* Exeter Hispanic Texts 13. Exeter, UK: U of Exeter, 1976.

Grunwald, M. "Elijah's Chair." *The Jewish Encyclopedia.* 1903. London: Funk, 1901–1905. 5: 128–29.

Hair, J. L. *Jezebel.* New York: Vantage, 1953.

Hanscombe, Gillian E. "Jezebel: Her Progress." *Bread and Roses: An Anthology of*

Works Cited

Nineteenth- and Twentieth-Century Poetry by Women Writers. Ed. Diana Scott. London: Virago, 1982. 246–47.

Harbaugh, Thomas Chalmers. *Plucky Phil of the Mountain Trail; or, Rosa, the Red Jezebel.* Beadle's and Adam's Half Dime Lib. 8.231. New York: Beadle, 1881.

Harden, Donald. *The Phoenicians.* Ancient Peoples and Places 26. London: Thames, 1962.

Hardy, Thomas. "Jezreel: On Its Seizure by the English under Allenby, September 1918." 1918. *The Complete Poetical Works of Thomas Hardy.* 1984. Ed. Samuel Hynes. 5 vols. Oxford: Clarendon, 1982–1995. 2: 333–34.

———. *Tess of the D'Urbervilles.* 1891. New York: Norton, 1965.

Haskins, Susan. *Mary Magdalen: Myth and Metaphor.* New York: Harcourt, 1993.

Heavysege, Charles. *Jezebel: A Poem in Three Cantos. Saul and Selected Poems.* 1868. Introd. by Sandra Djwa. Toronto: U of Toronto P, 1976. 339–68.

[Helms, Jesse]. "Jesse's World." *Newsweek* 5 Dec. 1994: 24.

"Henry VIII." *Biography.* Introd. Peter Graves. Arts and Entertainment Network. June 1996.

Herm, Gerhard. *The Phoenicians: The Purple Empire of the Ancient World.* New York: Morrow, 1975.

Hesky, Olga. *The Painted Queen.* London: Anthony Blond, 1961.

Higgins, F. R. "Song for the Clatter-Bones." *Chapters into Verse.* Ed. Robert Atwan and Laurance Wieder. Oxford: Oxford UP, 1993. 1: 249.

The Holy Scriptures. Philadelphia: Jewish Pub. Soc., 1917.

Homer. *The Iliad.* Trans. E. V. Rieu. Baltimore: Penguin, 1950.

———. *The Odyssey.* Trans. E. V. Rieu. Baltimore: Penguin, 1961.

Hood, Thomas. "A Tale of a Trumpet." *The Comic Poems of Thomas Hood.* London: Ward, n.d. 10–31.

Horace. "Art of Poetry." *Criticism: The Major Texts.* Ed. W. J. Bate. New York: Harcourt, 1952. 51–58.

Hughes, Ted. "The Dogs Are Eating Your Mother." *Birthday Letters.* New York: Farrar, 1998.

The Interpreter's Bible. Ed. George Arthur Buttrick. 12 vols. 1954. New York: Abingdon, 1951–1957. Vol. 3.

Jackson, Holbrook. Introduction to *Salome: A Tragedy in One Act.* By Oscar Wilde. London: Limited Editions Club, 1938.

Jeter, Ida. "*Jezebel* and the Emergence of the Hollywood Tradition of a Decadent South." *Southern Quarterly* 19 (1981): 3–4, 31–46.

Rev. of *Jezebel,* by Dorothy Clarke Wilson. *Library Journal* 80 (1955): 2612.

———. *New York Times* 4 Dec. 1955: 57.

Rev. of *Jezebel,* by Richard Pryce. *New York Sun* 8 Feb. 1913: 4.

Rev. of *Jezebel's Daughter,* by A. R. Craig. *New York Times* 5 May 1935: 18.

Johannsen, Albert. *The House of Beadle and Adams and Its Dime and Nickel Novels: The Story of a Vanished Literature.* 2 vols. Norman: U of Oklahoma P, 1950.

Josephus. *Jewish Antiquities.* Trans. H. St. J. Thackeray, Ralph Marcus, and Louis H. Feldman. 1930–1965. Loeb Classical Lib. 9 vols. Cambridge: Harvard UP, 1926–1965. Vols. 4–9.

Joyce, James. *Finnegans Wake.* New York: Viking, 1939.

Keach, Benjamin. *Distressed Sion Relieved, or The Garment of Praise for the Spirit of Heaviness.* London, 1689.

Kellerman, Faye. *Serpent's Tooth.* New York: Avon, 1997.

Kingsland, Dorothea. Rev. of *A Modern Jezebel* by Irene Nemirovsky. *New York Times* 7 Mar. 1937: 7.

Klaidman, David. "The Starr Wars Drag On." *Newsweek* 26 Oct. 1998: 47.

Knox, John. *The First Blast of the Trumpet against the Monstrous Regiment of Women.* 1558. Reprinted in *The English Experience: Its Record in Early Printed Books Published in Facsimile* 471. New York: Da Capo, 1972.

Krutch, Joseph Wood. "Drama: Tempest and Sunshine." *Nation* 3 Jan. 1934: 28.

Lally, Gwen. *Jezebel: A Play.* 1912. London: Humphreys, 1918.

Lee, Robert G. *Pay-Day—Someday.* Grand Rapids, MI: Zondervan, 1957.

Lindsay, Vachel. "A Curse for the Saxophone." *Spokesman-Review* 16 Dec. 1924: 50–53.

Loewenthal, L. J. A. "The Palms of Jezebel." *Folklore* 83 (1972): 20–40.

Longfellow, Henry Wadsworth. *Christus: A Mystery. The Complete Writings of Henry Wadsworth Longfellow.* 11 vols. Boston: Houghton, 1904. 5:19–527.

Longford, Sixth Earl of [Edward Arthur Henry Pakenham]. *The Vineyard: Being the Story of Elijah, Ahab and Jezebel.* Dublin: Hodges, 1943.

MacCallum, M. W. *Queen Jezebel: Fragments of an Imaginary Biography in Dramatised Dialogue.* Sydney, Austral.: Angus, 1930.

MacFall, Haldane. *The Wooings of Jezebel Pettyfer.* New York: Knopf, 1925.

Margalith, Othniel. "The Kuelabim of Ahab." *Vetus Testamentum* 34 (1984): 228–32.

Masefield, John. "A King's Daughter: A Tragedy in Verse." 1923. *Verse Plays.* New York: Macmillan, 1925. 209–313.

McCarthy, Mary. Rev. of *Jezebel's Daughter,* by A. R. Craig. *Nation* 19 June 1935: 720.

McDowall, H. M. *Jezebel: A Tragedy.* Oxford: Blackwell, 1924.

McHugh, Roland. *Annotations to "Finnegans Wake."* Baltimore: Johns Hopkins UP, 1980.

McLaws, Lafayette [Emily Lafayette]. *Jezebel: A Romance in the Days When Ahab Was King of Israel.* Illus. Corwin K. Linson. Boston: Lothrop, 1902.

Merchant, Natalie. "Jezebel." *Our Time in Eden.* Prod. Paul Fox. Christian Burial Music, 1992.

Metzger, Bruce M., and Michael D. Coogan, eds. *The Oxford Companion to the Bible.* Oxford: Oxford UP, 1993.

Meyers, Carol. *Discovering Eve: Ancient Israelite Women in Context.* New York: Oxford UP, 1988.

Middleton, Scudder. "Jezebel." 1924. *Prize Poems: 1913–1929.* Ed. Charles A. Wagner. New York: Boni, 1930. 156–58.

Midrash Rabbah. Trans. H. Freedman and Maurice Simon. 2nd ed. 10 vols. London: Soncino, 1951.

Milton, John. "Samson Agonistes." *John Milton: Complete Poems and Major Prose.* Ed. Merritt Y. Hughes. Indianapolis: Odyssey, 1957. 593.

M'Neile, Hugh. *Jezebel: Speech of the Rev. Hugh M'Neile, at Market Drayton, Salop, December 19, 1839.* London: The Protestant Assoc., 1840.

Monjo, F. N. *The Jezebel Wolf.* Illus. John Schoenherr. New York: Simon, 1971.

Moultrie, John. "The Black Fence." *Poems.* New ed. London: Macmillan, 1876. 254–63.

Nashe, Thomas. "In Time of Pestilence." *The Oxford Book of English Verse.* Ed. Arthur T. Quiller-Couch. Oxford: Clarendon: 1919. 263.

Nathan, Robert. *Jezebel's Husband and the Sleeping Beauty.* New York: Knopf, 1953.

Nathanson, Barbara Geller. "Lilith." *The Oxford Companion to the Bible.* Ed. Bruce M. Metzger and Michael D. Coogan. New York: Oxford UP, 1993. 437.

Nemirovsky, Irene. *A Modern Jezebel.* Trans. Barre Dunbar. New York: Holt, 1937.

The New Oxford Annotated Bible with the Apocryphal/Deuterocanonical Books. Ed. Bruce M. Metzger and Roland E. Murphy. New York: Oxford UP, 1991.

Nickerson, Kate. *Ringside Jezebel.* New York: Original Novels, 1953.

Olyan, Saul. "2 Kings 9:31—Jehu as Zimri." *Harvard Theological Review* 78 (1985): 203–7.

Oppenheim, E. Phillips. "Jezebel of Valley Farm. 1926." *The Works of E. Phillips Oppenheim: Nicholas Goade, Detective.* New York: Review of Reviews, 1929. 182–204.

The Oxford Study Bible: Revised English Bible with the Apocrypha. Ed. M. Jack Suggs, Katharine Doob Sakenfeld, and James Mueller. New York: Oxford UP, 1992.

Rev. of *The Painted Queen,* by Olga Hesky. *Spectator* 30 June 1961: 960.

———. *Times Literary Supplement* 14 July 1961: 429.

Parker, Simon B. "Jezebel's Reception of Jehu." *Maarav* 1 (1978): 67–78.

Peake, A. S. "Elijah and Jezebel. The Conflict with the Tyrian Baal." *Bulletin of the John Rylands Library* 11 (1927): 296–321.

Works Cited

Peters, Catherine. *The King of Inventors: A Life of Wilkie Collins.* London: Secker, 1991.

Pickett, Fuchsia. *The Next Move of God.* Orlando: Creation, 1994.

Pope, Alexander. "Rape of the Lock." *Eighteenth-Century English Literature.* Ed. Geoffrey Tillotson, Paul Fussell, Jr., and Marshall Waingrow. New York: Harcourt, 1969. 568–78.

Potok, Chaim. *Wanderings: Chaim Potok's History of the Jews.* New York: Knopf, 1983.

Pryce, Richard. *Jezebel.* Boston: Houghton, 1913.

Quick, Catherine S. "Jezebel's Last Laugh: The Rhetoric of Wicked Women." *Women and Language* 16 (1993): 44–48.

Racine, Jean. *Complete Plays.* Trans. Samuel Solomon. 2 vols. New York: Random, 1967. Vol. 2.

Ratcliff, Nora. *Jezebel. Nelson's Theatrecraft Plays.* Ed. Nora Ratcliff and John Bourne. London: Nelson, 1939. 81–94.

Rawlinson, George. *History of Phoenicia.* London: Longmans, 1889.

Richardson, Samuel. *Pamela; or Virtue Rewarded.* 1740. New York: Norton, 1958.

Robbins, Tom. *Skinny Legs and All.* New York: Bantam, 1990.

Robertson, Noel. "The Ritual Background of the Dying God in Cyprus and Syro-Palestine." *Harvard Theological Review* 75 (1982): 313–59.

Robins, Denise. *Jezebel.* Rev. ed. Bath: Chivers, 1977.

Robinson, J. *The First Book of Kings.* Cambridge, UK: Cambridge UP, 1972.

Rofé, Alexander. "The Vineyard of Naboth: The Origin and Message of the Story." *Vetus Testamentum* 38 (1988): 89–104.

Schatz, Thomas. "'A Triumph of Bitchery': Warner Bros., Bette Davis and Jezebel." *Wide Angle* 10 (1988): 16–29.

Selvidge, Marla J. *Woman, Violence, and the Bible.* Lewiston, NY: Mellen, 1996.

Shakespeare, William. *The Complete Works of Shakespeare.* Ed. David Bevington. 4th ed. New York: HarperCollins, 1992.

Shelley, Percy Bysshe. "Charles the First." 1824. *Shelley: Poetical Works.* Ed. Thomas Hutchinson. Oxford: Clarendon, 1967. 488–507.

Sheridan, Frances Chamberlaine. *Memories of Miss Sidney Bidulph.* 1761. N.p.: 1961. 3: 220–322.

Sheridan, Richard Brinsley. *Six Plays.* Ed. Louis Kronenberger. New York: Hill, 1957. 1–84.

Slaughter, Frank Gill. *The Curse of Jezebel: A Novel of the Biblical Queen of Evil.* Garden City, NY: Doubleday, 1961.

———. Interview. *Contemporary Authors.* New Revision Ser. 5: 493. Detroit: Gale Research, 1985.

Smelik, Klaas A. D. "The Literary Function of 1 Kings 17, 8–24." *Pentateuchal and Deuteronomistic Studies: Papers Read at the XIIIth Iosot Congress.* Ed. C[hristian] Brekelmans and J[ohan] Lust. Bibliotheca Ephemeridum Theologicarum Lovaniensium 94. Leuven, Belgium: Leuven UP, 1990. 239–43.

Speed, Samuel. "On Beauty." *Prison-Pietie: Or, Meditations Divine and Moral.* London, 1677. 41–42.

Squires, Edith Lombard. *Queen Jezebel. Poet Lore* 40 (1929): 615–26.

Standish, Robert. *The Prince of Storytellers: The Life of E. Phillips Oppenheim.* London: Davies, 1957.

Stockbridge, Dorothy. *Jezebel: A Play. Contemporary One Act Plays, 1921.* Ed. Frank Shay. Cincinnati: Kidd, 1922. 541–69.

Swinburne, Algernon Charles. *Bothwell: A Tragedy.* London: Chatto, 1874.

Symons, Arthur. "Jezebel Mort." *Jezebel Mort, and Other Poems.* London: Heinemann, [1931].

Talmud, The Babylonian. Ed. I. Epstein. 17 vols. London: Soncino, 1938.

Telushkin, Joseph. *Jewish Literacy.* New York: Morrow, 1991.

Trenchard, Warren C. *Ben Sira's View of Women: A Literary Analysis.* Brown Judaic Studies 38. Chico, CA: Scholars, 1982.

Trible, Phyllis. "Exegesis for Storytellers and Other Strangers." *Journal of Biblical Literature* 114 (1995): 3–19.

———. "The Odd Couple: Elijah and Jezebel." *Out of the Garden.* Ed. Christina Büchmann and Celina Spiegel. New York: Fawcett, 1994. 166–79.

Tupper, Martin F[arquhar]. "Czar Peter." *Three Hundred Sonnets.* London: Hall, 1860. 138.

Urquhart, Fred. *Jezebel's Dust.* London: Methuen, 1951.

Van Der Meulen, E., and C. S. Hulst. *An Epistle to Ahab King of Israel.* 1911. [Grand Rapids, MI: Lyon, Kymer, Palmer], n.d.

Weber, Thomas H. "Sirach." *The Jerome Biblical Commentary.* Ed. Raymond E. Brown, Joseph A. Fitzmyer, and Ronald E. Murphy. Englewood Cliffs, NJ: Prentice, 1968. 1: 541–55.

Webster, John. *The Duchess of Malfi.* 1623. *Stuart Plays.* Ed. Arthur H. Nethercot, Charles R. Baskerville, Virgil B. Heltzel. New York: Holt, 1971. 311–61.

Welsh, Robert Gilbert. *Jezebel. The Forum* 53 (1915): 647–60.

Wheeler, Edward L. *The Black Hills Jezebel; or, Deadwood Dick's Ward.* Beadle's and Adam's Half Dime Lib. 8.201. New York: Beadle, 1881.

White, Fred M. *A Society Jezebel.* London: Ward, 1917.

Wiesel, Elie. *Five Biblical Portraits.* Notre Dame, IN: U of Notre Dame P, 1981.

Wilcox, Ella Wheeler. "Devils." *Poems of Affection.* London: Gay, 1920.

Williams, Isaac. *Female Characters of Holy Scripture: In a Series of Sermons.* London: Rivingtons, 1873.

Wilson, Dorothy Clarke. *Jezebel.* New York: McGraw, 1955.

Yadin, Yigael. "The 'House of Ba'al' of Ahab and Jezebel in Samaria, and That of Athalia in Judah." *Archaeology in the Levant: Essays for Kathleen Kenyon.* Ed. Roger Moorey and Peter Parr. Warminster, UK: Aris, 1978. 127–35.

Young, Stark. "Jezebel." *New Republic* 3 Jan. 1934: 226.

Ziolkowski, Jan M. *Jezebel: A Norman Latin Poem of the Early Eleventh Century.* Humana Civilitas 10. New York: Lang, 1989.

Index

෧෨

Aaron, 45
Abednego, 133
Abel, 64, 142
Abraham, xiv, 30, 34, 45, 53
Abram. *See* Abraham
Absalom, 85
Adam, 19–21
Adonis, 34
Aeneas, 40
Agrippina, 115
Ahab, xiii–xvi, 3–15, 18–19, 25, 28, 34–35,
    39–45, 47–50, 55–74, 76–78, 81–82, 84–86,
    88–92, 98–99, 102, 104–13, 124, 127, 132–35,
    137, 142–44, 154, 156, 159, 164–70, 172–73,
    175–78, 180–81
Ahasuerus, 19, 61
Ahaziah, 9, 70, 74–78, 86, 90, 110
Ahijah, 66
Akhenaton, 79
Alcott, Louisa May, 117
Allenby, Edmund, 159
Amasa, 85
Ambrose, Saint, 98
Amos, 12, 83–84, 91, 180
Anat, 34
Anderson, Flavia, 109–11
Anth-Ya'u, 36
Antichrist, 103
Aphrodite, 27
Arden, Elizabeth, 137
Arnaz, Desi, 188
Arthur, Chester A., 187–88

Asherah, 6, 34–37, 39, 45, 47
Ashtoreth, 11, 112, 167, 176
Astarte, 6, 34–35, 37, 83, 110–11, 134, 138,
    170–71
Athaliah, 18, 25, 27, 40, 71, 90–91, 100, 110,
    125, 166, 168, 170, 178, 181
Atwood, Margaret, 129–32, 163
Augustine, Saint, 16
Aytoun, William E., 158

Baal, 3–4, 6–9, 12–13, 15, 18, 25, 31–37, 39,
    43–50, 71–72, 74–76, 83–84, 89–92, 105,
    107–11, 113–14, 133–34, 142, 144, 158, 165,
    167, 169, 175–76, 179, 181
Baal-zebub, 9, 74–75
Baasa. *See* Baasha
Baasha, 66, 85
Babylon, 5, 21, 37, 54, 109, 147, 151
Babylonia. *See* Babylon
Bakker, Tammy Faye, 138
Ball, Lucille, 188
Barak, 18
Barbor, H. R., 176–77
Barlow, George, 152–53
Barnard, P. Mordaunt, 168–70
Barton, Elizabeth, 99
Bathsheba, 28, 68, 105, 151
Battle of Bunker Hill, 129
Bayne, Peter, 167–68
Beadle's and Adams's Half Dime Library,
    117–19, 120, 122, 163
Beaumont, Joseph, 141–42

Beliyyaal, 62

Ben-hadad, 59, 71, 144, 169

Ben Sira, Jesus, 16–18, 20–21, 80

Bialik, Hayim Naham, 13–14

Bickersteth, Edward Henry, 146

Bidkar, 170, 178

Boaz, 23

Boleyn, Anne, 99

Bonifacio, Juan, 164–65

Booth, John Wilkes, 148

Borgia, Lucrezia, 105

Boyz II Men (musical group), 150

Brand, Christanna. *See* Lewis, Mary

Brathwait, Richard, 141–42

Bremkamp, Gloria Howe, 113–14

Brontë, Charlotte, 116

Browning, Robert, 155–56

Burke, Edmund, 147

Cain, 64, 148, 170

Campbell, Joseph, 19–20, 37–38, 115

Canaan, 5, 7, 9, 12–13, 31–32, 34, 36, 38, 48, 56, 58, 84, 109, 111, 158

Carmel, Mount, 4, 7, 42, 44, 51, 54–56, 67, 69, 71, 75, 88–89, 108, 110, 134, 142, 154, 169, 176, 178, 180

Catto, Max, 107–9

Chapman, Charles Hiram, 183–84

Chaucer, Geoffrey, 141

Christ. *See* Jesus

Church Fathers: Christian, 98; Greek, 16

Clark, Jonas, 106

Cleopatra, 3, 80, 83, 106, 173

Clinton, William Jefferson, xv

Coleridge, Samuel Taylor, 140

Collins, Patricia Hill, 121–22

Collins, Wilkie, 119–20

Comédie-Française, 166

Comstock, Anthony, 183–85

Congreve, William, 182–83

Crabbe, George, 147–48

Craig, Alan Robert, 124–25

Creation stories, 21

Crowley, Aleister, 153–55

Dagon, 22, 34

Dante, 141

David (king), 11, 13, 23, 45, 67–69, 85, 166, 170, 173

Davis, Bette, xvii, 185–87

Davis, Owen, Sr., 185–87

Dead Sea Scrolls, 16

Deborah, 18, 28, 83

Decalogue. *See* Ten Commandments

deconstructionism, 28

Delilah, 22, 24–25, 27–28, 105

Deuteronomist, xvi, 5–6, 10–11, 13, 25, 27–28, 33, 35–36, 38–39, 41–42, 47–48, 51, 54–56, 58–59, 61–69, 72, 77–79, 82–84, 86–87, 91, 93, 98, 108, 114, 138, 172, 178

devil, 3, 146, 154, 188. *See also* Lucifer; Satan

diaspora, 36

Dickens, Charles, 119–20, 184

Dido, 40

divine right of kings, 9, 25, 29, 58

doctrine of the Fall, 19

Donne, John, 102, 136, 140

Downey, Fairfax, 127–28

Drusilla, 105

Dryden, John, 182–84

Edward VI, 99–100

Eithobal. *See* Ethbaal

Ekron, 75

El, 34, 89

Elah, 86

Elijah, xv, 4, 12, 14, 17, 31, 35–36, 38–56, 59, 63–67, 69–70, 72–78, 87–89, 92, 99, 101, 103, 108–10, 112–13, 132–35, 141–44, 152, 154–55, 159, 165, 167–70, 173, 176–78, 180–82

Elisha, 43, 54, 56, 59, 64, 71, 76–77, 92, 114, 165

Elizabeth I, 99

Elizabeth II, 137

Elohim, 31. *See also* God (of Israel); Jehovah; Lord; Yahweh

Enoch, 75

Ephraem Syrus, Saint, 98

Esau, 144

Eshmun, 34

Esther (queen), 19, 23, 26, 28, 61–62, 166

Ethbaal, 7–9, 18, 25, 39–40, 57–58, 107, 109, 113, 168, 169–71

Eve, 3, 19–21, 26

Faulkner, William, 123–24, 150
Fielding, Henry, 115, 183
Fonda, Henry, 186
Fonda, Jane, 79
Francis II, 101
Frangipane, Francis, 105–6
Frankau, Pamela, 107–9

Garrick, David, 183
gehenna, 13
Gideon, 67, 89
Gilboa, Mount, 69
God (of Israel), xiii–xiv, 4, 6, 8–9, 11, 13–15,
    18–19, 21–57, 59, 62–69, 71–77, 80–93,
    100, 103–4, 105, 108–13, 132–35, 142,
    144–46, 149, 154–55, 157–58, 166–69,
    171–74, 176, 178–79, 181–82, 184–86. *See
    also* Elohim; Jehovah; Lord; Yahweh
Goddard, Paulette, 182
golden calf, 51, 91
Goodman, Christopher, 100
Goulding, Edmund, 187
Gregory the Great (pope), 23–24
Griffin, Nigel, 164–65
Grunwald, M., 53

Hadad, 34
Hair, J. L., 110–11
Half Dime novels. *See* Beadle's and
    Adams's Half Dime Library
Haman, 19, 23, 62, 105
Hanscombe, Gillian E., 159–60
Harbaugh, Thomas Chalmers, 117–19
Hardy, Thomas, 158–59
Hawthorne, Nathaniel, 150
Heat, Horton, 150
Heavysege, Charles, 142–43
Hector, 10
Helen of Troy, 10, 174
Hellman, Lillian, 187
Helms, Jesse, 97–98
Henri II, 99
Henry VIII, 99, 148
Henson, Jim, 188
Hercules, 104

Herem-bethel, 36
Herman, Mount, 59
Herod, 25–26, 146, 171
Herodias, 26, 105, 151
Hesky, Olga, 133–35
Hezekiah, 67
Hiel, 14
Higgins, F. R., xvii, 145–46
Hilkiah, 39
Hiram, 46
Hollywood, xvi, 182, 186–89
Holofernes, 24
Homer, 3, 88
Hood, Thomas, 148
Horace, 140
Horeb, Mount, 31, 50–54, 75–76, 103. *See
    also* Sinai, Mount
Hosea, 12, 14, 91, 171
Hughes, Ted, 160–61
Huldah, 18
Hulst, C. S., 143–44
human sacrifice, 33, 46–47, 179
Hutchinson, Anne, 101–2

Imlah, 167
Innocent I (pope), 16
Isaac, 18–19, 144
Isaiah, 12, 21, 79
Ishbaal, 7
Ishtar, 37
Ishum-bethel, 36
Israel, xiii–xiv, 1–12, 14–15, 18–19, 22–24, 26,
    34–36, 39–42, 44–67, 69–72, 74–79, 81–83,
    85–86, 88–92, 98, 108–15, 129, 132–34,
    137–39, 141, 143–44, 167–83, 185

Jacob, 18, 89, 144
Jael, 24, 26
James, Jesse, 117
James I, 102
Jehoiada, 71, 90
Jehoram, 70–71, 76–78, 84–86, 114, 172–73,
    179
Jehoshaphat (father of Jehu), 91
Jehoshaphat (king of Judah), 71–72, 114
Jehovah, 113, 132, 167, 179, 182. *See also* Elo-
    him; God (of Israel); Lord; Yahweh

Jehu, xiii, xv, 3–4, 10, 17, 27, 47, 54, 67, 70–71, 76–79, 81–93, 109–11, 114, 121, 125, 130, 135, 137, 145, 154, 159, 165, 170–74, 177–80

Jephthah, 142

Jeroboam, 8, 40, 66, 74, 76

Jerome, Saint, 98

Jesus, 23, 26, 105, 173, 185

Jezebel: advertising links to, xvi; appearance of, 78–81, 92, 93; in balcony window, 78, 82–85, 93; and conflict with Elijah, 44–48; and conflict with Elisha, 54; death of, xiii, 87, 93; and feminism, 27; influence on Ahab, 14–15; lack of respect for Hebrew laws of, 58, 61, 63, 67–69; marriage of, xiii–xvi, 3–4, 6, 8, 9–15, 18, 25, 34; meaning of name, 6–7; outlaws circumcision, 53; political astuteness of, xiv; polytheism of, xiii–xvi, 3–4, 6, 12; as representative of evil, xvi; sexual connections of, xv, 3, 14, 17; similarity to Elijah, 49, 75; treatment in drama, 163–89; treatment in poetry, 140–62; treatment in prose, 97–139

Jezebel butterfly, 79

Jezreel, xiii, xvii, 4, 10, 48–50, 55–56, 59–60, 62, 64–66, 73, 76–78, 81, 85, 87–88, 90–92, 108, 130, 142, 145, 159, 170, 173, 177, 179, 186

Joab, 68, 85

Joan of Arc, 184

Joash, 90

Job, 63, 75

Job's wife, 105

Johnson, Samuel, 147

John the Baptist, 25, 146

John the Divine, 26

Jonathan, 7

Joram. *See* Jehoram

Joseph, 11, 21, 22, 30, 79

Josephus, 26, 40–41, 63, 89

Joshua, 9, 23, 38, 51–52

Josiah, 18

Joyce, James, xvii, 126–27

Judah (person), 23

Judah (region), xiv, 10, 12, 18, 37, 50, 70–72, 77, 80–81, 89–91, 110, 114, 166, 178

Judas Iscariot, 51, 142, 148

Judith, 24

Justina, 98

Kali, 37

Keach, Benjamin, 147

Kellerman, Faye, 132

Kennedy, Edward, 97–98

KMFDM (musical group), 150

Knox, John, xvii, 100–102, 158, 163

Kournikova, Anna, xvi

Kronos, 34

Lally, Gwen, 170–71

Latouche, John, 187

Leah, 43

Le Borg, Reginald, 182

Lee, Robert G., 104

Leonidas, 79

levirate laws, 23

Lewinsky, Monica, xv

Lewis, Mary, 128

lex talionis. See talion laws

Lilith, 20–21, 145, 171

Lindsay, Vachel, 148–49

Linson, Corwin K., 132

Longfellow, Henry Wadsworth, 157

Lord, 9–11, 13–14, 22–24, 30, 41–47, 52, 57, 65–67, 71–74, 76–77, 83, 88, 90–91, 102–3, 124, 135, 146. *See also* Elohim; God (of Israel); Jehovah; Yahweh

Los Alamos, xv

Lot, 151

Louis XIV, 166

Lucifer, 126, 145–46. *See also* devil; Satan

Luke, 23, 44

MacCallum, M. W., 178–79

MacFall, Haldane, 120

Mary (mother of Jesus), 104, 136

Mary Magdalene, 23–24

Mary of Guise, 100–101

Mary, Queen of Scots, 100–101, 158, 163

Mary Tudor, 99–101, 158

Marzeah, 83–84

Masefield, John, 173–75

McDowall, H. M., 175–76

Index

&

McLaws, Lafayette, 132–33
Medea, 115
Medici, Catherine de, 98–99, 101, 105
Medici, Lorenzo de, 98
Melkaart, 34
Menander of Ephesus, 39
Merchant, Natalie, 150
Meribbaal, 7
Meshach, 133
Messalina, 115
Micaiah, 167
Middleton, Scudder, 149–50
Milcom, 11
Miss Piggy, 188
M'Neile, Hugh, 103–4
Moab, 34, 76
Monjo, F. N., 129
Moore, Douglas, 187
Moses, 11, 30–31, 41, 45, 48, 50–52, 64–65, 67, 90
Mot, 84
Mother Goddess, 38, 138
Moultrie, John, 158

Naboth, xv, 4, 9, 14, 17, 23, 25, 27, 55–70, 77–78, 81, 86–88, 92, 98–99, 105, 108–10, 112–13, 119–20, 133–35, 141–44, 148, 165, 168–70, 172–74, 176–79, 181, 186
Naomi, 23, 179
Napoleon, 159
Nathan, 68
Nathan, Robert, 181–82
Nebat, 8, 66, 74, 76
Nebuchadnezzar, 133
Nefertiti, 79
Nemirovsky, Irene, 125–26
Nero, 148
Nickerson, Kate, 128–29
Nineveh, 62, 181–82
Nut, 37

Obadiah, 41–45, 77, 113, 167, 176, 178, 180–81
Omri, 7, 9–10, 12, 44, 54, 56, 66, 73, 85–86, 90, 133, 178
Onca, 34
Oppenheim, E. Phillips, 122–24
O'Shea, Kitty, 105

Ostara, 37
Ovid, 84
Ozias, 24

Pakenham, Edward Arthur Henry, 180
Paris (France), 125, 151
Paris (husband of Helen), 10
Parton, Dolly, 188
Passover, 53
Pfeiffer, Michelle, 188
pharaoh, 21, 30, 48
Philistia, 22, 75
Phoenicia, xiii–xiv, 3–4, 6–11, 15, 23, 29, 32, 34, 37, 41–42, 45, 50, 54, 58, 79, 83–84, 112, 138, 145, 158, 167, 171, 175, 179
Pickett, Fuchsia, 106
Plath, Sylvia, 161
Potiphar's wife, 21–22, 27, 79, 105, 151
Potok, Chaim, 35
Priapus, 151
Principal, Victoria, 79
Promised Land, xii–xiv, 5–6, 18, 30–32
Pryce, Richard, 135–36
Putnam, Israel, 129

Rachel, 43
Racine, Jean-Baptiste, 165–68, 189
Rahab, 23, 26
Ramoth-gilead, 71–73, 76–77, 84, 153–54
Ratcliff, Nora, 179–80
Ravnitzky, Yehoshua Hana, 13–14
Rebekah, 18–19, 28, 43
Renee of Hollywood, xvi
Richardson, Dorothy, 159
Richardson, Samuel, 115
Robbins, Tom, 136–38
Robins, Denise, 112–13
Roosevelt, Theodore, 183
Ruth, 12, 23, 28, 57

Saint Bartholomew's Day Massacre, 99
Salome, 26, 121, 146, 171
Samaria, 4, 8–12, 27, 33, 35, 40, 44–45, 47, 64, 66, 71, 73, 74–75, 80, 83, 90, 108, 133–34, 137–38, 142, 160, 173
Samson, 22
Sarah, 26, 28, 43, 124–25

Satan, 3, 45, 105, 137. *See also* devil; Lucifer
Saul, 7, 51, 59, 67, 142, 173
Selznick, David O., 185
Septuagint, 49
Shadrach, 133
Shakespeare, William, xvii, 82, 104, 118, 142, 144, 156, 166, 170, 176, 182–83
Shalmaneser III, 10
Shelley, Percy Bysshe, xvii, 158
Shemer, 10
Sheridan, Frances Chamberlaine, 116
Sidon, 4, 7–8, 25–26, 34, 40–41, 58, 74, 176, 178, 180
Sinai, Mount, xiv, 13, 31, 37. *See also* Horeb, Mount
Sisera, 24, 83
Solomon, 8, 11, 13, 24, 27, 40, 46, 67, 71, 151, 168
Speed, Samuel, 147
Squires, Edith Lombard, 177–78
Starr, Kenneth, xv
Strauss, Richard, 26
Svareff, Vladimir. *See* Crowley, Aleister
Swinburne, Algernon Charles, 119, 183
Sydyk, 34
Symons, Arthur, 156

talion laws, 65–66, 87–88
Tamar, 23, 151
Tanata, 34
Tanith, 34
Ten Commandments, 57, 65
10,000 Maniacs (musical group), 150
Thatcher, Margaret, 160
Thermopylae, 79
Trollope, Anthony, 119
Tupper, Martin Farquhar, 157
Tutankamen, 79

Ugarit, 58, 86, 89
Uriah, 68
Urquhart, Fred, 136

Van Der Meulen, E., 143–44
Vashti, 61
Venegas, Miguel, 164
Venus, 151
Victoria, 103–4
Virgin Mary. *See* Mary (mother of Jesus)
Voltaire, 68, 166
Vulgate, 98, 164–65

Warner, Fred, 185–87
Warner of Rouen, 150
Washington, George, 129
Webster, John, 86
Welch, Raquel, 79
Welsh, Robert Gilbert, 171
Wheeler, Edward L., 117–18
White, Fred M., 122
widow of Zarephath, 41–42, 50, 74. *See also* Zarephath
Wiesel, Elie, 15, 60
Wilcox, Ella Wheeler, 145
Wilde, Oscar, 26
Williams, Isaac, 102–3
Williams, Tennessee, 187
Wilson, Dorothy Clarke, 111
Wyler, William, 185

Yahweh, xiii, 4–6, 10–12, 18, 22–23, 26, 29, 31–37, 39–41, 44–52, 54–55, 57, 59, 65, 67–69, 71–72, 74–76, 90–92, 103, 110, 114, 133–34, 137–38, 144, 146, 165, 167, 179. *See also* God (of Israel); Jehovah; Lord
Yeats, William Butler, 153

Zarephath, 41–42, 50, 74, 180
Zeresh, 105
Zeus, 38, 75
Zidon. *See* Sidon
Zimri, 84–86, 89, 103, 113, 135
Ziolkowski, Jan, 151

Janet Howe Gaines has been on the English department faculty at the University of New Mexico since 1981, where she has received a Distinguished Service Award. She specializes in the Bible as literature, teaches Hebrew, and is currently the executive director of Hillel, the Foundation for Jewish Life, on Campus.